Interior Design Visual Presentation

Interior Design Visual Presentation

A Guide to Graphics, Models, and Presentation Techniques

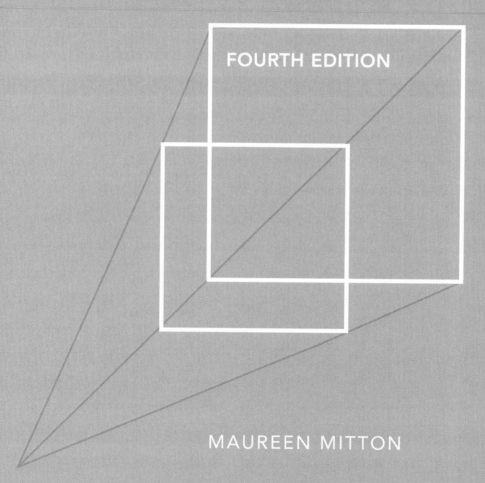

FOURTH EDITION

MAUREEN MITTON

WILEY

JOHN WILEY & SONS, INC.

Library of Congress Cataloging-in-Publication Data:

Mitton, Maureen.
  Interior design visual presentation : a guide to graphics, models, and presentation techniques / Maureen Mitton.
-- 4th ed.
      p. cm.
  Includes index.
  ISBN 978-0-470-61902-5 (pbk.); ISBN 978-1-118-17164-6 (ebk); ISBN 978-1-118-17166-0 (ebk); ISBN 978-1-118-17323-7 (ebk); ISBN 978-1-118-17324-4 (ebk); ISBN 978-1-118-17325-1 (ebk)
  1. Interior decoration rendering. 2. Interior decoration--Design. 3. Graphic arts. I. Title. II. Title: Guide to graphics, models, and presentation techniques.
  NK2113.5.M58 2012
  729.028--dc23

                              2011030356

Printed in the United States of America

10   9   8   7   6   5   4   3   2   1

Contents

Acknowledgments

This book, like the previous editions, compiles the work of many hands (and keyboards) and conversations. It has been made possible by the generous contributions of numerous people, to whom I would like to express my gratitude.

First, I must acknowledge my current and former students, who have taught me volumes and who continue to give me the energy to keep going. This edition includes new work by the following talented and hardworking current and former students: Nicole Banaszewski, Kelly Greff, Veronica McCracken, Katie Oja, Alecia Plaetz, Laura Purcell, Holly Sivula, and Jessica Smith.

I must also thank all of the former students who contributed work to earlier editions: Tiffany Baca, Nicole Banaszewski, Laura Blanchard, Tina Bucher, Ciarah Coenen, Laura Eysnogle, Ellie Feenstra, Stephanie Holmblad, Megan Gruner, Amber Liestman, Jenna Michels, Laura Purcell, Sunny Reed, Vicky Salzsieder, and Mary Wawra. Kristy Bokelman, Dan Effenheim, Denise Haertl, Leanne Larson, Anne (Cleary) Olsen, Ardella Pieper, Justin Thomson, and I thank former exchange student Julian Hensch, as well as Laura Sudbrock, Ilka Schnelle, Jessica Tebbe, and Dirk Olbrich, whose work was featured in previous editions.

Melissa Brewer contributed CAD drawings to previous editions, and Katey Fortun came through with fine Revit work in the face of some daunting roadblocks.

I have been amazed and touched by the generosity of members of the design community who shared time and contributed projects. Traci Lesneski and the staff at Meyer, Scherer & Rockcastle, Ltd. (MS&R) generously allowed me to review projects and contributed excellent project work, as they have for each edition. For this and previous editions, the staff at Cuningham Group Architecture contributed time and a range of projects and process work. Jim Smart of Smart Associates graciously contributed work to previous editions that is also included here.

Conversations with my friend Lynn Barnhouse were instrumental in developing the first and second editions. Previous editions included generous contributions of time and work by Jane Rademacher; Thom Lasley; Thomas Oliphant; Jim Moeller, Janet Lawson, of Janet Lawson Architectural Illustration; and Harris Birkeland.

I am thrilled to be able to include examples by Michelle Morelan, a talented designer and illustrator whose work has a wonderful, fresh quality. A special thanks to Matthew Saunders, a gifted illustrator and designer, for his digital and manual renderings and drawings, which enrich this edition immensely.

I must acknowledge and thank my current and former University of Wisconsin–Stout colleagues. Courtney Nystuen, a wonderful teacher and architect, contributed in many ways to all editions. Thanks to Ambica Prakash for graciously allowing the publication of her illustrations of graphic design concepts.

Jack Zellner contributed work to this and the previous editions. Additionally, some typically excellent student work from Kristine Recker's courses has been included in this edition and previous editions. Shelley Pecha kindly (and quickly) contributed to this edition. Bill Wikrent and the staff (including Andrew Bottolfson and Katie Hladilek) at Learning Technology Services contributed all of the photography included, unless otherwise noted.

Thank you to Margaret Cummins, Paul Drougas, Mike New, Lauren Poplawski, and Kerstin Nasdeo at John Wiley & Sons.

Thank you to Andrew Miller for bringing clarity and precision to my manuscript.

My immediate family always pays a price for my time at the keyboard, and I thank them for their patience and support: thanks to Roger, Anna, and Luc.

Introduction

The first edition of this book was intended as a primer on interior design visual communication, one that presented a range of styles and techniques. The goal for that and each subsequent edition has been to provide students and practitioners with up-to-date information on visual presentation techniques. Like earlier editions, this book identifies the methods used in the visual presentation of interior spaces and articulates them in written and visual language. Various phases of the design process are discussed in order to reveal the connection between process and presentation. Some often overlooked basic principles of graphic design and portfolio design are also discussed.

Research for this edition made clear that today's designers must have both good hand- and digital-drawing skills. Quickly created perspective drawings offer the benefit of providing designers with a visualization tool early in the design process, before finalized design drawings are completed. In addition, skills learned in drawing by hand transfer directly to computer modeling. The ability to create quick perspective sketches in client conferences and team meetings is a highly useful—something I have heard many times from those hiring designers. For these reasons, numerous examples of quick sketching techniques are included.

The focus here is on quick, estimated sketching and quick modeling (using SketchUp) because these skills are useful to all designers. My approach to rendering is similar: all designers need go-to quick rendering skills serviceable in a range of situations. My purpose is to provide an overview of accessible approaches to drawing, modeling, and rendering that will serve as a foundation for design students and then create a comfort level with drawing and rendering so that those skills can be used throughout the design process.

As this edition goes into production, designers continue to present projects using traditional presentation boards, and those are covered in detail in this edition. Information is also provided about digital presentations methods, as many designers are creating completely digital and virtual presentations. Clearly, we are at a time of transition, where new methods are employed by some and traditional methods are favored by others; both are covered in detail in this edition.

As with earlier editions, many of the examples included here were executed by undergraduate design students. I've included them because I want students to see real examples of developing skills. It is important for all designers to develop drawing and sketching skills. Drawing and model making should not be reserved for the final presentation of fully developed designs. Rather, sketching, drawing, and model making must be ways of seeing and exploring throughout the design process—from beginning to final presentation. I own up to my desire to get interior designers to draw (and draw and draw): it is the best way to learn to visualize and develop good work.

Examples of work done by professional illustrators, digital illustrators, and model makers are also included in order to demonstrate what is being done in current practice by specialists. The work is beautiful and depicts what top professionals can produce. We can learn from this work and allow it to influence our own design drawings and in-process presentations.

While much has changed since the first edition of this book was published—particularly that related to digital technology—so many things have stayed consistent, especially regarding the process of design and the complex, yet flexible ways of thinking required of a professional designer. Interior design continues to be a profession populated by bright, creative individuals who must call upon a broad range of talents and skills in everyday practice. While technology has made many things easier and faster, today's designers have to know more—and possess more skills—than at any previous time. I hope this book will help today's designers acquire some of the many skills required in current practice.

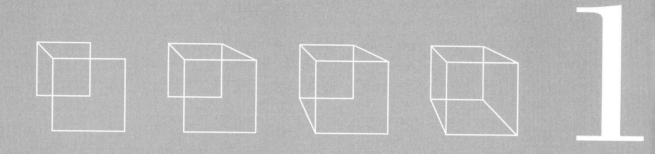

An Introduction to Drawing for Interior Design

Interior design is a multifaceted and ever-changing discipline. The practice of interior design continues to evolve due to technological as well as societal changes.

The sentences above were written roughly thirteen years ago, for the introduction to the first edition of this book, but they continue to hold true today. Digital technology continues to influence—and to catalyze—the ongoing evolution of design practice. Today's interior designers use software for two-dimensional drawing, parametric modeling, digital rendering, and digital imaging, and make use of word processing, spreadsheet, and presentation programs as well.

In addition to undergoing continual, rapid technological advancement, the profession of interior design has also grown in scope and specialization, and in the range of design practiced. The profession's growth, combined with the development of educational standards, registration, and licensing, have increased its legitimacy as a serious professional discipline.

Constant change in society and in one's profession can be overwhelming and a bit frightening; it is therefore useful to consider the elements that have remained stable in this evolving profession. In many ways, the design process itself is a constant, whether it is practiced with a stick in the sand, a technical pen, or a powerful computer running special software. There are many stories about designers drawing preliminary sketches on cocktail napkins or on the back of a paper bag, and these anecdotes lead us to a simple truth: design drawing is a key part of the design process.

Professional designers conduct research and generate piles of information, then wrap this all together with inspiration and hard work in what is referred to as the *design process* to create meaningful and useful environments. An enduring and key factor in interior design is that human beings—and other living creatures—occupy and move within interior spaces. To create interior environments, professional designers must engage in a process that involves *research, understanding, idea generation, evaluation,* and *documentation*—all significant constants in an ever-changing world.

This book covers the drawing and presentation elements used in *design communication* throughout the design process. These processes and basic concepts are consistent, whether generated manually or by computer. Practicing designers currently use computers for most finalized design drawings as well as for many in-process drawings; manual drawings are usually used earlier in the design process or to create quick, idea-oriented sketches throughout the process as needed.

This chapter covers what is often referred to as drafting, as well as other forms of two-dimensional graphics. The term *drafting* refers to measured drawings done with specialized drawing tools or computers. (Detailed information about drawing and drafting tools, as well as related media, can be found in appendix 1.)

Drawings created in the preliminary stages of the design process are often rough sketches and may be done by hand. As designs are refined, there is a need for highly accurate, measured, and detailed drawings, and these are most commonly generated via computer. Put another way, as a given design is refined, the drawings for that design are also refined: the design process is one of refinement, as is the drawing process. Figures 1–1a through 1–1c illustrate drawing refinement occurring during the design process.

This chapter presents an overview of the most common drawings used in interior design practice. The information presented is meant as an overview, not a definitive drawing or drafting reference. Subsequent chapters cover the other forms of drawings and design graphics used in sketching, as well as other forms of idea generation.

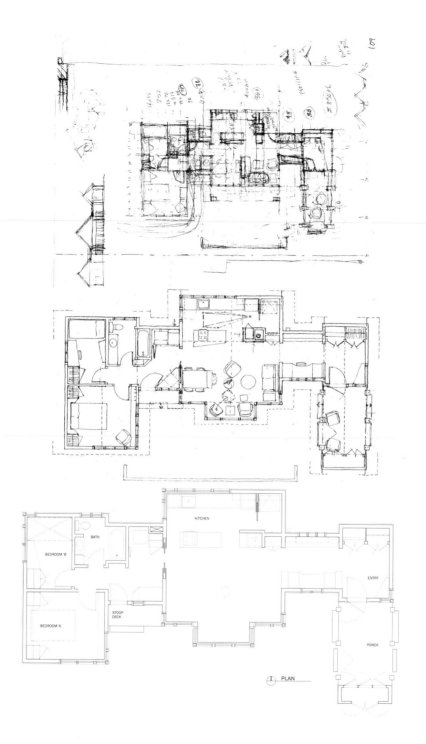

FIGURES 1–1A THROUGH 1–1C
Drawings are refined as the design process moves forward in a continual process of refinement, as one can see from early exploration sketches (1–1a), to more refined (1–1b) to the finalized design drawn using AutoCAD (1–1c). DESIGN AND SKETCHES BY COURTNEY NYSTUEN; AUTOCAD DRAWING BY SHELLEY PECHA

The practice of interior design requires the creation and use of various types of drawings. These can be divided into three broad categories based on purpose.

Interior Design Drawings Types and Purposes

1. IDEATION
   Conceptual or preliminary drawings that allow the designer to explore ideas and work conceptually, often in the form of sketches.

2. COMMUNICATION
   These drawings allow the designer to communicate to others, including members of the design team, the client, end users, consultants, and other professionals, usually through presentation drawings.

3. CONSTRUCTION
   This type of drawing conveys the technical information required for construction through construction documents or working drawings. This book focuses on the first two types of drawing: those used for exploration and presentation or for graphic communication of ideas.

To create the appropriate type of drawing with the level of detail required, begin by asking what the purpose of the drawing is. For example, if ideation is the goal, then the drawings should be sketchy and executed quickly by hand, using few (or no) drawing tools.

Interestingly, as parametric modeling software becomes more advanced, students and designers tend to do more quick sketching by hand in order to flesh out ideas, and then use the loose ideation sketches as a reference when modeling the project digitally. In my work with students, for example, the more we use software such as Revit, which requires you to make decisions as you model digitally, the more we use hand sketches. In other words, Revit requires that you know what you are modeling and understand it as a three-dimensional form. So pre-sketching by hand is often necessary early in the design and drafting process

This chapter focuses on the drawings used most for communication and construction, but designers do many other types of drawings, from diagrams to perspective sketches. Diagrams are covered in chapter 2, and perspective drawing is covered in chapters 3, 4, and 5.

Understanding Orthographic Projection Drawings

Information about tools used in hand-drawing and drafting can be found in appendix 1.

Unlike ideation sketches, presentation drawings and construction documents must use certain standard drawing conventions in order to clearly communicate and delineate the proposed design; these often involve drafting in scale. Unlike fine art drawing, design drawing requires adherence to conventions, proportional scale, and accuracy of line. Design drawings are highly standardized so that they can carry universal meaning. Or as one early reviewer of this book put it, "Design drawing is much like a language; the drawings must convey the designer's meaning clearly."

The design drawings most commonly used in scaled delineation of interior environments are *floor plans, interior elevations, sections,* and *reflected ceiling plans.* These drawings, called *multiview orthographic projections,* are created by projecting information about an object onto an imaginary plane known as the *picture plane.* This direct projection of an object's dimensions allows orthographic projections to retain both shape and proportion, making these drawings accurate and precise.

Multiview orthographic projections create fragmentary views of an object, resulting in the need for multiple drawings (hence the "multiview" portion of the name). Because of their fragmentary nature, orthographic projections therefore become parts of a system and are mutually dependent on one another. By their nature, these orthographic projections appear flat and lack the three-dimensional quality of perspective drawings. One way to visualize orthographic projection is to imagine an object enclosed in a transparent box. Each transparent plane of the enclosing box serves as the picture plane for that face of the object.

The view through the top plane of the enclosing box is called a *plan.* In a plan view, only those elements seen when looking directly down at the object are drawn. Figure 1–2 depicts a roof plan.

The views through the picture planes that form the sides of the enclosing box are called *elevations.* Elevations depict only what is visible when the object is viewed directly through the side picture planes. Figure 1–3 is an exterior elevation.

A *section* portrays a view of the object or building with a vertical plane sliced through it and removed. One way of understanding section views is to imagine that a very sharp plane has been inserted into the object or building, cutting neatly into it and revealing the structure and complexity of the object's form (see Figure 1–4).

A *floor plan*, also known as a *horizontal section*, portrays a view of the building with a horizontal plane sliced through it and removed, exposing the thickness of the walls and the elements below the cut line, such as floor finishes and furniture (see Figure 1–5).

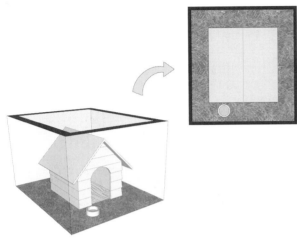

FIGURE 1–2
Roof plan. When an object is enclosed in a glass box, each plane of the box can serve as a picture plane. The view drawn through the top plane (picture plane) creates a plan view—in this case a roof plan.

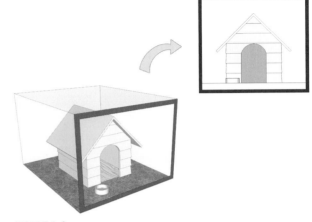

FIGURE 1–3
Elevation. The view drawn through the picture plane enclosing the side of the box is called an elevation.

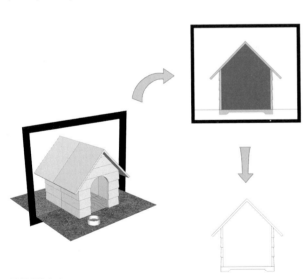

FIGURE 1–4
Section. A section is a view of an object with the picture plane slicing neatly through it.

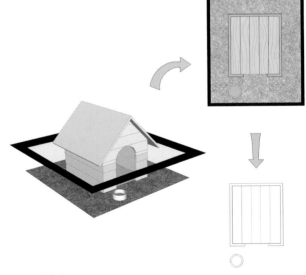

FIGURE 1–5
A floor plan is a view of the building from above, with a horizontal plane sliced through it and removed to expose the thickness of the walls. FIGURES 1–2 THROUGH 1–5 DRAWN BY CIARAH COENEN

Orthographic projection drawings are an abstraction of reality and use specific conventions to delineate space and materials. Items such as walls, doors, windows, property boundaries, and references to other drawings are represented by very specific graphic symbols or combinations of lines. Figures 1–6a through 1–6c illustrate some graphic notations used in these types of drawings, including wall lines, door and window symbols, and reference and notation symbols.

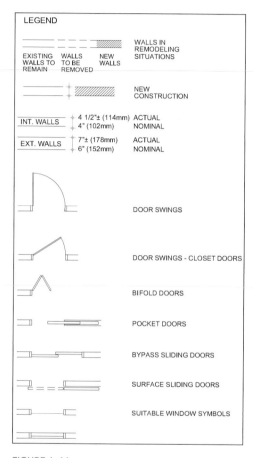

FIGURE 1–6A
Common graphic notations used in orthographic projection drawings. SHELLY PECHA

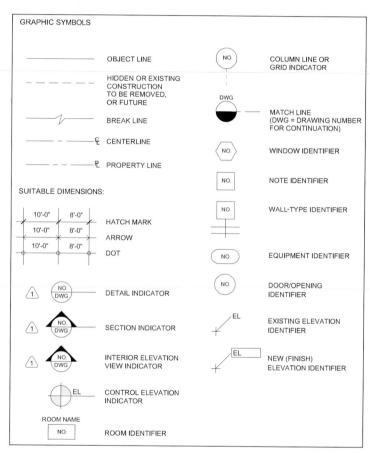

FIGURE 1–6B
Graphic symbols used for references and notes. Items shown with the numeral 1 near them are reference symbols; these typically include a number on top of another number. The number on top refers to the drawing number, and the lower number refers to the sheet the drawing can be found on. SHELLY PECHA

FIGURE 1–6C

Graphic symbols
used for lighting and
electrical informa-
tion. SHELLY PECHA

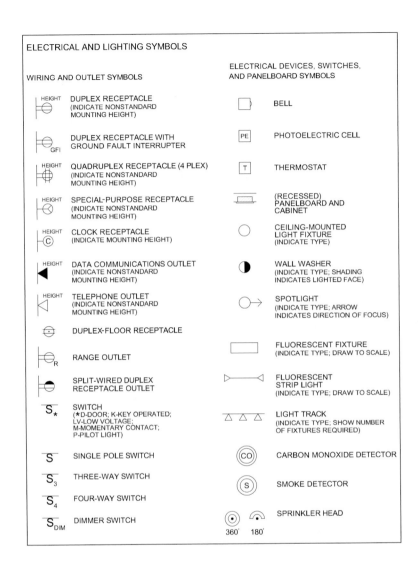

Orthographic Projection Drawings for Interior Environments

The special orthographic projection drawings used in the delineation of interior environments are also based on the concepts discussed above. These drawings impart information particular to interior construction.

Floor Plans

Floor plans are also called *horizontal building sections* because they are drawn as though a horizontal cut has been made through the building (typically between 3′-6″ and 5′-6″ above the floor), as shown in Figure 1–7. Cutting into the building at this location exposes the thickness of walls and other structural elements, shows windows and doors, and can reveal floor finishes and furnishings, all of which are located below the location of the cut.

In the United States, floor plans are most often drawn at a scale of ⅛″ = 1′-0″ or ¼″ = 1′-0″, although this varies according to project conditions. Larger-scale floor plans are useful for the presentation of complex or highly detailed spaces. Smaller-scale floor plans are required for large projects and are also used as key plans in complex presentations. In creating floor plans using metric measurements, a scale of 1:50 is relatively common; it is somewhat similar to ¼″ = 1′-0″ scale (the ratio is precisely 1:48). Architectural drawings—other than small-scale interior-related drawings such as the floor plans mentioned—are commonly drawn using a metric scale of 1:100. (More information about the use of scale and reading various scale devices can be found in appendix 1.)

Floor plans must convey significant spatial relationships with consistent graphic conventions. The conventions for those are listed below.

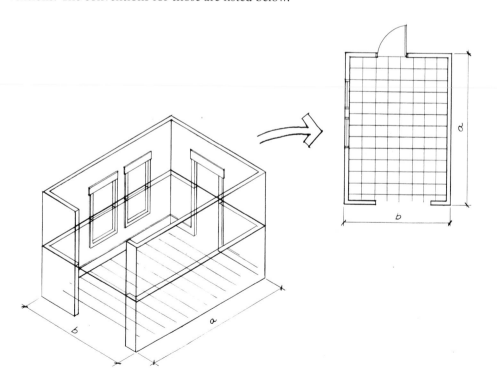

FIGURE 1–7
A floor plan is created when the picture plane cuts through the building horizontally, at 3′-6″ and 5′-6″ above floor level.

Plan Drawing and Line Weight Conventions (See also Figures 1–8a through 1–8c.)

Various line weights are used to convey depths and qualities of form.

In standard floor plans, the boldest line weight is used to outline those elements that have been cut through and are closest to the viewer (such as full-height wall lines).

An intermediate line weight is employed to outline objects that lie below the plane of the cut but above the floor plane, such as fixtures, built-ins, and furnishings.

A finer line weight is used to outline the surface treatment of floors and other horizontal planes, such as tile and wood grain.

Objects that are hidden (such as shelves) or above the plane of the cut are dashed or ghosted in a manner that is consistent throughout the presentation.

Standard doors are drawn open at 90 degrees to the wall and are often shown with the arc of their swing. The door frame and the space it requires must be considered in the drawing of the door system; the dimensions of the frame itself must be dealt with as well.

Nonstandard doors, such as smaller swinging closet doors, bifold doors, sliding doors, and pocket doors are drawn in a manner consistent with their construction, as shown in Figure 1–6a.

Windowsills are typically outlined, often with a lighter line weight at the sill only. Window frames and sheets of glass are shown at various level of detail, as the scale allows.

Stairs are generally shown broken off past the height of the plane of the cut; this is signified with a special cut or break line, as shown in Figure 1–8a. An arrow should be included to indicate the direction of the stairs from the level of the floor plan, with the word up (UP) or down (DN) adjacent to the directional arrow.

A title, north arrow, and some type of scale notation should be included on all floor plans. Scale notation can be stated numerically (e.g., ¼″ = 1′-0″). The use of a graphic scaling device, which allows for the reduction, enlargement, and electronic transmission of drawings, is often necessary.

Symbols relating the floor plan to additional orthographic views or details are often drawn on the floor plan and serve as cross-references.

Figures 1–8a and 1–8b are examples of town house floor plans drawn using Auto-CAD and employing standard conventions and reference symbols. Figure 1–8c is an enlarged portion of the floor plan showing detailed information. Figures 1–9a and 1–9b are examples of the same town house floor plans drawn using Revit.

FIGURE 1–8A

The lower-level floor plan of a town house employing standard drafting conventions.

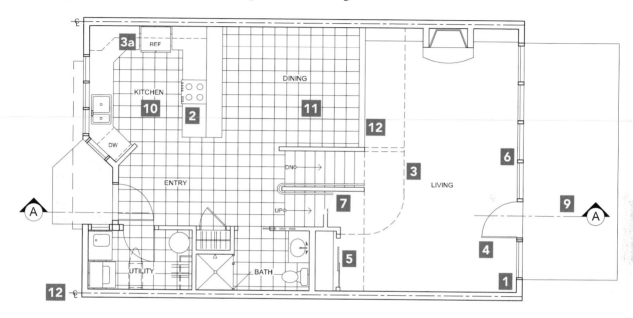

1. The boldest lines indicate the location of cut; full-height walls are bold. Lower walls may be shown in lighter line weights.

2. Fixtures, cabinetry, and finish materials are drawn with progressively lighter lines as they recede from the cut location.

3. Elements that are above or below the cut line, such as cabinets (3a) and soffits, or that are hidden, such as dishwashers, are indicated with dashed lines.

4. Standard doors are drawn open at 90 degrees, with the arc of the swing shown; the door's full swing can also be depicted to ensure that nothing impedes it.

5. Specialized doors, such as smaller closet doors (shown), bifold doors, sliding doors, and pocket doors are drawn in a way that indicates size and construction.

6. Window glass and sill lines are shown, often with a lighter-weight line than walls.

7. Stairs are broken off past the line of the cut; a special break line is used.

8. A title, north arrow, and scale notation are required on all plans. Because this drawing was reduced, a standard written scale was omitted; instead, a graphic scale device is included.

9. This is a section reference symbol. The arrow indicates the view direction of the section.

10. This is an elevation reference symbol. The arrow indicates the direction of the elevation view. The number indicates the particular drawing that is referenced.

11. Flooring materials are shown as required (using a light line weight).

12. This is a centerline, indicating the centerline of the shared wall in the town house.

FIGURE 1–8B

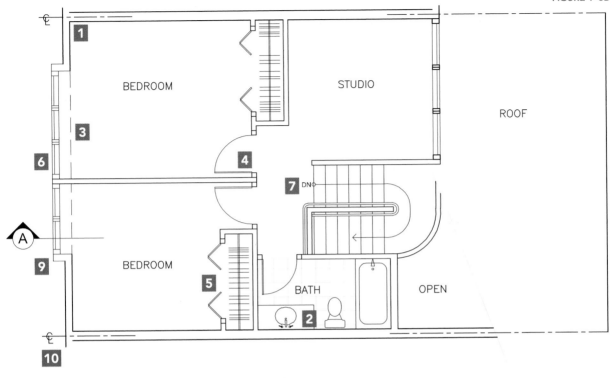

UPPER-LEVEL PLAN

1. The boldest lines indicate the location of cut; full-height walls are bold. Lower walls may be shown in lighter line weights.

2. Fixtures, cabinetry, and finish materials are drawn with progressively lighter lines as they recede from the cut location.

3. Elements that are above or below the cut line, such as cabinets and soffits, or that are hidden, such as dishwashers, are indicated with dashed lines.

4. Standard doors are drawn open at 90 degrees, with the arc of the swing shown; the door's full swing can also be depicted to ensure that nothing impedes it.

5. Specialized doors, such as smaller closet doors (shown), bifold doors, sliding doors, and pocket doors are drawn in a way that indicates size and construction.

6. Window glass and sill lines are shown, often with a lighter-weight line than walls.

7. Stairs are broken off past the line of the cut; a special break line is used. Because this is a view from the top floor, no break line is required.

8. A title, north arrow, and scale notation are required on all plans. Because this drawing was reduced, a standard written scale was omitted; instead, a graphic scale device is included.

9. This is a section reference symbol. The arrow indicates the view direction of the section.

10. This is a centerline, indicating the centerline of the shared wall in the town house.

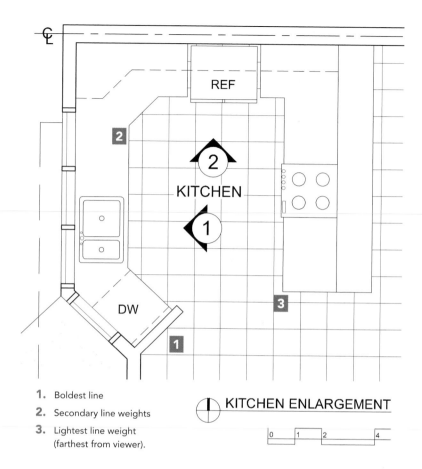

FIGURE 1–8C
Varying line
weights for floor
plans. FIGURES 1–8A
THROUGH 1–8C:
DESIGN BY COURTNEY
NYSTUEN; DRAWN BY
MELISSA BREWER AND
SHELLEY PECHA

REF

2

2

KITCHEN

1

DW

3

1

1. Boldest line
2. Secondary line weights
3. Lightest line weight
   (farthest from viewer).

KITCHEN ENLARGEMENT

0   1   2   4

Successful floor plan presentation drawings require a thorough understanding of drafting conventions. Presentation floor plans may be drawn fastidiously with tools or sketched freehand. Regardless of the drawing style, presentation floor plans must be accurate and drawn to the appropriate scale so that they communicate the design and can be used by the designer as the project progresses. Presentation floor plans are enhanced by the use of tone, value, color, and other graphic devices. The graphic enhancement of floor plans is discussed in greater detail in Chapters 6 and 7. Additional examples of plans for commercial projects can be found at the end of this chapter.

FIGURE 1–9A
and 1–9B
Revit-generated
floor plans of the
town house proj-
ect shown in Fig-
ures 1–8a through
1–8c. DRAWN BY
KATEY FORTUN

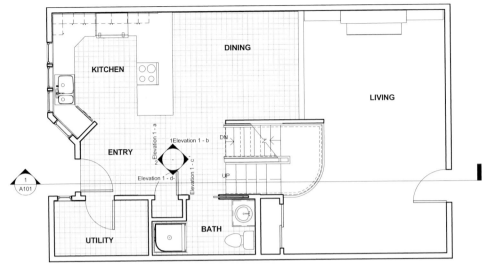

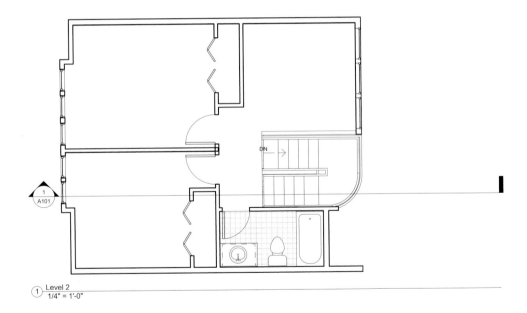

Interior Elevations

Just as exterior elevations are created to reveal exterior elements and features, interior elevations reveal a building's interior features. To understand the creation of interior elevations, imagine yourself inside the room you are drawing, directly facing one wall, with a large sheet of glass (the picture plane) inserted between you and the wall. The interior elevation can then be created by outlining (i.e., projecting onto the picture plane) the wall's significant features. Each wall of the room can be drawn in elevation by projecting what is visible as you face that wall directly, as illustrated in Figure 1–10.

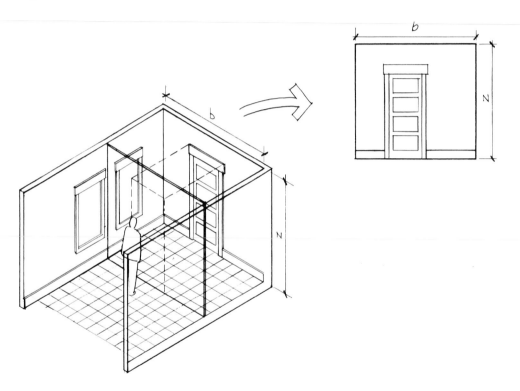

FIGURE 1–10
In drawing interior elevations, the picture plane is inserted between the viewer and wall(s). What is visible through the picture plane is drawn in elevation.

Interior elevations are used extensively in professional practice (see Figures 1–11 and 1–12). Successful elevations must follow the drafting conventions in the following list.

Interior Elevation Drawing and Line Weight Conventions (See also Figures 1–11 and 1–12.)

Interior elevations must clearly depict all interior architectural elements in a consistent scale.

Interior elevations are typically drawn in a scale ranging from ¼″ = 1′-0″ to 1″ = 1′-0″. Elevations drawn to depict accessories, equipment, cabinetry, fixtures, and design details are often drawn at ⅜″ = 1′-0″ or ½″ = 1′-0″. Millwork and other highly complicated elevations are often drawn at ½″ = 1′-0″ or larger.

Elevations require the use of differing line weights to clearly communicate spatial relationships.

Typically, any portion of walls cut through, as well as those closest to the viewer, are drawn using a bold line weight.

Elements become progressively lighter in line weight as they recede from the picture plane.

Some designers draw the ground line the boldest, with those lines representing the top and sides of the wall drawn just slightly lighter in weight.

Drawing interior elevations by hand or digitally using two-dimensional drafting programs requires a clear understanding of the concepts mentioned here and can be difficult for beginning students to master; therefore, additional examples are presented at the end of this chapter (see Figures 1–18a, 1–18d, 1–19a, and 1–19c). Revit and other parametric modeling programs can create highly accurate interior elevations. Although these modeling programs basically draw the elevations for you, an understanding of elevations is nonetheless required to obtain the intended view, as indicated in Figure 1–12.

Interior elevations are an excellent vehicle for developing and refining interior details. For elevations to work well in visual presentations, they must be clearly keyed, noted, or referenced to the floor plan. Regardless of the referencing method, titles must be included beneath all elevations, and the scale should always be noted. Like floor plans, elevations used for design presentations vary greatly from those used for construction. Figure 1–13 is a preliminary elevation sketch, created to convey design elements in the early phases of a professional project.

FIGURE 1–11

Kitchen elevations for the town house shown in Figures 1–8a through 1–9b.
DRAWN BY SHELLEY PECHA

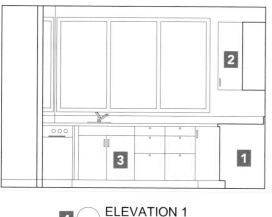

ELEVATION 1

0 1 2 4

ELEVATION 2

0 1 2 4

1. Portions of walls cut into or closest to the viewer are bold.

2. Receding elements are drawn with progressively lighter lines.

3. In elevations including cabinetry and/or millwork, details such as countertops, door frames, and hardware should be included.

4. Interior elevations require titles, reference symbols (names or numbers), and scale notation (see also Figure 1-6b).

Level 2
8' - 0"

Level 1
0' - 0"

1 Elevation 1 - b
1/2" = 1'-0"

FIGURE 1–12

This elevation was created using Revit. It represents the area shown in Figure 1–11, elevation 1. While a properly created Revit model can generate accurate elevations, the correct placement of the elevation symbol relative to the viewing location is still necessary. DRAWN BY KATEY FORTUN

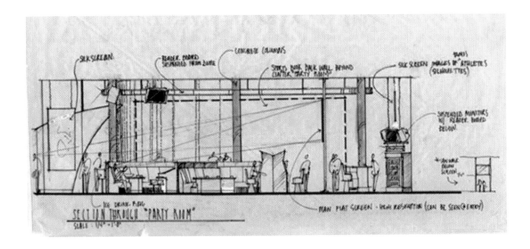

Elevations used for construction drawings must contain significant dimensions and appropriate technical information, as illustrated at the end of this chapter.

Sections

As previously described, a building section is a view created as though a vertical plane has cut through the building and been removed. Unlike interior elevations, which depict only what appears inside the interior, sections can expose the structure of the building. Section drawings should include the outline of the structural elements as well as the internal configuration of the interior space. Sections require varied line weights to describe depths and spatial relationships. It is typical to show what is cut through, and therefore closest to the viewer, in the boldest line weight; receding features and details are drawn using progressively lighter line weights.

Carefully consider the most useful location(s) of a building to show in section. The section should be cut through the building as a single continuous plane. Sections should expose and convey important interior relationships and details such as doors, windows, changes in floor level, ceiling heights, and, in some cases, finish material locations.

Design and presentation sections differ greatly from construction sections, which include technical information about building systems. In contrast, design and presentation sections focus on form, finish materials, and the definition of interior space. For sections to work well in visual presentations, they must be clearly keyed, noted, or referenced to the appropriate floor plan. Generally, sections are referenced to the floor plan through the use of a symbol that denotes the locations of the vertical cut. Figure 1–14 is an example design section for the town house project.

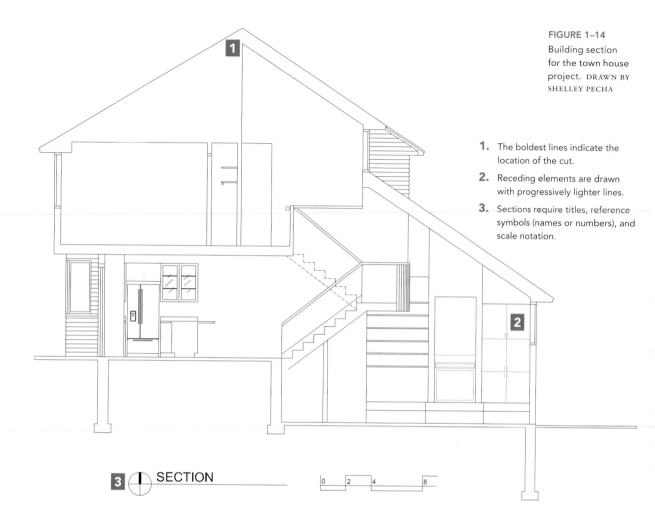

FIGURE 1–14
Building section
for the town house
project. DRAWN BY
SHELLEY PECHA

1. The boldest lines indicate the location of the cut.

2. Receding elements are drawn with progressively lighter lines.

3. Sections require titles, reference symbols (names or numbers), and scale notation.

SECTION

0   2   4   8

Reflected Ceiling Plans

Reflected ceiling plans are often used in conjunction with floor plans, elevations, and sections to communicate interior design. Reflected ceiling plans transmit important information about the design of the ceiling, such as materials; the layout and locations of light fixtures; items such as sprinklers, diffusers, and grilles; and ceiling heights. A reflected ceiling plan is drawn as though a giant mirror on the floor were reflecting the elements located on the ceiling. Using reflective imagery means the ceiling plan will have exactly the same orientation as the floor plan.

Ceiling plans used for presentation and those used for construction differ. Ceilings plans created for construction are typically highly technical and include a great deal of information. Reflected ceiling plans used in design presentations can be simplified to include basic ceiling lighting information, ceiling heights, and finish materials, as shown in Figure 1–15. Precisely measured, complex technical ceiling plans are required for construction (as illustrated at the end of this chapter).

FIGURE 1–15
Simple reflected ceiling plan for the town house project.
DRAWN BY SHELLEY PECHA

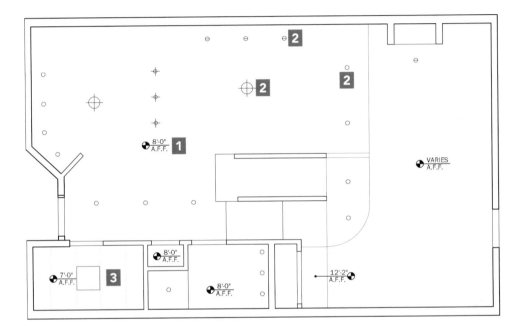

REFLECTED CEILING PLAN

1. Ceiling heights are noted and enclosed in a symbol.

2. Light fixture locations are noted using various symbols and are keyed to a legend.

3. Finish materials such as gypsum board, wood, and ceiling tiles are indicated in scale.

4. Reflected ceiling plans require titles, north arrows, and scale notation.

Reflected ceiling plans require legends (keyed to the symbols used); in this example, the legend has been omitted.

Together, floor plans, elevations, sections, and ceiling plans communicate information about the quality of an interior environment. Because these drawings are abstracted, fragmented versions of three-dimensional form, they depend on one another to communicate effectively.

The orthographic projections covered in this chapter relate directly to the communication and design of interior space. Differing versions of orthographic projections are used for construction and presentation, but they are used in one form or another on virtually all projects.

Additional types of orthographic drawing are used to communicate the features of buildings and building sites. Site plans, foundation plans, demolition plans, roof plans, framing plans, exterior elevations, wall sections, and design details are also used in the design of buildings. Designers of interior space must be knowledgeable about the nature of these drawings, how they are created, and how they relate to the interior architecture of a building.

Lettering

In the days before CAD, floor plans, elevations, and sections contained notes and dimensions written in a standardized style of hand lettering. Today, computer lettering and type can be generated by labeling machines and applied to hand-drawn orthographic projections, presentation boards. In addition, all of the commonly used CAD and modeling programs permit consistent, standardized type to be located appropriately on a drawing.

Although hand-lettering skills are not used to the extent that they were in the past, designers still create quick sketches, preliminary design details, and some presentation drawings by hand. For the sake of visual consistency, developing hand-lettering skills is crucial.

There are some basic rules for lettering design drawings, as well as some stylistic elements that influence letterform; these are outlined in Figure 1–16.

Dimensions

Dimensions, required on most construction drawings, are also sometimes needed on drawings used for presentation purposes. The decision to include them is based on the project and the presentation's audience. The following is a list of dimensioning conventions.

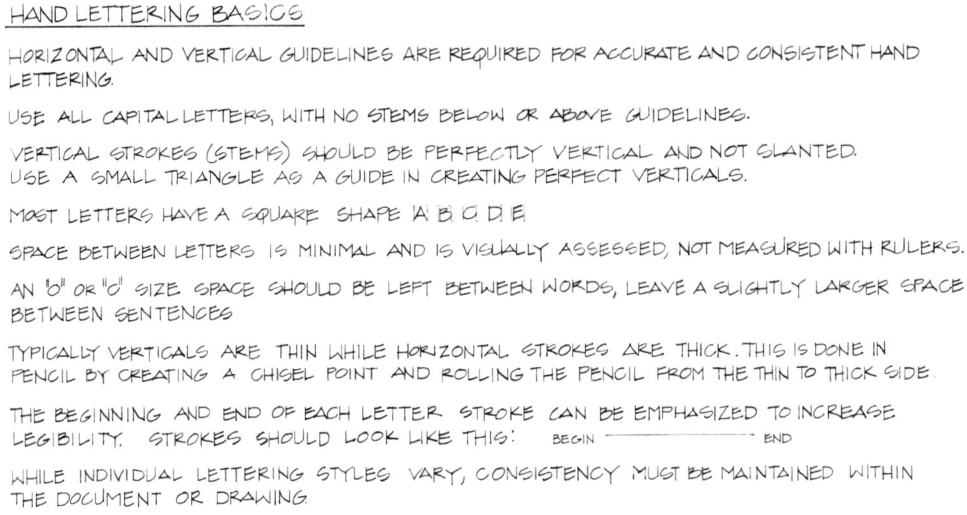

FIGURE 1–16

Hand-lettering
reference.

HAND LETTERING BASICS

HORIZONTAL AND VERTICAL GUIDELINES ARE REQUIRED FOR ACCURATE AND CONSISTENT HAND LETTERING.

USE ALL CAPITAL LETTERS, WITH NO STEMS BELOW OR ABOVE GUIDELINES.

VERTICAL STROKES (STEMS) SHOULD BE PERFECTLY VERTICAL AND NOT SLANTED. USE A SMALL TRIANGLE AS A GUIDE IN CREATING PERFECT VERTICALS.

MOST LETTERS HAVE A SQUARE SHAPE 'A' 'B' 'C' 'D' 'E'

SPACE BETWEEN LETTERS IS MINIMAL AND IS VISUALLY ASSESSED, NOT MEASURED WITH RULERS.

AN 'O' OR 'O' SIZE SPACE SHOULD BE LEFT BETWEEN WORDS, LEAVE A SLIGHTLY LARGER SPACE BETWEEN SENTENCES

TYPICALLY VERTICALS ARE THIN WHILE HORIZONTAL STROKES ARE THICK. THIS IS DONE IN PENCIL BY CREATING A CHISEL POINT AND ROLLING THE PENCIL FROM THE THIN TO THICK SIDE.

THE BEGINNING AND END OF EACH LETTER STROKE CAN BE EMPHASIZED TO INCREASE LEGIBILITY. STROKES SHOULD LOOK LIKE THIS: BEGIN ——————— END

WHILE INDIVIDUAL LETTERING STYLES VARY, CONSISTENCY MUST BE MAINTAINED WITHIN THE DOCUMENT OR DRAWING

Rules and Conventions for Creating Dimensioned Drawings

When included, dimensions must be accurate, complete, and readable, and are generally listed in feet *and* inches: write *2´-4˝*, for example, rather than *28˝*, except for dimensions of less than a foot, which can be written either *11˝* or *0´-11˝*. Dimensions should be located so that they are underlined by the dimension line; place them so that the reader does not have to rotate the sheet to read them. For standard construction, dimensions and dimension lines are located outside of the object (such as the building), as shown in Figure 1–17a. Specific dimensions are placed close to the particular object they are related to, while overall distances are placed in the position farthest from the construction, as shown in Figure 1–17a. Openings except for masonry openings (MO), such as windows and doors, are dimensioned to centerlines or to rough frame openings (RO). Dimension things once and only once; repetition from one drawing to another can lead to discrepancies. Dimensions typically run from the outside of exterior walls to the centerline of interior walls. Where interior tolerances are critical, dimensions can be run from the face of the finished wall to the face of the other finished wall ("paint to paint"), as shown in Figure 1–17b. This type of dimension can be employed for interior design projects created within existing architecture. When dimensioning walls for the interior renovation of an existing office or retail space, for example, it is common to dimension only the paint-to-paint dimensions rather than the exterior to centerline dimensions, as shown in Figure 1–17b.

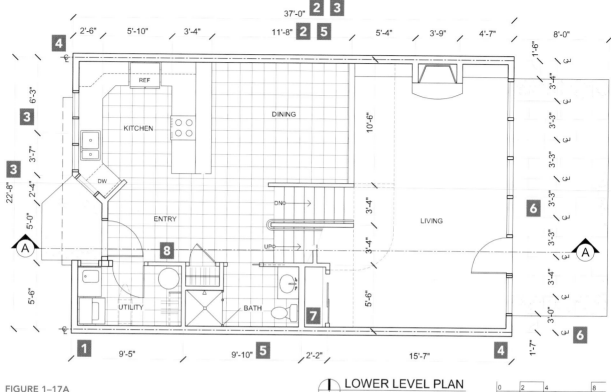

FIGURE 1–17A

A dimensioned lower-level floor plan for the town house project, employing standard conventions for locating interior and exterior dimensions outside the plan boundaries.

LOWER LEVEL PLAN

1. Dimension lines and leader lines should be lighter than wall lines or objects measured.

2. Horizontal written dimensions sit above the dimension lines, so they are underlined by the dimension line, as shown, or are written in a break in the dimension line.

3. Dimensions should be located so that the reader need not rotate the sheet or turn in upside down to read them.

4. Leader lines run from the building location being dimensioned to the dimension lines. Leader lines should not touch the building; instead, they should be drawn slightly away from it.

5. Dimensions are written in feet and inches unless they are less than a foot, in which case either inches alone or a notation of 0 feet and the number of inches may be used.

6. Dimensions measured from centerlines must be clearly indicated. Windows are commonly measured to centerlines or rough openings, as shown.

7. Exterior walls (and plumbing walls) are shown as nominal 6″ thick; their actual measurement is 6½″ to 7½″.

8. Interior walls are shown as nominal 4″ thick; their actual measurement is typically 4½″.

Additional examples of dimensioned drawings can be found in Figures 1–18b, 1–18d, 1–19b, and 1–19c.

FIGURE 1–17B

A portion of a dimensioned upper-level floor plan for the town house project delineating conventions for interior paint-to-paint (or finish-to-finish) dimensions. FIGURES 1–17A AND 1–17B: DESIGN BY COURTNEY NYSTUEN; DRAWN BY MELISSA BREWER AND SHELLEY PECHA

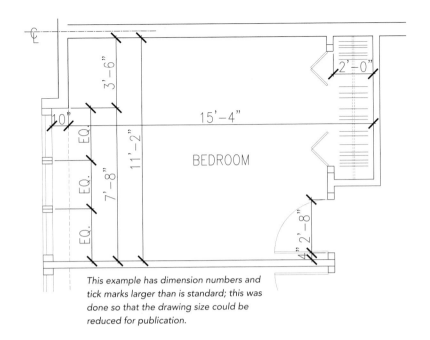

This example has dimension numbers and tick marks larger than is standard; this was done so that the drawing size could be reduced for publication.

FIGURE 1–18A

A floor plan for a professional restaurant design project. This is part of a set of construction documents. (Figures 17b through 17d are part of this set.)

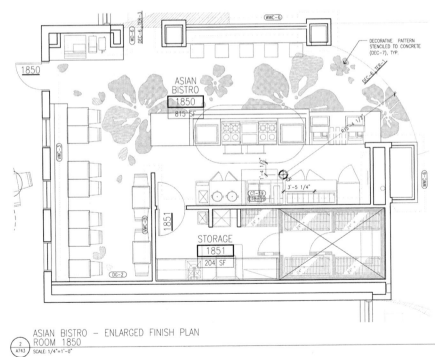

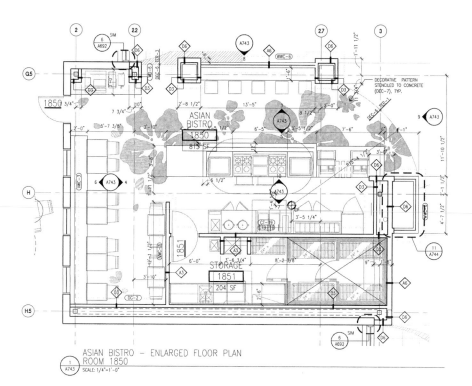

FIGURE 1–18B

A dimensioned floor plan for the project featured in the previous figure.

ASIAN BISTRO – ENLARGED FLOOR PLAN
ROOM 1850
SCALE: 1/4"=1'-0"

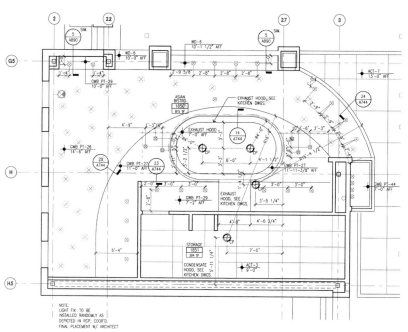

FIGURE 1–18C

A reflected ceiling plan for the project featured in the previous figure.

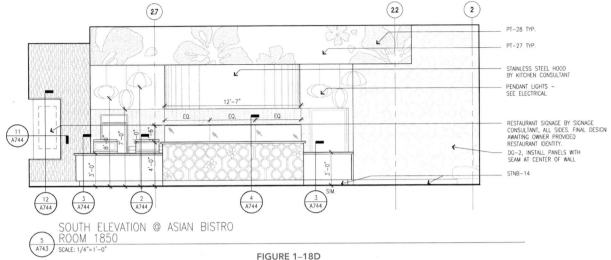

PT-28 TYP.

PT-27 TYP.

STAINLESS STEEL HOOD
BY KITCHEN CONSULTANT

PENDANT LIGHTS –
SEE ELECTRICAL

RESTAURANT SIGNAGE BY SIGNAGE
CONSULTANT, ALL SIDES. FINAL DESIGN
AWAITING OWNER PROVIDED
RESTAURANT IDENTITY.

DG-2, INSTALL PANELS WITH
SEAM AT CENTER OF WALL

STNB-14

SOUTH ELEVATION @ ASIAN BISTRO
ROOM 1850
SCALE: 1/4"=1'-0"

FIGURE 1–18D

Elevations for the project featured in the previous figure.
FIGURES 1–18A THROUGH 1–18D BY CUNINGHAM GROUP ARCHITECTURE, P.A.

FIGURE 1–19A

A floor plan for a professional restaurant design project. This is part of a set of construction documents. (Figures 19b and 19c are included in this set.)

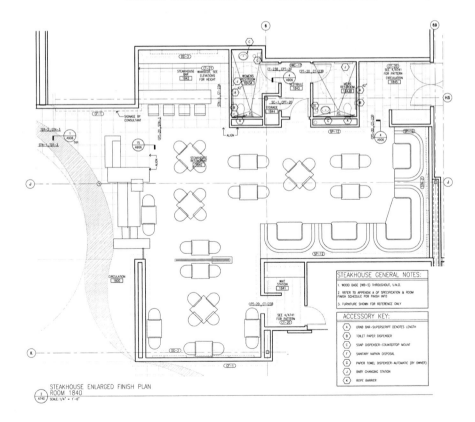

STEAKHOUSE GENERAL NOTES:

1. WOOD BASE (WB-5) THROUGHOUT, U.N.O.
2. REFER TO APPENDIX A OF SPECIFICATION & ROOM FINISH SCHEDULE FOR FINISH INFO
3. FURNITURE SHOWN FOR REFERENCE ONLY

ACCESSORY KEY:

Ⓐ GRAB BAR-SUPERSCRIPT DENOTES LENGTH
Ⓑ TOILET PAPER DISPENSER
Ⓒ SOAP DISPENSER-COUNTERTOP MOUNT
Ⓕ SANITARY NAPKIN DISPOSAL
Ⓖ PAPER TOWEL DISPENSER-AUTOMATIC (BY OWNER)
Ⓙ BABY CHANGING STATION
Ⓚ ROPE BARRIER

STEAKHOUSE ENLARGED FINISH PLAN
ROOM 1840
SCALE: 1/4" = 1'-0"

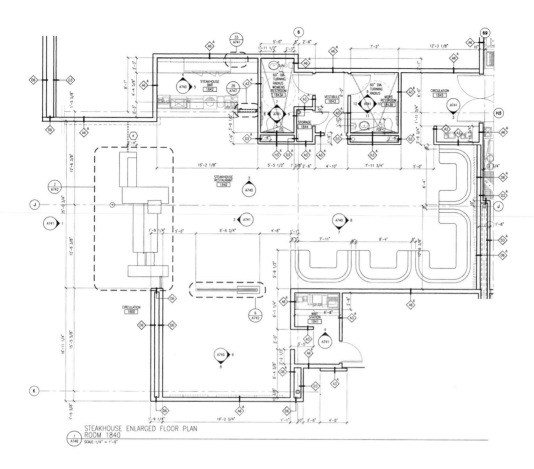

FIGURE 1–19B

A dimensioned floor plan for the project featured in the previous figure.

STEAKHOUSE ENLARGED FLOOR PLAN
ROOM 1840
SCALE: 1/4" = 1'-0"

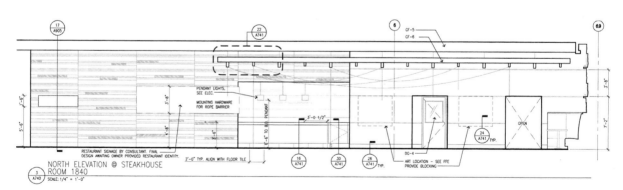

NORTH ELEVATION @ STEAKHOUSE
ROOM 1840
SCALE: 1/4" = 1'-0"

FIGURE 1–19C

Elevations for the project featured in the previous figure.

FIGURES 1–19A THROUGH 1–19C BY CUNINGHAM GROUP ARCHITECTURE, P.A.

Ongoing Software Advances

Until very recently, Autodesk's AutoCAD was the most widely used CAD program in commercial interior design and architectural firms in the United States. AutoCAD is a vector-based graphics drawing program in which primitive elements such as lines, polylines, arcs, and text serve as the foundation for more complex objects. Current versions of AutoCAD allow for two- and three-dimensional design and drafting and can serve as a basis for industry-specific products such as Autodesk Architecture. AutoCAD LT is a scaled-down, less costly version of AutoCAD that does not include full three-dimensional drawing capabilities, certain presentation graphics, sheet-set management, or certain other elements.

Autodesk Revit Building is quickly becoming industry standard software for commercial interior design and general architectural practice. Revit is building information modeling (BIM) software that allows for parametric modeling and drafting. An advantage of BIM software is its ability to create coordinated, consistent, computable information about a building project. With BIM, changes made in one view are automatically integrated into related drawings and schedules—in contrast to AutoCAD, which requires that drawings be cross-referenced for this to occur.

Another advantage to using Revit and similar software is that buildings are modeled as three-dimensional entities; once an accurate model is generated, it is relatively simple to create plans, sections, and elevations, as well as wonderful three-dimensional (perspective) views. In addition, in Revit, rendering occurs as an integrated element within the model (as discussed in Chapter 7).

Other types of CAD software used by design firms throughout the world include MicroStation (developed by Bentley), which generates two- and three-dimensional vector graphic objects and elements. ArchiCAD (developed by Graphisoft) is BIM software used in architectural, facilities management, and interior design practices and employs "smart," data-enhanced parametric objects; these, in turn, generate the basic structure and elements that come together to create the building.

Designers and sales professionals specializing in kitchen and bath design, as well as those involved in residential design and furniture sales, use a program called 20–20 Design. This software facilitates two-dimensional drawing and planning as well as the generation of three-dimensional views that can be used for client presentations and that can incorporate manufacturers' product information into drawings.

There are a number of software programs used specifically for three-dimensional modeling and rendering. Google's SketchUp is commonly used in interior design; it is covered in detail in chapter 5.

Although the software and hardware used in design and design presentations continues to evolve, the conceptual basis for orthographic drawings and drafting conventions is the same whether they are created by hand or through the use of digital tools. Similarly, the meaning communicated by a floor plan is the same whether the drawing is created by hand or with the use of any of the range of CAD programs available. Therefore, this book covers the concepts behind the drawings rather than supplying detailed information about the software used to create them.

REFERENCES

Ching, Frank. *Architectural Graphics, 5th ed.* Hoboken, NJ: John Wiley & Sons, 2009.

———. *A Visual Dictionary of Architecture.* New York: John Wiley & Sons, 1995.

Forseth, Kevin, and David Vaughn. *Graphics for Architecture.* New York: John Wiley & Sons, 1998.

Kirkpatrick, Beverly, and James Kirkpatrick. *AutoCAD for Interior Design and Space Planning Using AutoCAD 2005.* Upper Saddle River, NJ: Prentice Hall, 2005.

Kilmer, Otie, Rosemary Kilmer, and Stephen Hanessian. *Construction Drawings and Details for Interiors: Basic Skills.* Hoboken, NJ: John Wiley & Sons, 2001. A good introduction to drafting concepts and to drawings for construction documents.

Liebling, Ralph. *Architectural Working Drawings.* 4th ed. Hoboken, NJ: John Wiley & Sons, 1999. Contains some valuable information about drafting and drawings for construction documents.

Porter, Tom. *Architectural Drawing.* New York: Van Nostrand Reinhold, 1990.

Smith, C. Ray. *Interior Design in 20th-Century America: A History.* New York: Harper & Row, 1987.

U.S. Metric Association (USMA). FAQ: Frequently Asked Questions about the Metric System. *http://lamar.colostate.edu/~hillger/faq.html.*

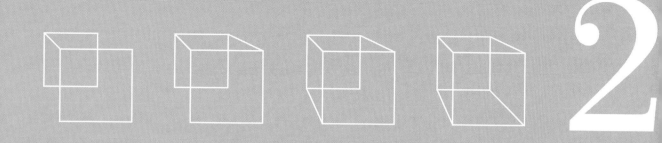

The Design Process and Related Graphics

Because the reasons for communication may change as a project advances, design communication and the design process are inextricably linked. Having a thorough understanding of the process of design means the appropriate form of communication can be successfully employed at the appropriate time. To that end, this chapter covers the design process and related design communication methods.

The design process is complex, and designers must communicate different aspects (and potential outcomes) of the process to clients and consultants at various points along the way. Like professionals, students must present in-process projects to team members, instructors, and guest critics. Visual presentations must vary to accommodate the process of design and to communicate both process and outcome.

In *Interior Design Illustrated* (2004), Francis Ching identifies three basic stages of design process.

Analysis involves defining and understanding the problem.

Synthesis involves the formulation of possible solutions.

Evaluation involves a critical review of the strengths and weaknesses of the proposed solutions.

These three basic stages of the design process are used by design practitioners in a variety of disciplines. *Industrial designers, graphic designers, exhibition designers*, and others often engage in a similar process. But the actual interior design process and project phases are distinct, and they are more elaborate than these three basic stages may indicate.

For the purpose of contractual organization, the process of design engaged in by architects and interior designers in the United States has been divided into basic project phases, spelled out here in a list derived from the American Institute of Architects (AIA) Owner-Architect Agreement for Interior Design Services and the American Society of Interior Designers (ASID) Interior Design Services Agreement.

Interior Design Project Phases

Programming

Schematic design

Design development

Construction documentation

Bidding or negotiation

Contract administration

Table 2–1 identifies generally accepted project phases and visual presentation methods.

William Peña, Steven Parshall, and Kevin Kelly, writing in *Problem Seeking* (1987), conclude that the actual design process takes place in the first three project phases. They state that "programming is part of the total design process but is separate from schematic design." The authors classify schematic design and design development as the second and third phases of the total design process, respectively. This chapter is an exploration of the three phases of the design process identified by Peña, Parshall, Kelly, and others, and a study of the drawings and graphics used to communicate, document, inform, and clarify the work done during these phases.

PROJECT PHASE	TYPICAL TASKS AND ACTIVITIES	TYPICAL MEANS OF VISUAL PRESENTATION
Programming, also known as pre-design	In-depth analysis and documentation of needs, requirements, goals, and objectives. Can include identification of space and adjacency requirements analysis; asset assessment; specialized needs assessments; codes and accessibility research; identification of conceptual and thematic issues, as well as analysis of architectural or site parameters and analysis of scheduling and budget.	Most often written information compiled in a programming report. Often includes problem identification, diagrams, charts, and matrices, and may include some orthographic drawings and early fit studies. May also include preliminary scheduling graphics.
Schematic design, also known as the preliminary design phase	Preliminary conceptual, spatial, and technical design of project. Includes preliminary space planning, often using relationship diagrams matrices, bubble diagrams, blocking diagrams, stacking and fit plans, as well as initial furnishings, fixtures, and equipment design and layout. Development of project's conceptual and thematic issues. Color, material, and finish studies. Preliminary code review. Preliminary budgetary information.	Graphic presentation of preliminary design. Can include relationship diagrams, blocking and fit plans, preliminary space plan(s), preliminary furnishing and equipment layouts, preliminary elevations and sections, preliminary 3-D drawings, preliminary color and materials studies, and study models. Presentation may also include graphic presentation of conceptual and thematic issues using sketches, diagrams, and mixed media.
Design development	Refinement of finalized design. Includes space plan and design of interior construction elements and details. Often involves incorporation of lighting, electrical, plumbing, and mechanical systems design, as well as data and telecommunication systems integration. Often includes millwork design and detailing. Also includes color, materials, and finish selection. Design and specification of furnishings, fixtures, and equipment, as well as refinement of budgetary and scheduling information.	Finalized, refined design presentation incorporating all necessary components of design. Graphic presentation of finalized design can include conceptual diagrams; space plan(s); and plan(s) for furnishings, fixtures, and equipment, as well as elevations, sections, and ceiling plans; 3-D drawings; colors, materials, and finish samples; scale models; and mock-ups. Multimedia presentations can incorporate all of these elements plus sound and animation.

TABLE 2–1

Project Phases and Related Visual Presentation Methods

PROJECT PHASE	TYPICAL TASKS AND ACTIVITIES	TYPICAL MEANS OF VISUAL PRESENTATION
Construction documentation	Preparation of drafted, working drawings and/or contract documents. Includes preparation of drawings, schedules, details, and specifications, as well as coordination and integration of consultant's documents. Can include preparation of specialized equipment and furnishings documents for bidding by purchasing agents. May include purchasing documents.	Preparation of contract documents. Often includes submission to general contractor(s) and purchasing agents for bid and to appropriate agencies for plan check.
Bidding or negotiation	Assist in review of bidding.	Limited visual presentation/design communication for this phase.
Contract administration	Guide and review construction and installation. Can include periodic site visits and creation of progress reports. Coordination and review of shop drawings and sample submittals. May include clarification and interpretation of drawings, as well as review of billing and payment. Preparation of punch list. May include move coordination and supervision of furnishings, fixtures, and equipment installation.	Primarily written and verbal communication with contractors, agencies, and clients. May include scheduling, budgetary, and administrative graphics.

Adapted from the AIA Owner-Architect Agreement for Interior Design Services and the ASID Interior Design Services Agreement.

Programming

The experienced, creative designer withholds judgment, resists preconceived solutions and the pressure to synthesize until all the information is in. He refuses to make sketches until he knows the client's problem…. Programming is the prelude to good design.

—William Peña, Steven Parshall, and Kevin Kelly in *Problem Seeking* (1987)

Programming, also known as pre-design or strategic planning, involves a detailed analysis of the client's (or end user's) needs, requirements, goals, budget, and assets, as well as an analysis of any architectural or site parameters and constraints. Information gathered about the user's needs and requirements is often documented in written form, whereas architectural or site parameters are often communicated graphically through orthographic projection. These two distinct forms of communication, verbal and graphic, must be brought together in the early stages of design.

Some firms employ professionals to work as programmers and then hand the project over to designers. It is also common for project managers and designers to work on project programming and then continue to work on the design or management of the project. Programmers and designers could be seen as separate specialists, given the distinctions between programming (analysis) and design (synthesis). However, many firms and designers choose not to separate these specialties or do so only on very large or programming-intensive projects.

In practice, programming varies greatly depending on the type and size of the project and on the quantity and quality of the information supplied by the client (or end user). In some cases, clients provide designers with highly detailed written programs. In others, clients begin with little more than general information or simply exclaim, "We need more space because we are growing very fast," or even, "Help! We are out of control." In situations such as the latter, research and detective work must go into creating programming information that will allow for the development of successful design solutions.

It is difficult to distill or summarize the programming process. Clearly, the programming required for a major metropolitan public library is very different from that needed in a small-scale residential renovation. Instead, let's consider what programming requirements all projects relating to interior environments share.

All projects require a careful analysis of space requirements for current and future needs, as well as an analysis of work processes, adjacency requirements, and organizational structure (or lifestyle and needs-assessment factors in residential design). Physical inventories and asset assessments are needed to evaluate existing furniture and equipment as well as to plan for future needs. Building code, accessibility, and health and safety factors must also be researched as part of the programming process.

In addition to this primarily quantitative information, there are aesthetic requirements. Designers must also identify the project's cultural and sociological aspects. All of these should be researched and can be documented in a programming report that is reviewed by the client and used by the project design team. When possible, a problem statement—a concise identification of key issues, limitations, objectives, and goals that provides a clearer understanding of the project—should be included with the programming report. With the programming report complete, designers can begin the job of synthesis and continue the design process.

Diagrams and Programming Analysis Graphics

Before continuing a discussion of programming, a description of the use and importance of diagrams and visual notes—especially in the preliminary phases of design—is necessary. In *Visual Notes for Architects and Designers* (1995), Norman Crowe and Paul Laseau have defined a diagram as

> …a simple, rapid method for representing the underlying structure or relationships in either a physical setting, physical design or in the process by which something operates. Diagrams help make sense out of a complex whole.…

Diagrams can be considered "graphic thinking" (Paul Laseau, *Graphic Thinking for Architects and Designers*, 2001) and can distill written project information graphically in ways that are useful to the designer or design team. Many diagrams serve as a sort of visual brainstorming session, allowing visual information to be recorded quickly during design ideation and sorted through later. Put another way, diagrams are a useful way to get ideas outside of our heads and onto paper so they can be refined—and used—down the line.

Many of the types of diagrams designers use can serve as a bridge between information uncovered in the programming phase of a project and the creation of ideas generated in the schematic or preliminary design phase. Most diagrams employ symbols that serve as abstract representations of information or ideas. In architecture and interior design, these most commonly include the representation of relationships, adjacencies, size and area, and context (see Figures 2–1 through 2–3). In some cases, early diagrams are abstractions of preliminary plans.

More examples of diagrams and preliminary design graphics can be found at the end of this chapter.

In addition to using them for idea generation, clients, consultants, and designers may also utilize diagrams and graphic analysis as a way to understand and gain insight into programming data and information. Some tips for creating successful presentation diagrams are illustrated in Figures 2–4 and 2–5. Diagrams, charts, matrices, and visual imagery are easier to comprehend than pages of written documentation; it is helpful to develop ways of sorting and simplifying programming information so that it can be easily assimilated.

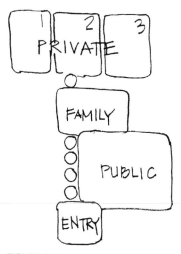

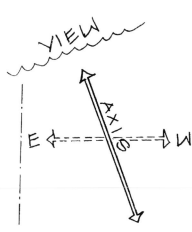

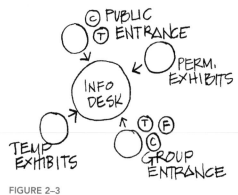

FIGURE 2–1

A diagram showing the relationships between the various spaces in a dwelling.

FIGURE 2–2

A diagram showing the possible relationships within a building site.

FIGURE 2–3

A diagram showing the relationships between entrances, exhibition spaces, and an information desk for use in presentations and for ideation.

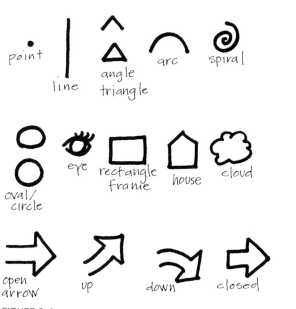

FIGURE 2–4

These are some basic shapes typically used—in combination—in diagrams. Arrows or horizontal and vertical lines are often used to link these shapes.

FIGURE 2–5

These are some common types of diagrams used for conveying information and relationships, and for ideation. They are employed in addition to bubble diagrams, blocking diagrams, and others shown throughout this chapter.

Many designers obtain early programming data and incorporate it into graphic worksheets. Using a flip-chart pad, brown kraft paper, or other heavy paper, programmers can generate large, easy-to-read graphic documents that can be understood easily by the client, who is then able to comment on or approve them. Even the eventual project designers often find such sheets useful for project documentation.

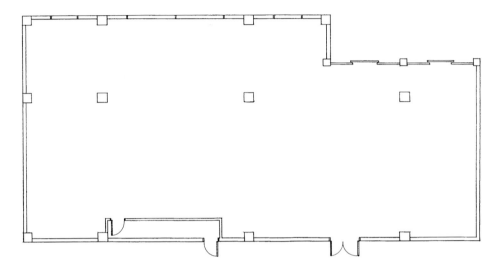

The book *Problem Seeking* provides an additional technique for recording information generated in the early stages of programming graphically: the use of analysis cards, which facilitate comprehension, discussion, clarification, and feedback. The cards are drawn from interview notes and early programming data. Based on the premise that visual information is more easily comprehended than verbal information, the cards contain simple graphic imagery with few words and concise messages.

Residential projects generally require less intensive programming graphics. Programming is a significant element of the residential design process; however, the relationships, adjacencies, and organization of the space are often simpler than in large commercial and public spaces. The following discussion therefore focuses primarily on commercial design, where a significant amount of visual communication of programming information is often required.

A sample project is used to illustrate some of the design process concepts covered in this chapter. Table 2–2 contains programming information for the sample project. Figure 2–6 is a floor plan for the sample project, and Figure 2–7 illustrates some program-based diagrams for the project.

ECO
TOYS Programming Information

TABLE 2–2

Programming
Information for the
Sample Project

Company History:
Eco Toys is a young, dynamic company. Larry Leader, the company president started the company in 1985. The company designs and produces toys for preschoolers, using recycled plastic products. Eco Toys has enjoyed tremendous success and growth in the last five years. Owing to recent growth, the company must move to larger, better organized design and marketing offices.

Company Structure and Organization:
The president is at the center of all company operations and constantly interacts with all members of his staff. Mr. Leader depends a great deal on his assistant Steve Stable. Although Mr. Leader is in touch with all levels of operation, he has set up the company in a horizontal organizational structure. This means that all members of the Eco Toys staff have equal status and power and are seen as important contributors to the organization. The design of the space should reflect the organizational structure of the company.

General Requirements:
Because of the non hierarchical organizational structure, all workstations must be exactly the same size. As a means of encouraging team meetings and sharing within departments small (8' x 8') individual workstations have been requested. As a result of complicated egress conditions, the existing door locations must be retained.

Department Information and Requirements:

Entry/Reception: Very public, must visually represent company's mission. Requires reception desk with work surface and transaction counter, task seating. Guest seating for 6. Must allow space for movement of children into toy test center. Must be near conference room, toy test center and close to marketing dept.
Conference Room: Very public and attractive, seating for 10 at tables with additional seating available. Requires multimedia center. View if possible. Immediately adjacent to toy test center (with visual connection), close to reception, and near marketing dept.
Toy Testing Center: Open and flexible space for use by 4 - 6 preschool age children. Must be visually connected to conference room and adjacent to entry and conference room.
Design Dept.: 2 designers and 2 assistants. All individual work spaces must accommodate CADD station, plus layout space, 2 file drawers, and handy reference storage. Adjacent to model shop; a messy, noisy, enclosed space -120 sq. ft. min. Adjacent to engineering dept. Nearby team meeting space with casual seating for 4, room for plotter, display area, and filing.
Marketing Dept.: 2 marketing managers and 1 assistant. All individual work spaces must accommodate a P.C., 2 file drawers, and handy reference storage. Must have adjacent team space with table and seating for 5. Must be near conference room, toy test and reception area.
Engineering Dept.: 2 engineers. All individual work spaces must accommodate CADD station, and lay-out space, two file drawers, and handy reference storage. Must be adjacent to design dept. and near design team space.
Accounting Dept.: 2 accountants. Individual work spaces must accommodate a P.C. and printer, 2 file drawers, and handy reference storage. Requires some privacy and no major interaction with other departments, with the exception of the President.
President: Pres. plus assistant (2 total); must accommodate P.C. and printer, 2 file drawers, and handy reference storage. President to have small conference table (to seat 4). Near all depts. and break room.
Break Room: Generous counter space, base and wall cabinets, sink, refrig., microwave, and commercial coffee makers. Seating for 8 minimum.
Copy/Mail: Room for copy machine and adjacent 5 lineal ft. of collating space, room for 16 mailboxes, paper, and supply storage. Convenient to corridor.
Storage: Generous heavy-duty shelving. Must be enclosed and private, requires shelving and ventilation for Local Area Computer Network.

FIGURES 2–7A and 2–7B

Examples of preliminary diagrams for the sample project.

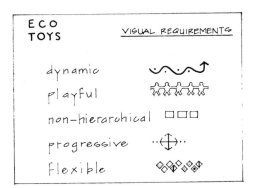

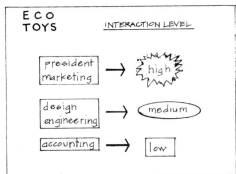

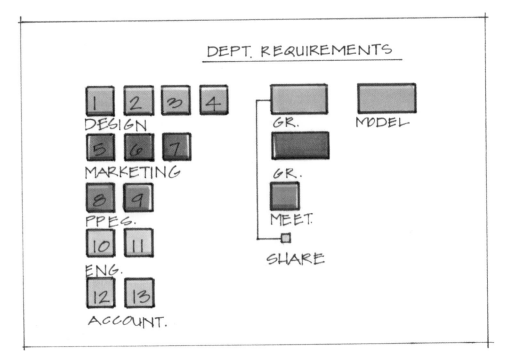

Programming Matrices

Matrices are another useful programming tool; they incorporate a wealth of information into an easily understood visual aid. An *adjacency matrix* is commonly used as a means of visually documenting spatial proximity, identifying related activities and services, and establishing priorities. The complexity of adjacency matrices varies in relation to project requirements. Large-scale, complicated projects often require highly detailed adjacency matrices. Figures 2–8 and 2–9 illustrate two types of adjacency matrices.

A *criteria matrix* can distill project issues such as needs for privacy, natural light, and security into a concise, consistent format. Large-scale, complex design projects may necessitate numerous detailed, complex matrices, whereas smaller, less complex projects may only need simple ones. Criteria matrices are used in residential design projects and in the programming of public spaces. In smaller projects. criteria matrices can be combined with adjacency matrices. Figure 2–10 illustrates a criteria matrix that includes adjacency information. Special types of matrices are used by designers on particular projects. A blank version of the criteria matrix illustrated here can be found in appendix 2.

ECO TOYS

1	RECEPTION											
2	CONFERENCE											
3	TOY TEST											
4	PRESIDENT											
5	DESIGN											
6	MARKETING											
7	ENGINEERING											
8	ACCOUNTING											
9	MODEL SHOP											
10	BREAK ROOM											
11	COPY/MAIL											
12	STORAGE											

LEGEND
- ▲ Major Adjacency
- ◣ Minor Adjacency
- ◇ Not Related

FIGURE 2–8

Simple adjacency matrix for the sample project. BY MELISSA BREWER

ECO TOYS

	RECEPTION	CONFERENCE	TOY TEST	PRESIDENT	DESIGN	MARKETING	ENGINEERING	ACCOUNTING	MODEL SHOP	BREAK ROOM	COPY/MAIL	STORAGE
RECEPTION	·	●	●	○	○	◑	○	○	X	○	○	○
CONFERENCE	●	·	●	○	○	◑	○	○	X	○	○	○
TOY TEST	●	●	·	○	○	◑	○	○	X	○	○	○
PRESIDENT	○	○	○	·	◑	◑	◑	◑	○	◑	○	○
DESIGN	○	○	○	◑	·	○	◑	○	●	○	○	○
MARKETING	◑	◑	◑	◑	○	·	○	○	○	○	○	○
ENGINEERING	○	○	○	◑	◑	○	·	○	○	○	○	○
ACCOUNTING	○	○	○	◑	○	○	○	·	○	○	○	○
MODEL SHOP	X	X	X	○	●	○	○	○	·	○	○	○
BREAK ROOM	○	○	○	◑	○	○	○	○	○	·	○	○
COPY/MAIL	○	○	○	○	○	○	○	○	○	○	·	○
STORAGE	○	○	○	○	○	○	○	○	○	○	○	·

LEGEND
- ● Major Adjacency
- ◑ Minor Adjacency
- ○ Not Closely Related
- X Undesirable

FIGURE 2–9

Another type of adjacency matrix for the sample project. BY MELISSA BREWER

FIGURE 2–10

A combination
criteria and adja-
cency matrix, which
was computer gener-
ated. Appendix 2
includes a blank
version of this matrix
for student use. BY
LEANNE LARSON

	ECO TOYS	Adjacencies	# of Dept Members	Seating Req's	Public Access	Privacy	Plumbing	Data/Phone	Special Req's	Comments
1	Reception	② ③ 6	1	6 min	●			●	Y	Visually rep mission; used by adults & children; "dynamic & playful"
2	Conference	① ③ 6		10+	●			●	Y	"Dynamic & playful"; multimedia center; multiple lap-top /computers
3	Toy Test	① ②		4-6	●			○	Y	Used by preschoolers; open, flexible, playful
4	President	5 6 7 8 10	2	4				●	Y	PC, printer, 2 file drawers, ref storage for each 8' x 8' work space
5	Design	⑨ ⑦	4	4 min				●	Y	CADD, lay-out, 2 file drawers, ref storage for each 8' x 8' work space
6	Marketing	① ② 3	3	5 min				●	Y	PC, printer, 2 file drawers, ref storage for each 8' x 8' work space
7	Engineering	⑤	2					●	Y	CADD, lay-out, 2 file drawers, ref storage for each 8' x 8' work space
8	Accounting	4	2			●		●	Y	PC, printer, 2 file drawers, ref storage for each 8' x 8' work space
9	Model Shop	⑤				○	●	○	Y	Messy & noisy; enclosed
10	Break Room	4		8 min			●	○	Y	Relaxing & inviting; gen counters; refrig, microwave, sink, coffee makers req
11	Copy/Mail							○	Y	5 lineal feet collating space; 16 mailboxes; storage
12	Storage					●			Y	Generous heavy-duty shelving; ventilation

Legend

①	Major Adjacency	○	Secondary Requirement
1	Minor Adjacency	Y	Yes, See Comments
●	Mandatory Requirement	X	Undesirable

Programming graphics, such as project worksheets, diagrams, and a variety of
matrices, are widely used in interior design practice. These are presented to the client or

end user for comment, clarification, and approval. Many of these graphics are refined, corrected, and improved upon during the programming process and are eventually included in the final programming report.

Schematic Design

With the programming phase completed and the problem clearly stated, designers can begin the work of synthesis and problem solving can begin. The creation of relationship diagrams is the first step in the schematic (or preliminary) design of a project. Relationship diagrams allow designers to digest and internalize the programming information. They also permit designers to begin to use graphics in order to better understand the physical qualities of the project.

One such diagram explores the relationship of functional areas to one another and uses information completed on the criteria and adjacency matrices. This type of one-step diagram may be adequate for smaller commercial and residential projects; larger-scale, complex projects often require a series of relationship diagrams. Diagrams of this type do not generally relate to architectural or site parameters and are not drawn to scale. Most specialized or complex projects need additional diagrams that examine issues such as personal interaction, flexibility, and privacy requirements.

Bubble Diagrams

As relationship diagrams begin to incorporate and account for requirements and adjacencies, they can become refined into *bubble diagrams*, which take the project one step further in the schematic design process. Bubble diagrams often approximate the actual architectural parameters (or building space) in rough scale. They may also incorporate elements identified in criteria and adjacency matrices through the use of graphic devices keyed to a legend. Figures 2–11a through 2–11c are a sequence of bubble diagrams for the sample project.

A primary purpose of these early schematic diagrams is to generate a number of options. Brainstorming many ideas is highly advisable. Designers with years of experience use brainstorming techniques, as should students of design. Successful design requires sparks of creativity in every project phase, and such sparks are fostered by nurturing idea generation. Rarely does the first try (or even the first several) beget a masterpiece or even a workable solution. It is often the combination of several diverse schemes that eventually generates a good solution.

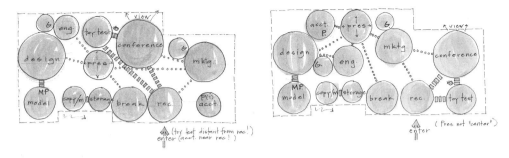

FIGURE 2–11C
Final, successful
bubble diagram for
the sample project.

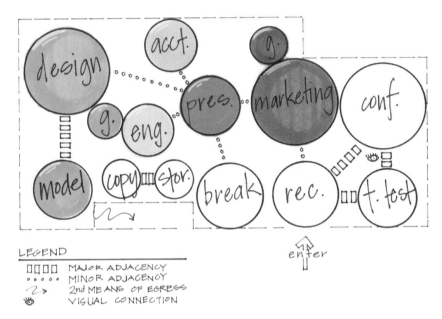

LEGEND

⯀⯀⯀⯀	MAJOR ADJACENCY
∘∘∘∘∘	MINOR ADJACENCY
↝	2nd MEANS OF EGRESS
👁	VISUAL CONNECTION

Blocking Diagrams

Bubble diagrams are part of a continuous process of refinement. One diagram may have useful components that can be combined with elements of another. As this process of refinement continues, designers often proceed to *blocking diagrams.*

Before design students move to blocking diagrams, they benefit from the creation of *space studies*, also known as *area prototype sketches*. Each area or function—including furniture and equipment—is sketched in scale. These sketches can then be used to roughly identify spatial use in the blocking diagram. Space study sketches are also helpful in the design of systems furniture, allowing students to explore possibilities and gain insight into the use of these products. (See Figures 2–12a through 2–12c for examples of space studies.)

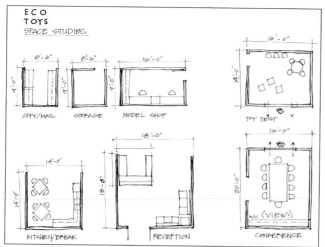

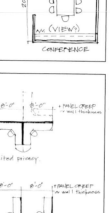

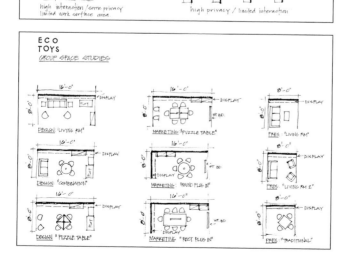

FIGURES 2–12A
through 2–12C
Space studies for
the sample project.
These individual
spaces can be used
as individual "blocks"
when creating block-
ing plans.

The Design Process and Related Graphics

Blocking diagrams can be generated on tracing paper taped over a scaled, drafted floor plan of the existing or proposed building. In rare cases, projects do not involve the use of existing architectural parameters because the interior space will dictate the final building form. In such cases, bubble diagrams and blocking plans are sometimes the genesis for the eventual building plan. It is increasingly common for designers to use CAD software to begin the blocking plan process and then continue to use it throughout the rest of the design process. Some designers find that space planning on CAD is frustrating and therefore plot out a CAD drawing and draw by hand on tracing paper placed over the CAD plot.

Blocking diagrams are usually drawn to scale and relate directly to the architectural parameters or the existing building plan. Blocking plans are generally drawn with each area or function represented by a block of the appropriate square footage; circulation areas are often blocked in as rectilinear corridors. Figures 2–13a and 2–13b are blocking diagrams. Additional blocking diagrams can be found in Figures 2-18b, 2-20a, and 2-20b.

Some experienced designers move quickly to blocking diagrams, foregoing the use of bubble diagrams, whereas others dislike the blocky, confining nature of blocking diagrams. Many designers develop a personal system of schematic diagrams that combines bubble and blocking diagrams. Although the approach and graphic quality of schematic diagrams used by individual designers vary greatly, the underlying purpose is consistent: designers use these diagrams to move from verbal and simplified graphic notation toward true scale and the eventual realization of architectural form.

Fit and Stacking Plans

A *fit plan* can be considered a further refinement of the blocking diagram. The fit plan is basically a test to determine whether the requirements and needs clarified in programming fit into a given space. In some cases, fit plans are drawn up when a client reviews a piece of real estate or a potential site. In others, fit plans are drawn up to indicate the way a proposed office tower may eventually be laid out. These types of fit plans are generated for both real estate professionals and end users.

In still other situations, the fit plan is part of the final stage of the space-planning process. For this reason, fit plans often contain to-scale drawings of furniture and equipment as a means of testing the space plan for fit and for client review.

A *stacking plan* is used when a project occupies more than one floor of a building; it examines the interrelationships of departments or work group locations. Stacking plans are generally created early in the design process as a means of evaluating the use of each floor before refined space planning is begun.

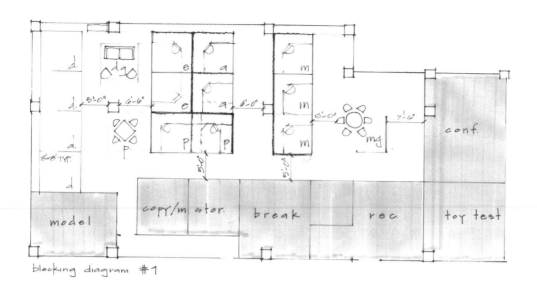

blocking diagram #1

FIGURES 2–13A
and 2–13B
Blocking diagrams
for the sample proj-
ect. Note that these
blocking diagrams
focus on the layout
of individual work
spaces, as the other
spaces are fixed.

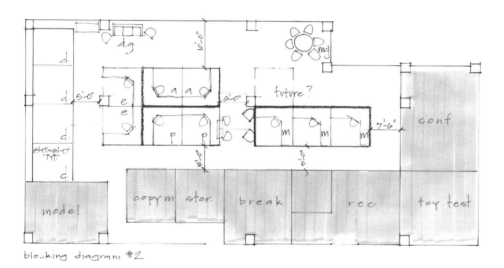

blocking diagram #2

Conceptual Design

The schematic design phase is when designers explore symbolic representation for the conceptual foundation of a project. Although relationship, bubble, and blocking diagrams represent functional and spatial requirements, they may do little to illuminate a project's conceptual nature. It is therefore useful to employ an abstract diagram or graphic device to represent the conceptual qualities of a project.

One means of illustrating conceptual project themes is the *design parti*. Francis Ching, in *A Visual Dictionary of Architecture* (1995), defines a parti as "the basic scheme or concept for an architectural design represented by a diagram." A design parti can take a wide range of forms, from a highly simplified graphic symbol to a more complex plan diagram. Some designers use a conceptual diagram such as a parti as an aid in bringing together the functional and conceptual components of a design. The parti, or another conceptual diagram, can be used throughout the design process as a conceptual anchor for the project. Designers sometimes employ the parti extensively, and it may become the foundation for the design and appear as a logo or project icon on all presentation graphics.

A formal design parti is not sought for all design projects. Most projects do, however, include a considerable number of thematic issues. Views, geography, climate, building context and site, functional requirements, and cultural issues may contribute to the project on a conceptual level. The existing building form often dictates project constraints in the design of interior environments. Most designers therefore articulate and explore conceptual and thematic issues early in the schematic phase of a project. Some designers find it useful to create three-dimensional conceptual studies in the form of models (see chapter 6). In professional practice, the methods of presentation of conceptual components of a project are varied and highly personal, and involve both verbal and graphic notations.

Space planning and conceptual development are discussed separately here. In design practice, however, these elements are brought together in the early stages of project design. Bubble diagrams often incorporate conceptual elements, and a design parti can serve as an organizational anchor in the space-planning process. The schematic or conceptual design phases are a continuous process of refinement whereby all elements are brought together. Figures 2–14a and 2–14b are conceptual sketches that might be generated during the drawing of blocking diagrams.

As the project evolves and blocking diagrams make way for a schematic space plan, it is helpful to consider the totality of the design through the use of *preliminary elevations*. Much like early perspective studies, preliminary elevations facilitate a more complete understanding of a space's total volume. Preliminary elevations can be used as a means of ideation or idea generation; it is therefore useful to undertake more than one approach to the elevations. Two such preliminary elevations of varying approaches for the design shown in the blocking diagram in Figures 2–14a and 2–14b are found in Figure 2–15.

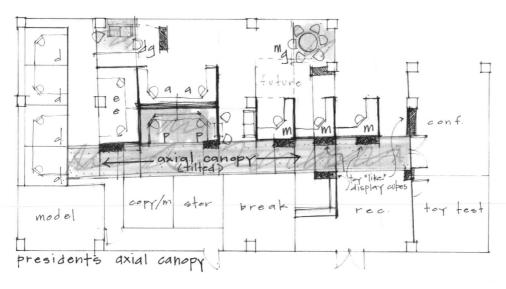

FIGURES 2–14A
AND 2–14B
Conceptual block-
ing diagrams for
the sample project.
Typically, the parti
is used to develop
the space plan from
its earliest inception
forward—from early
bubble and blocking
diagrams to the final
space plan. In this
example, however,
the parti is used
more as an overlay.

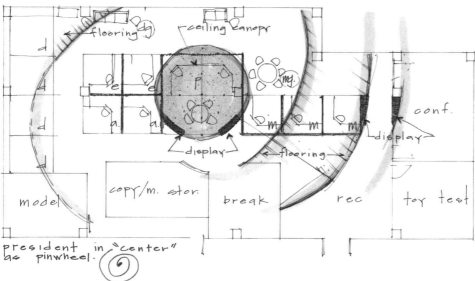

Mood and Inspiration Boards

In developing an aesthetic or conceptual direction for a project, some designers create *mood boards* or inspirational boards. These boards perform a function similar to visual notation; they are another form of visual language that can help set the visual direction of the project.

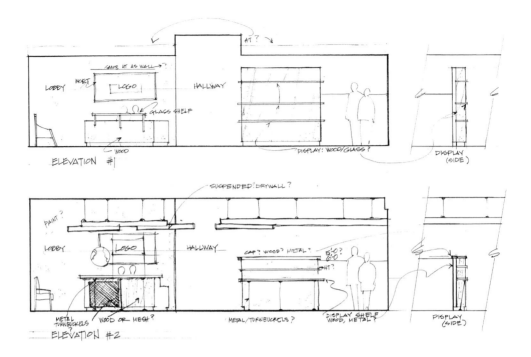

The term *mood board*, which evolved from the world of advertising and branding, has been defined by the Association for Qualitative Research as "a form of visual stimulus material, usually comprising large boards covered with images (often cut from magazines) and designed to represent a mood, atmosphere or feeling." In advertising and product development, these boards are presented to research subjects and focus groups as a type of stimulus material.

Interior designers do not always share these boards with clients and end users; some use them in-house only, to develop and define an aesthetic direction for a project. But others do utilize them to communicate this direction early on to clients or end users. In most cases, this type of board serves as a preliminary mechanism for getting a feel or visual direction for a project very early on. Different firms have differing names for these boards and varying ways for crafting and developing them.

While the name, mechanics, and audiences may vary, designers create such boards to allow them to remain unspecific about the project's final materials, details, and furnishings while setting a direction for the way the materials will look or feel, and perhaps to suggest a general color palette. The boards therefore often include other defining visuals, which are also represented vaguely.

FIGURE 2–16
Mood or inspiration board for the sample project. Photoshop was used to color sample the images in order to create a potential palette. In some cases, a traditional paper collage version can be created in place of a digital version; the idea of selecting inspirational or mood images to jump-start the visual direction of a project is consistent, regardless of the use of software.

These boards may be made using traditional collage technique, whereby printed images from a variety of sources are neatly cut and pasted onto a surface such as foam board or Gatorfoam board. Or they can be composed using graphic imaging software such as Photoshop, or InDesign, as illustrated in Figure 2–16. This type of software allows for images to be cropped, enlarged, and reduced easily. In addition, graphic imaging software offers the ability to pick or sample colors from images and then use them to create a digital palette.

Occasionally, the boards are used in conjunction with a preliminary presentation of materials samples to communicate a project's evolution, as shown in Chapter 9.

Schematic Presentation Graphics

The preliminary design(s) created through this process of continual refinement must be evaluated by the designer or design team as well the client for the project to continue successfully. The presentation of the preliminary design may be informal or very formal, depending on the nature of the project, the purpose of the presentation, and its audience.

The audience for a preliminary presentation may include the client, consultants, real estate professionals, and those with financial interests in the project. Prior to the creation of any presentation, always assess the audience for the presentation; identifying and understanding this audience is imperative to the quality of the communication.

To address members of the design team or design consultants, a presentation may consist of rough sketches and multiple layers of paper. Designers and most consultants are familiar with orthographic drawings and can wade through some confusing and messy drawings and notes. Many clients, however, require easy-to-understand graphic images to understanding the schematic presentation. And the client must comprehend the preliminary design to evaluate and approve it, which is necessary for the project to continue successfully.

The preliminary client presentation must communicate the underlying project research and the constraints that have led to the preliminary design. These include preliminary budgetary, scheduling, and programming information, and research on appropriate building codes. At a minimum, the preliminary schematic design presentation requires a floor plan to communicate the space plan. When the project involves more than one floor, each floor plan and stacking plan is included in the preliminary presentation.

The floor plan should be drawn to scale and include a north arrow and titles. If the designers wish to communicate several design schemes, the various floor plans must be labeled clearly with some sort of notation system, such as "Scheme 1" or "Concept 1." Any additional drawings presented, such as elevations and sections, should include appropriate titles and scale information (see Figures 2–17a through 2–17c). For many projects, a color-coded version of the program can be helpful in communicating adjacencies and other relationships and clarifying design decisions (see Figure 2–17b).

FIGURE 2–17A

Schematic presentation floor plan (line drawing) for the sample project.

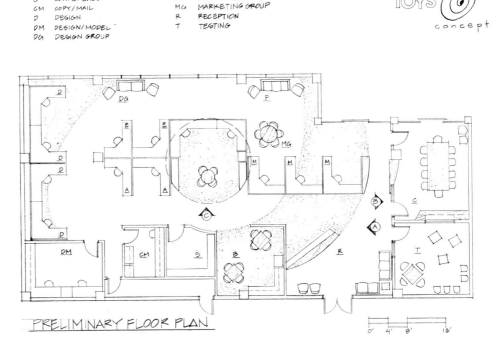

FIGURE 2–17A

Schematic presentation floor plan (line drawing) for the sample project.

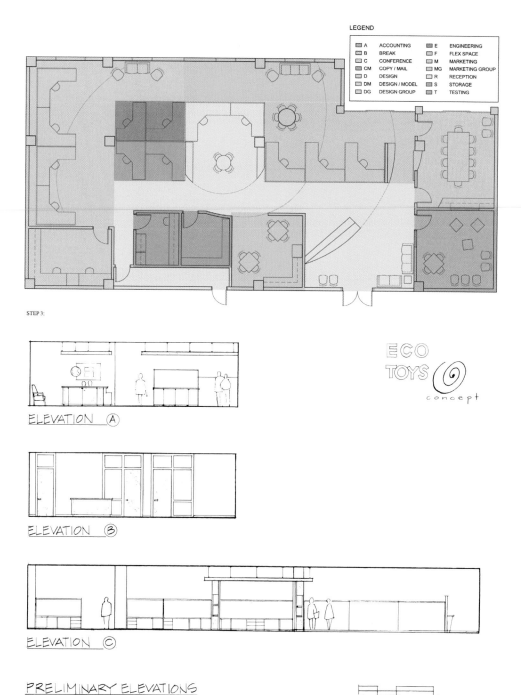

FIGURE 2–17B

Schematic presentation floor plan colored in Photoshop to indicate departmental groupings and adjacencies. This type of color coding is a helpful presentation communication tool. Instructions for using Photoshop to create this type of image can be found in chapter 7.

LEGEND

A	ACCOUNTING		E	ENGINEERING
B	BREAK		F	FLEX SPACE
C	CONFERENCE		M	MARKETING
CM	COPY / MAIL		MG	MARKETING GROUP
D	DESIGN		R	RECEPTION
DM	DESIGN / MODEL		S	STORAGE
DG	DESIGN GROUP		T	TESTING

STEP 3:

ELEVATION Ⓐ

ELEVATION Ⓑ

ELEVATION Ⓒ

PRELIMINARY ELEVATIONS

ECO TOYS Ⓞ
concept

FIGURE 2–17C

Schematic presentation elevations for the sample project.

0' 4' 8' 16'

The Design Process and Related Graphics

Some preliminary presentations include programming information, floor plans, and minimal additional graphics; other projects require preliminary presentations that include additional drawings, such as elevations, sections, and preliminary perspective drawings, as well as models and materials samples. The following chapters cover some of these additional forms of preliminary presentation. A successful presentation of the preliminary schematic design communicates information to the client and other interested parties and allows for input, comments, criticism, and approval.

Figures 2–18a through 2–20c are examples of elements from professional schematic design elements.

FIGURES 2–18A through 2–18E

Design drawings, graphics, samples, models, and presentation elements for a professional project. The "project design principles" were arrived at after many visioning sessions and discussions with the client about their culture, values, goals, and expectations; these were condensed and communicated in the "design principles" board (Figure 2–18a) and used as a touchstone throughout the project. Budgetary, planning, and other design decisions were consistently tied to these principles and reflected in later presentation tools.

Many hand sketches were generated (one is illustrated in Figure 2–18b) in order to study the relationships between the "solids" of rooms and the "voids" of circulation areas and paths (including stairways) to find the best means of fostering connectivity among departments. The use of daylight and the creation of simple, clearly articulated pathways were fundamental concerns and were studied in many varying plans. These studies reflect many of the issues and concerns expressed in the design principles and led to design decisions reflected in later floor plans (2–18c) and sections (2–18d) that illustrate stair design and floor-to-floor relationships, as well as perspective views (2–18e). BY MEYER, SCHERER & ROCKCASTLE, LTD.

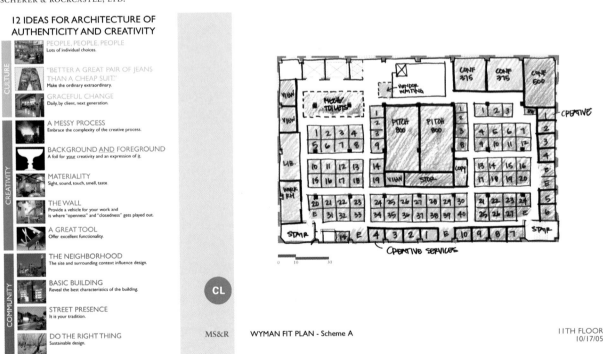

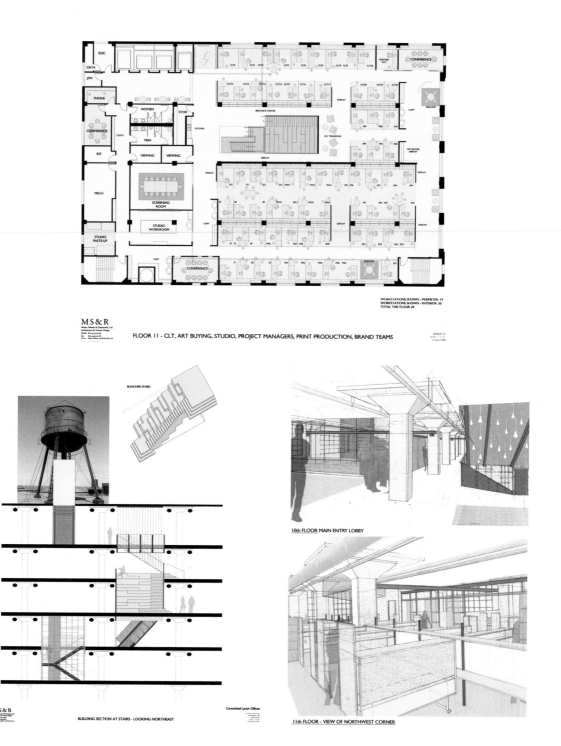

WORKSTATIONS SHOWN - PERIMETER: 19
WORKSTATIONS SHOWN - INTERIOR: 50
TOTAL THIS FLOOR: 69

MS&R

FLOOR 11 - CLT, ART BUYING, STUDIO, PROJECT MANAGERS, PRINT PRODUCTION, BRAND TEAMS

BLEACHER STAIRS

10th FLOOR MAIN ENTRY LOBBY

MS&R

BUILDING SECTION AT STAIRS - LOOKING NORTHEAST

Carmichael Lynch Offices

11th FLOOR - VIEW OF NORTHWEST CORNER

The Design Process and Related Graphics

**FIGURES 2–19A
through 2–19C**

A range of design drawings and presentation elements for a professional project. This undertaking began with some preliminary project concept sketches (2-19a and 2-19b), called "droodles" by their designer, Thom Lasley. Lasley then worked with a professional design illustrator to clarify and communicate the design with colored preliminary conceptual sketches. Harris Birkeland's sketches were used as a means of conveying the spirit of the design to the client early in the design process (2–19c).

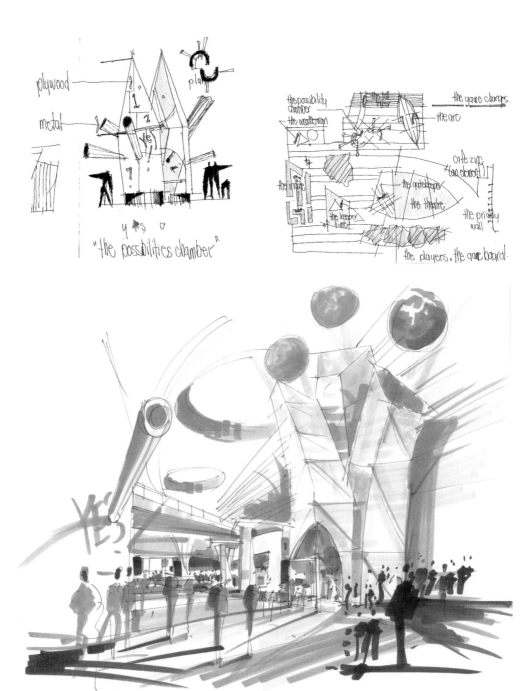

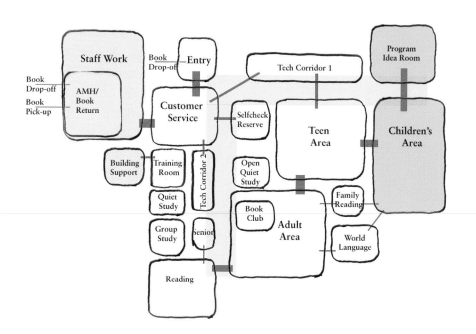

FIGURES 2–20A through 2–20D

A range of exploratory diagrams and drawings showing how relationships, adjacencies, and architectural elements evolved during the design of a library. BY MEYER, SCHERER & ROCKCASTLE, LTD.

CONTEXTUAL CARVING

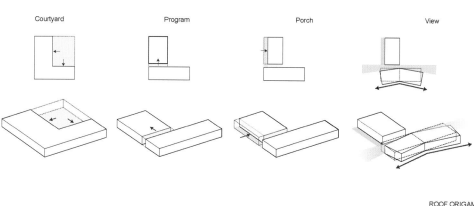

Courtyard   Program   Porch   View

ROOF ORIGAMI

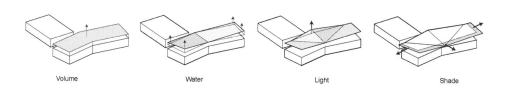

Volume   Water   Light   Shade

RELATIONSHIP DIAGRAM

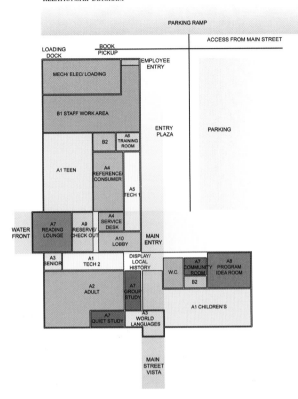

PARKING RAMP

ACCESS FROM MAIN STREET

LOADING DOCK

BOOK PICKUP

EMPLOYEE ENTRY

MECH/ ELEC/ LOADING

B1 STAFF WORK AREA

ENTRY PLAZA

PARKING

B2

A6 TRAINING ROOM

A1 TEEN

A4 REFERENCE/ CONSUMER

A5 TECH 1

WATER FRONT

A7 READING LOUNGE

A9 RESERVE/ CHECK OUT

A4 SERVICE DESK

A10 LOBBY

MAIN ENTRY

A3 SENIOR

A1 TECH 2

DISPLAY/ LOCAL HISTORY

W.C.

A7 COMMUNITY ROOM

A8 PROGRAM IDEA ROOM

B2

A2 ADULT

A7 GROUP STUDY

A1 CHILDREN'S

A7 QUIET STUDY

A3 WORLD LANGUAGES

MAIN STREET VISTA

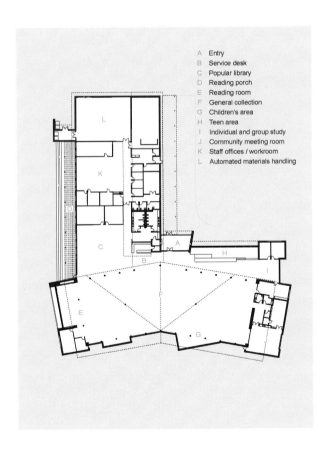

A   Entry
B   Service desk
C   Popular library
D   Reading porch
E   Reading room
F   General collection
G   Children's area
H   Teen area
I   Individual and group study
J   Community meeting room
K   Staff offices / workroom
L   Automated materials handling

BOUNDARY　　PATH　　CANYON　　INDIGENOUS PALETTE

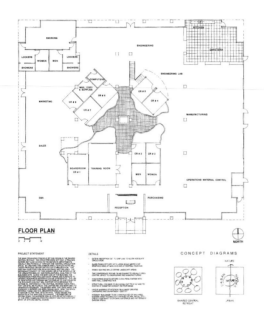

FLOOR PLAN

FIGURES 2–21A and 2–21B
Professional schematic design presentation. Note the parti diagrams at the lower right of Figure 2–21a. BY BRUCK ALLEN ARCHITECTS INC.

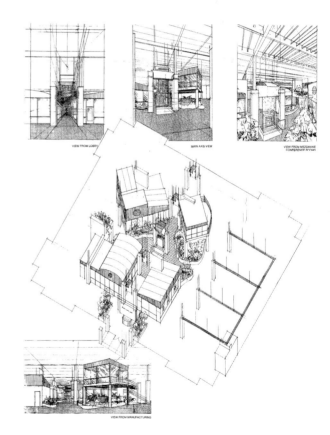

VIEW FROM LOBBY　　MAIN AXIS VIEW　　VIEW FROM MEZZANINE CONFERENCE ROOMS

VIEW FROM MANUFACTURING

This concept or mood board (2–20a) set an aesthetic direction for a library interior that is evident in a later presentation of materials (2–20b) and was used to create a mural in the library entry area. The palette on the right of Figure 2–22a, was created with Photoshop's color sampler (see chapter 9, Figure 9-26, for more information on working with Photoshop). BY MEYER, SCHERER & ROCK-CASTLE, LTD.

Designers usually come away from a preliminary presentation with lists of suggestions from the client. These range from minor corrections or clarifications to major changes in functional, conceptual, or aesthetic aspects of the design. The information generated by feedback to the first schematic presentation allows the designers to refine the design. Depending on project requirements and constraints and the number of changes requested by the client, more schematic presentations may be required. It is common for smaller, less complicated projects to receive quick general approval; larger projects can require many additional meetings and presentations before the client endorses the schematic design.

Great variety exists in the formality, visual quality, and quantity of information included in preliminary design presentations. There are many styles of presentation, and firms have varying standards. But certain elements remain consistent throughout. Designers communicate very clearly in early presentations and make sure that their clients understand the elements of the design presented. Most also describe the importance of clarifying the preliminary nature of the design. Many designers find that clients need time to settle into ideas—that pinning things down too early can be frightening and frustrating for them.

Design Development

The *design development* of a project involves finalizing the space plan and fully refining all the components of the design. All aspects of the design must come together and be resolved and completed in this phase of the project. The phase following design development is *construction documentation*, which involves preparing the project for construction. In large firms, the project is often handed from the design team to the production team upon completion of design development.

Design development drawings are drafted accurately and to scale. Some designers create design development drawings that are somewhat sketchy, and others create extremely precise, highly detailed drawings. In either case, the entire volume of a space must be explored and refined to ensure a successful design project and a smooth transition into the construction documentation phase of the project.

The presentation made upon the completion of the design development phase is the project's comprehensive final design presentation. This presentation must include every possible element of the design to ensure clear communication of the final design. Orthographic drawings—including detailed floor plans, ceiling plans, detailed elevations, sections, and design details—are all part of such a presentation. In addition, technical drawings, millwork drawings and samples, materials samples, and furnishings and fixtures samples and images are often included.

Smaller projects often move quickly from schematic to design development and involve minimal presentations. More complex projects require many interim presentations, and weekly or biweekly design meetings are not uncommon. Some firms keep the contents of their presentations secret; others see them as a source of pride. There is no industry standard for the preparation of design development presentations, and they vary enormously, depending on the scope of the project and the working style of its designers.

Although design presentations reflect the concerns, aesthetics, and tastes of designer and client, communication is the one constant in their preparation. The final design presentation must communicate all elements of the design. For the project to move forward, the design must be understood and approved by the client. In addition to the client or end user, a wide range of individuals may have to review and approve the design.

The design of projects dependent on public funding, such as libraries and municipal buildings, often require public review; many need the design approval of municipal agencies or local community groups. Investors and consultants must often review design presentations before a project can move forward. All of these constituencies form the eventual audience for the design presentation, and understanding this audience is key to the successful communication of the design.

The following chapters offer information on additional visual devices employed in the design and presentation of projects. These are discussed separately for purposes of clarity, but all are used throughout the design process as a means of exploring and communicating a design.

REFERENCES

The Association for Qualitative Research. Glossary. Mood Boards. http://www.aqr.org. uk/glossary/index.shtml?term=moodboard.

Ballast, David. *Interior Design Reference Manual*. Belmont, CA: Professional Publications, 2006.

Ching, Francis. *Interior Design Illustrated*. 3rd ed. Hoboken, NJ: John Wiley & Sons, 2004.

———. *A Visual Dictionary of Architecture*. New York: John Wiley & Sons, 1995. A beautiful and inspiring book.

Crowe, Norman, and Paul Laseau. *Visual Notes for Architects and Designers*. New York: John Wiley & Sons, 1995. A great guide to various types of notational drawing.

Guthrie, Pat. *Interior Designers' Portable Handbook*. 2nd ed. New York: McGraw-Hill, 2004.

Harwood, Buie. "An Interior Design Experience Program, Part II: Developing the Experiences." *Journal of Interior Design* 22, no. 1 (May 1996):15–31.

Henley, Pamela. *Interior Design Practicum Exam Workbook*, 2nd edition. Belmont, CA: Professional Publications, 2002.

Karlen, Mark. *Space Planning Basics*. 2nd ed. Hoboken, NJ: John Wiley & Sons, 2003.

Koberg, Don, and Jim Bagnall. *The Universal Traveler*. 3rd ed. Menlo Park, CA: Crisp, 2003. A wonderful primer on creative thinking; it continues to be helpful after all these years.

Laseau, Paul. *Graphic Thinking for Architects and Designers*. New York: John Wiley & Sons, 2001. Another great book on graphic thinking and design graphics from Paul Laseau. Graphic thinking is described in detail in the volume's first chapter.

Peña, William, Steven Parshall, and Kevin Kelly. *Problem Seeking*. Washington, DC: AIA Press, 1987.

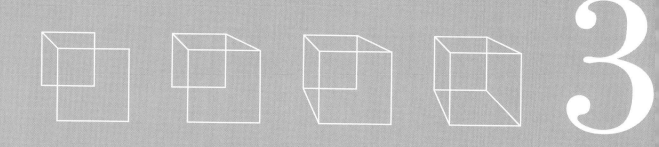

Paraline and Perspective Drawing Basics

Drawings depicting three-dimensional views differ greatly from orthographic drawings in that they offer a more natural view of space. These three-dimensional views (also known as *pictorial drawings* or *perspective drawings*) are useful at every phase of the design process as a way of examining and refining ideas; they should not be reserved merely for final project presentation.

Current interior design practice requires both hand-drawing and digital production skills for the creation of perspective views. In the early phases of design, hand-sketching and drawing are most helpful for creating quick sketches to brainstorm various options or to explore form. As a project moves forward and becomes more refined, digital modeling and three-dimensional perspective sketches are frequently used. This is not always the case, however; some designers and design firms work digitally from beginning to end, while others create most drawings by hand.

A need for strong hand-sketching skills continues despite the increased use of parametric modeling software such as Revit because parametric models require items to be fully understood as three-dimensional entities so they can be modeled successfully. Sketching items, elements, and components by hand gives the designer a clear understanding of them and thereby provides clarity in modeling. In addition, some designers use a combination of hand-sketched and computer-generated perspective imagery for project presentations. It is therefore important for students to develop both manual and digital drawing skills.

The primary focus of this chapter is quick sketching. Due to the evolution of parametric modeling and three-dimensional drawing programs, highly measured perspective drawings are used less commonly than they were when the first and second editions of this book were published. For those interested in learning more about creating measured perspective drawings, two methods can be found in chapter 4. Chapter 5 deals with generating quick digital models using SketchUp; information about how to create quick color renderings and about basic Photoshop rendering appears in chapter 6. Only cursory visual information is provided on more complex rendering programs, such as Revit and Cinema 4D. Further, in-depth study of those programs falls outside of the scope of this book; other publications with more information on them can be found in the References section of this and other chapters.

Unlike orthographic projections, three-dimensional views allow a large portion of an interior space to be depicted in a single drawing. This can help a designer explore the entire volume of the space and make design decisions accordingly. This type of drawing can also help clients understand the overall design of a project.

Pictorial drawings are created as line drawings (by hand or digitally) and may be used in presentations, or they may be rendered—again, either digitally or by hand. Information on rendering is available in chapter 6. Some quickly drawn perspective and paraline line drawings can actually communicate a design to an audience even without the addition of value or color rendering. The tools and materials used in pictorial drawings are similar to those used in orthographic projection drawings and the other forms of graphic communication. More information on such tools can be found in appendix 1.

Tracing paper is the most important material in the production of paraline and perspective drawings; its transparency and low cost make it a highly useful visualization tool. As a drawing becomes confusing, overlay a new sheet of tracing paper and trace necessary elements on the top sheet. A variety of colored pencils can be used to make sense of various lines and aid in the construction of three-dimensional drawings.

Paraline Drawings

Paraline drawings are quick and accurate ways to convey interior form. The construction method of these drawings is based on the relationship of three axes (x, y, and z). Although there are several types of paraline drawing, all share three common characteristics: Parallel lines are drawn parallel to one another, and these lines do not converge to vanishing points. Similarly, vertical lines are drawn as true verticals. Finally, paraline drawings are drawn using some method of proportional scale.

Plan Oblique Drawings

One type of paraline drawing commonly used in the communication of interior environments is known as a *plan oblique.* Figure 3–1 provides a quick reference of plan oblique construction. Plan obliques can be developed quickly because they are drawn

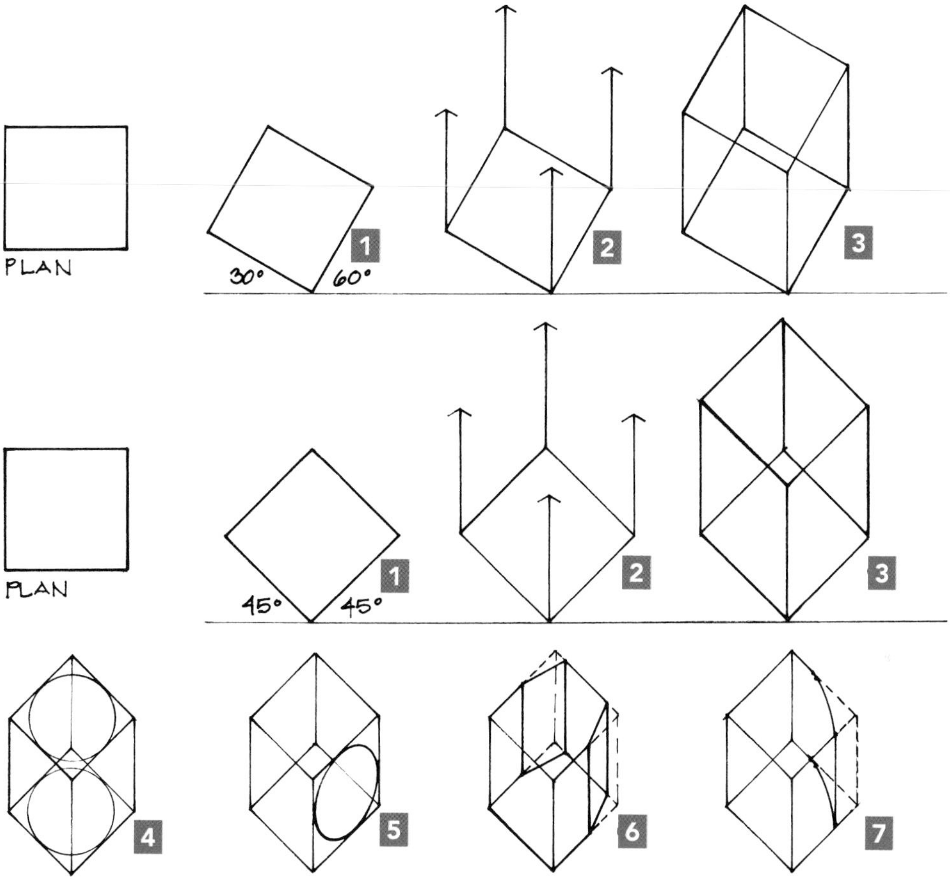

FIGURE 3–1
Quick Reference:
Plan Oblique
Construction

1. Rotate scaled plan to appropriate angles (shown here, 30 degrees/60 degrees and 45 degrees/ 45 degrees).

2. Draw vertical lines upward to the appropriate height in scale.

3. Draw lines parallel to the base plane (the floor plan) at the same angles as the plan.

4. Draw circles found on the plan and its parallel planes as circles.

5. Draw circles found on vertical planes as ellipses (see Figures 3-15 and 3-16 for information on ellipses).

6. Create an enclosing box to measure and locate non-axonometric lines.

7. Create an enclosing box to measure and plot irregular and curvilinear lines and planes.

by projecting directly off the floor plan. Drawing a plan oblique requires the rotation of the floor plan to appropriate angles as measured against a horizontal baseline. The most common angles of plan rotation or orientation are 30 degrees/60 degrees and 45 degrees/45 degrees, although plan obliques may be drawn at any two angles that together equal 90 degrees. Vertical elements are drawn by projecting locations vertically from the plan to the appropriate height. Horizontal elements are drawn using the same angles as those used in the orientation of the plan, as indicated in Figure 3–1.

The angle of rotation changes the orientation of these drawings; it must therefore be considered in their construction. Through the angle of rotation, the designer can both vary the view and emphasize different portions of the space. Plan obliques often employ some method of visual elimination of portions of walls to depict the space successfully. This is done through cutaway views or by ghosting in portions of walls, as shown in Figures 3–2 and 3–3.

Plan oblique drawings a simple and effective means of visualization for the designer. However, they can be confusing for clients who are not accustomed to viewing this type of drawing.

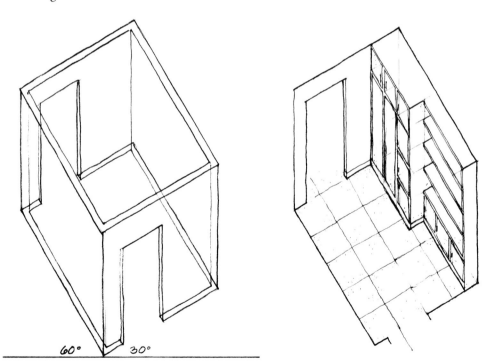

FIGURE 3–2
A plan oblique drawing of a residential storage area.

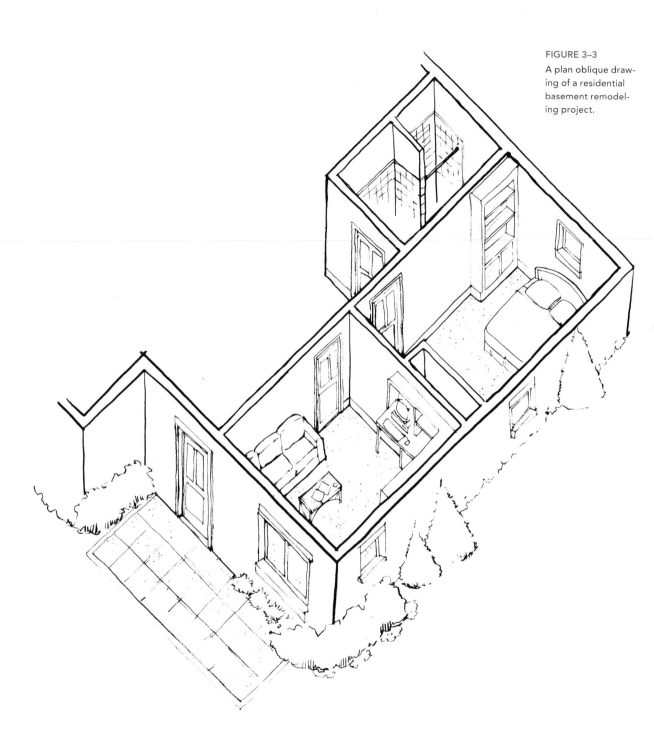

FIGURE 3–3
A plan oblique draw-
ing of a residential
basement remodel-
ing project.

FIGURE 3–4

A plan oblique draw-
ing of an office envi-
ronment (from the
Eco Toys project dis-
cussed in chapter 2).

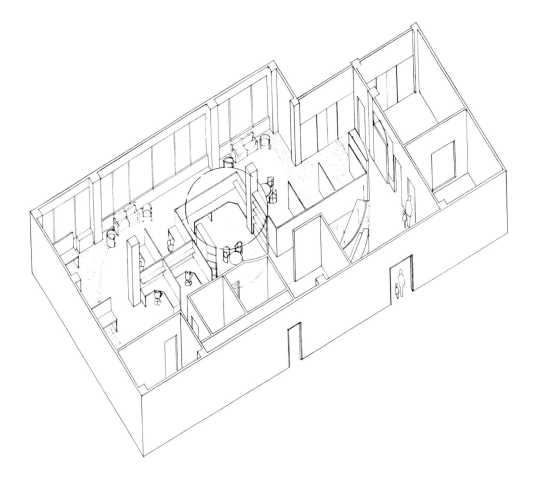

Isometric Drawings

An *isometric* is a paraline drawing based on the use of 30-degree angles. Unlike plan
obliques, isometrics cannot be constructed by simple rotation and projection of the
plan. Instead, they requires the reconstruction of the plan in scale with the two
ground-plane axes (*x* and *y*) at 30 degrees. All elements that are parallel to the ground
plane are drawn at 30 degrees. As in other types of paraline drawings, vertical elements
remain vertical in isometric drawings. Scale measurements can be made along any of
the three principal axes (*x*, *y*, and *z*). Figure 3–5 provides a quick reference of isometric
construction.

FIGURE 3–5
Quick Reference: Iso-
metric Construction

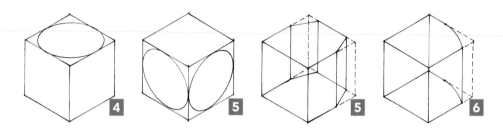

PLAN

1. Redraw plan, in scale, with x- and y-axes at 30 degrees.

2. Draw vertical lines upward to appropriate height in scale.

3. Draw lines parallel to the x- and y-axes at the same angles as plan.

4. Draw all circles as ellipses.

5. Create an enclosing box to measure and locate non-axonometric lines.

6. Create an enclosing box to measure and plot irregular and curvilinear lines and planes.

All circles and circular lines in isometric drawings are drawn as ellipses, and ready-made ellipse templates are available. (For additional information on ellipse construction, see Figures 3-15 and 3-16.) Isometric drawings offer a balanced view and the least distortion of any paraline drawing. They are also easy to create in most CAD programs. Figures 3–6a and 3–6b illustrate a method of drawing isometrics using AutoCAD.

Isometric drawings can be used at any phase of the design process as a means of communicating form and spatial relationships. Isometrics are also utilized in technical and construction documents. Although isometrics offer some advantages, they are somewhat inflexible and do not emphasize any particular portion of the space.

FIGURE 3–6A

Quick Reference:
Creating an Isometric
Drawing Using Auto-
CAD (Two-Dimen-
sional Environment)

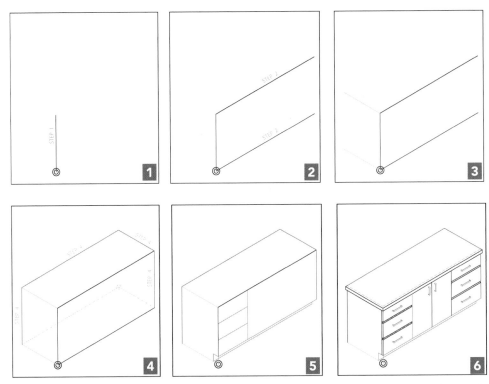

The drawing setup requires starting a new drawing in AutoCAD, right-clicking on polar tracking at the bottom of the toolbar, choosing the Settings option, and changing the Polar Angle Increment settings to 30 degrees. Then complete the following steps:

1. Draw a vertical line that is the desired height of the object using—in this case, 2´-6˝.

2. At the base of the object, draw the first (30-degree) angled line length (in this case, 5´-0˝); copy this line above at a parallel location to create the top of the object.

3. Draw the depth of the object by creating a 30-degree angled line in the desired dimension (in this case, 1´-10˝) at the bottom of the object, and repeat for the object's top parallel line.

4. Using the same 30-degree angles, complete the object by drawing the required lines. (Dashed lines show the hidden isometric lines.)

5. and 6. Add details. For the drawers, draw a line from the top of the unit to the bottom. Use the Divide command to divide the line into three equal parts, making sure Osnap Nodes are enabled.

Continue this method for additional cabinets and drawers. These instructions are continued in Figure 3–6b.

Note: Use copy lines rather than offsetting lines; offsetting does not follow the 30-degree angles.

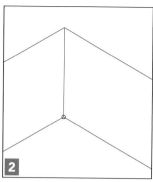
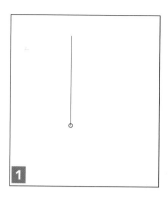

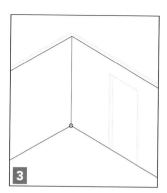
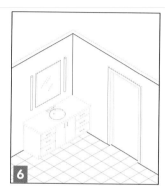

Upon completion of the previous steps, do the following:

1. At the starting point, draw an 8′-0″ line for the height of room.

2. At the starting point, draw lines for the base of the walls using the correct feet and inches. Copy the same lines upward 8′-0″ to create the tops of the walls.

3. Copy each top and base line over 3½″ to show wall thickness; add the door in the desired location.

4. Add detail to the door frame. Add wall fixtures in the desired locations.

5. Place the vanity in the room.

6. Copy the base

Continue this method for additional cabinets and drawers. These instructions are continued in Figure 3–6b.

Note: Remember to use the Aligned Dimension command for dimensioning items because the drawing is in Isometric Mode.

Perspective Drawings

Perspective drawing offers a natural view of interior space and for this reason is commonly used in design presentations. Many design students (and even some design professionals) have difficulty creating clear, natural-looking perspective drawings. This is unfortunate, because perspective sketching and drawing is an excellent design tool that can—and should—be used throughout the design process to generate and refine ideas. Quick perspective drawings are helpful visualization tools. An understanding of basic perspective principles and estimated sketching techniques allows designers to draw quickly and accurately, and to create fresh, attractive drawings. Using perspective drawing only in finalized design presentations can result in weak design projects and lost opportunities for discovery.

The ability to draw simply measured or estimated freehand perspectives permits the rapid expression of ideas, which then helps in the generation of new ideas and solutions. While the ability to produce laboriously created mechanical perspective drawings is important in design practice, equally relevant is the capability for expressing ideas quickly. Some CAD and modeling programs require that a design be complete and modeled or fully drawn prior to the generation of a three-dimensional view, underscoring the need to be skilled at quickly hand-drawn perspectives.

Perspective Basics

Creating successful pictorial drawings requires a working knowledge of the basic principles of perspective. These principles remain constant regardless of the method of drawing employed. Students should therefore become acquainted with the fundamental terms and principles of perspective drawing.

The Picture Plane

The *picture plane* is an imaginary transparent plane through which the area to be drawn is viewed and visualized as a giant sheet of glass standing between the viewer and the area to be drawn. The surface of the drawing paper represents this picture plane; understanding the paper surface as a metaphor for the picture plane is fundamental to good perspective drawing.

It is the relationship of an object to the picture plane (and to the location of the viewer) that creates a given perspective view for that object. For example, a box that has its front face (plane) parallel to the picture plane is in a position that creates a *one-point perspective* drawing (see Figure 3–7).

Turning the box so that the entire front corner is on edge in relation to the picture plane creates a *two-point perspective* view of the box (see Figure 3–8).

Tweaking the box so that only the top (or bottom) corner touches the picture plane creates a *three-point perspective* view of the box (see Figure 3–9).

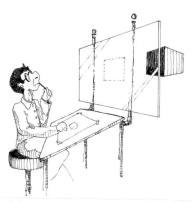

FIGURE 3–7
One-point perspective. A box drawn in one-point perspective has its front plane parallel to the picture plane.

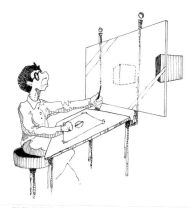

FIGURE 3–8
Two-point perspective. A box drawn in two-point perspective has its front corner viewed on edge in relation to the picture plane.

FIGURE 3–9
Three-point perspective. All planes of the box are oblique to the picture plane when viewed in three-point perspective. DRAWINGS FOR FIGURES 3–7 THROUGH 3–9 BY JUSTIN THOMSON

Although there are a number of nuances that create more complicated relationships, perspective concepts shared by all types of perspectives can be found in the following list and are illustrated in Figures 3–10 through 3–12.

Basic Perspective Concepts

Horizon Line (HL)

All three types of perspective employ a *horizon line* representing the viewer's eye level. A box held high above the viewer's eye level (horizon line) displays a view of the bottom of the box. As the box is moved below the eye level of the viewer, a view of the top of the box is possible.

Vanishing Point (VP)

In all types of perspective drawing, perspective lines converge to a *vanishing point* (or points, in two- and three-point perspectives).

Station Point (SP)

It is from the *station point* in space that the item or scene is seen by the viewer.

Cone of Vision (CV)

The *cone of vision* represents the angle of view, or sight range, of the viewer. A person cannot view all of a space at a given time; the cone of vision, or angle of view, represents the natural limits of human sight.

Elements that exist within the viewer's cone of vision can generally be drawn without excessive distortion. Those elements that exist outside the cone of vision become distorted and cannot be drawn successfully.

Diminution of Size

In perspective drawings, items decrease in size as they move away from the viewer; this is referred to as *diminution of size.* A box drawn correctly will appear larger when closest to the viewer and smaller as it moves away from the viewer. Because items diminish in size, they cannot be measured consistently in scale; therefore, a variety of methods of measurement have been devised.

One-Point Perspective

One-point perspective views portray an object or environment with one plane parallel to the picture plane. They also make use of one vanishing point, located along the horizon line, to which all perspective lines converge. The horizon line is a horizontal line that represents the viewer's eye level, usually between 5′ and 6′ from the floor. One-point perspective is the easiest type of perspective to draw because the entire plane that is parallel to the picture plane can be measured in scale. Figure 3–10 enumerates one-point perspective principles.

One-point perspective drawings are easy to construct because lines that are vertical in reality remain vertical, horizontal lines remain horizontal, and only lines indicating perspective depth are drawn converging to the vanishing point. However, one-point perspective views can be unnatural looking and become distorted. Despite their drawbacks, one-point perspective drawings are highly useful during the early stages of design and are often used by designers for idea generation.

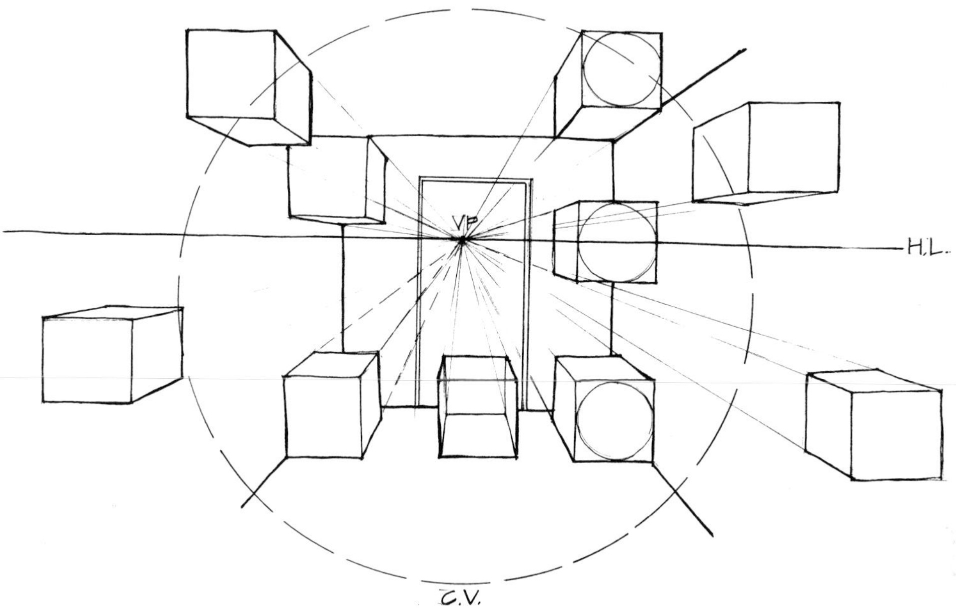

FIGURE 3–10
Quick Reference:
One-Point Perspec-
tive Principles

- Perspective lines converge to a single vanishing point (VP), located on the horizon line (HL).
- The front faces of the cubes and the back wall of a room are viewed parallel to the picture plane. Only those elements with faces touching the picture plane can be drawn in scale.
- One-point perspective drawings have true vertical, horizontal, and perspective (depth) lines.
- Items located outside of the cone of vision (CV) tend to appear distorted.
- Items appear to diminish in size as they recede from viewer, which makes boxes of the same size appear smaller when they are located in the rear of a room.

Two-Point Perspective

Two-point perspective drawings portray objects and volumes on edge in relation to the picture plane. In other words, two-point perspective depicts the primary faces of a volume oblique to the picture plane. This means that two-point perspectives offer a view of the front corner of objects or the rear corners of rooms and environments. In two-point perspective, an object's edge (or the corner of a room) is drawn first and can be used as a vertical measuring line from which perspective lines recede toward two vanishing points. The two vanishing points lie on the horizon line, one to the left and one to the right. As with one-point perspective drawings, the horizon line is always horizontal and represents the viewer's eye level. Figure 3–11 lists the principles of two-point perspective.

FIGURE 3–11

Quick Reference:
Two-Point Perspec-
tive Principles

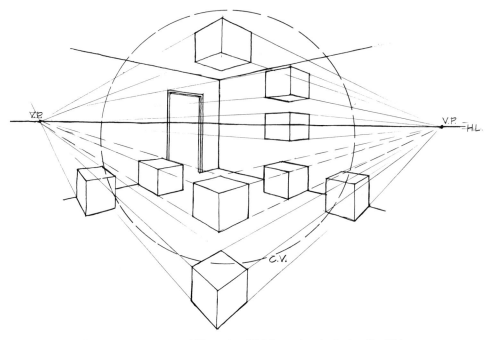

- Perspective lines converge to two vanishing points (VPs), located on the horizon line (HL).
- Boxes are viewed from the front corner, and rooms generally from the back corner, in relation to the picture plane.
- Two-point perspective drawings have true vertical lines and perspective (depth) lines.
- Only the front edge (or back edge) touching the picture plane can be measured in scale.
- Items located outside of the cone of vision (CV) tend to appear distorted.
- As with all forms of perspective, items appear to diminish in size as they recede from viewer, which makes boxes of the same size appear smaller when they are located in the rear of a room.

Apart from the horizon line and elements that lie along the horizon line, there are no horizontal lines found in accurate two-point perspective drawings. Instead, lines that are not true verticals converge to one of the two vanishing points. Only one vertical measuring line can be drawn in scale because perspective lines converge to two vanishing points, causing objects to look smaller as they recede from the viewer toward the vanishing points. Two-point perspective drawings can be tricky to measure and confusing to create. However, two-point perspective drawings appear more natural and suffer from less distortion than other types of perspective drawings.

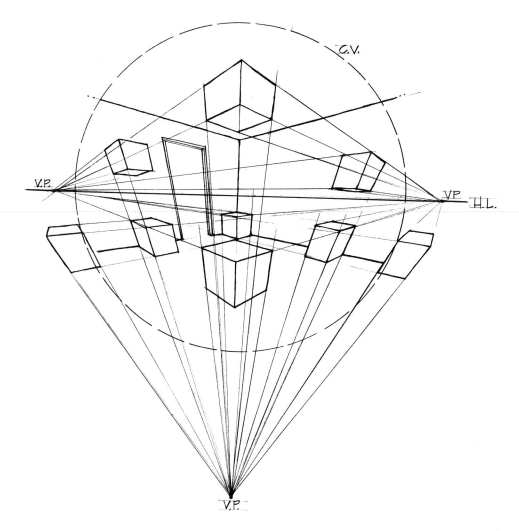

FIGURE 3–12

Quick Reference: Three-Point Perspective Principles

- Perspective lines converge to three vanishing points (VPs), two located on the horizon line (HL) and one usually above or below the horizon line.
- All planes of a box are oblique to the picture plane.
- All lines converge to a vanishing point.
- No portion of a three-point perspective drawing can be measured in scale.
- Items located outside the cone of vision (CV) tend to appear distorted.
- As with all forms of perspective, items appear to diminish in size as they recede from the viewer.

Paraline and Perspective Drawing Basics

77

Three-Point Perspective

Three-point perspective, which is not traditionally used in the illustration of interior space, portrays an object or volume with all its principal faces oblique to the picture plane. All lines in this type of perspective converge to vanishing points. Generally, three-point perspectives are constructed with two vanishing points on the horizon line, one to the left and one to the right, with an additional vanishing point above or below the horizon line. It is best to center the third vanishing point above or below the left and right vanishing points. Figure 3–12 is a quick reference to three-point perspective principles.

The use of three vanishing points creates highly dynamic drawings that may easily become distorted. Because all lines converge to vanishing points, no true-scale measuring line can be employed, so drawing three-point perspectives requires good visualization skills. Three-point perspective is most useful for portraying single objects, such as furniture or products, that by design should be dynamic, unusual, or attention grabbing. Three-point perspective creates a bird's-eye view (or worm's-eye view) and is also used in some types of animation.

Developing Visual Skills

To develop visual skills and learn to "see" in perspective, students should practice drawing simple square-looking boxes in one-, two-, and three-point perspectives. The key here is to create boxes that appear proportionally accurate. Figure 3–13 enumerates important principles of perspective sketching. Review the caption for Figure 3–13 carefully, as it covers distortion, the use of a vertical measuring line, diagonal division, and drawing slanting planes. See Figure 3–14 for additional information on drawing stairs in perspective using a *vanishing trace*.

Ellipses

Circles and curves are drawn as *ellipses* in perspective. An understanding of ellipses and how they are drawn can help you create natural-looking perspective drawings (see Figures 3–15 and 3–16). The following list covers important ellipse-related concepts; the captions to Figures 3–15 and 3–16 contain key information for drawing ellipses successfully.

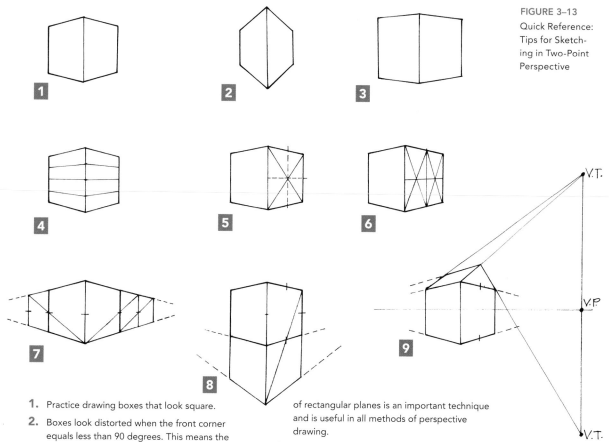

1. Practice drawing boxes that look square.

2. Boxes look distorted when the front corner equals less than 90 degrees. This means the vanishing points are too close together.

3. Boxes look distorted when the front corner equals greater than 140 degrees. This means the vanishing points are too far apart.

4. The front corner can be divided equally to serve as a measuring line. This line can be scaled and then used to measure portions of the object that recede toward the vanishing points. Vertical measuring lines allow you to measure of a drawing's vertical elements; in principle, this line is the only element of a drawing that can be accurately scaled.

5. Bisecting diagonals divide a square drawn in perspective. The intersection of diagonals drawn from corner to corner in a square locates the midpoint of that square. Rectangular planes are also divided in this manner. Diagonal subdivision

of rectangular planes is an important technique and is useful in all methods of perspective drawing.

6. Diagonals also divide rectangles.

7. Boxes can be extended using diagonals. Locate the midpoint of a single box or cube, and draw a diagonal from the bottom corner of the cube through the midpoint of the cube's far side. Then extend the diagonal from the midpoint to the top perspective line (the one that recedes to the vanishing point). Where the diagonal meets the perspective line of the original cube, draw a new vertical, creating a second square that is visually equal in perspective.

8. Diagonals can also extend a box vertically.

9. Slanting parallel lines converge at a common point. Francis Ching dubbed this point a vanishing trace, or VT, and it is directly below or above the vanishing point.

FIGURE 3–14
Sketching Stairs
in Two-Point
Perspective

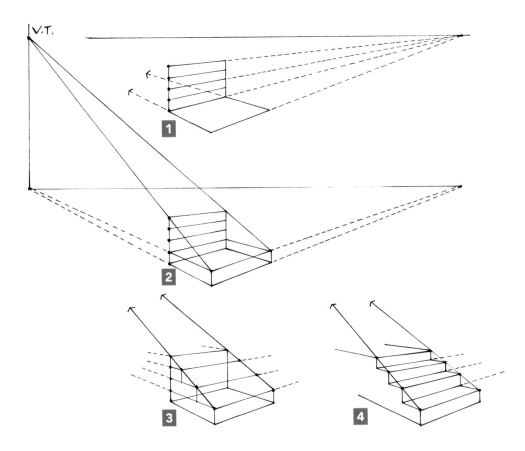

1. By measurement or estimation, plot the width
    and depth of the stairs on the floor plan. Locate a
    height plane by extending vertical lines to the
    appropriate height (the top of the stair run).
    Divide the height plane to create the appropriate
    number of risers.

2. Draw a line from the vanishing point through the
    height plane at the first riser measurement; this
    creates the first riser. Draw a diagonal line from
    the forward height of the first riser through the
    top of the height plane, and continue this
    diagonal until it is directly above the vanishing

    point; this is the vanishing trace. Draw a second
    diagonal from the vanishing trace to the location
    opposite the forward riser.

3. Draw lines from the vanishing point through each
    riser measurement on the height plane. Continue
    these lines until they intersect with diagonals;
    these are the forward riser locations.

4. Find the tread locations by extending vertical
    lines down to the next riser measurement; lines
    indicating treads converge to the appropriate
    vanishing point.

Drawing and Understanding Ellipses

The *major axis* is an imaginary line found at the widest part of an ellipse.

The *minor axis* is found at the narrow diameter of the ellipse.

An ellipse's major axis is longer than its minor axis.

The major and minor axes are always at right angles (90 degrees) to each other, regardless of the ellipse's position.

When found on horizontal planes such as floors and ceilings, an ellipse's major axis is horizontal.

The centerline of a cylinder or cylindrical object is drawn as an extension of the minor axis, which, therefore, always appears at a right angle to the major axis. The centerline of a complicated object, such as the axle of a wheel or the cylindrical base of a piece of furniture, can therefore be drawn as an extension of the minor axis.

Understanding the relationship between the minor and major axis and the location of the centerline can eliminate distortion in the drawing of circular forms in perspective. It also facilitates the freehand sketching of ellipses and the construction of complex linear perspectives.

Use of Enclosing Boxes

The ability to able to draw a square-looking box accurately is perhaps the single most effective tool in freehand perspective drawing. Once this skill has been developed, the box is drawn as an enclosing form, like a packing crate; then portions of the box can be subtracted to reveal the object within.

The relationship of an object to the horizon line becomes very important when sketching larger items, such as furniture. Because furnishings and larger items are typically viewed from a standing position, draw them with the horizon line at approximately 5′ above the floor (or 5′ above the surface that the items are sitting on). In constructing these drawings, create the horizon line with a scale figure depicted. The figure's eye level should align with the horizon line, as shown in Figure 3–17a.

FIGURE 3–15

Ellipses
(These ellipses
were drawn using
templates.)

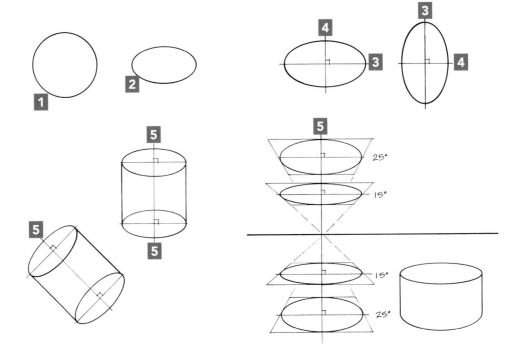

1. Circle.

2. Ellipse. In perspective drawings, circles are drawn as ellipses.

3. The major axis is an imaginary line found at the widest part of an ellipse.

4. The minor axis is an imaginary line found at the narrow diameter and is always at 90 degrees to the major axis. An ellipse's major axis is longer than its minor axis.

5. The centerline of a cylinder is drawn as an extension of the minor axis. The major and minor axes always appear at right angles (90 degrees) to each other, regardless of the position of the object.

6. When found on a horizontal plane such as a floor, the major axis is horizontal. The view of the ellipse varies according to the location of eye level (horizon line). Elliptical templates are used to approximate the various views more easily.

Developing a quick method for sketching human figures is very helpful. Steps for drawing these figures are shown in Figures 3–17a through 3–17c. Along with scale figures in proper relationship to the horizon line, estimation boxes can create a fairly accurate scale relationship.

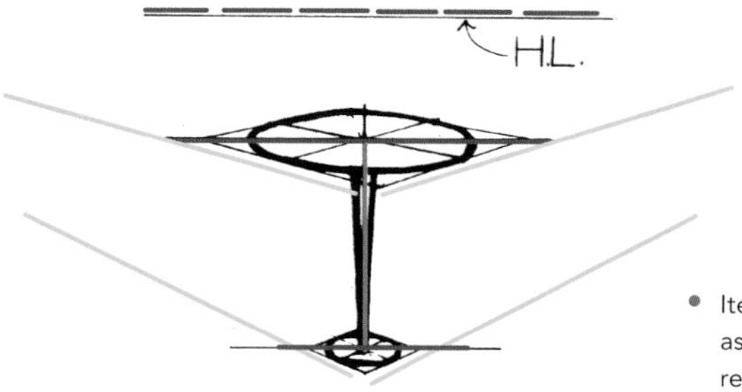

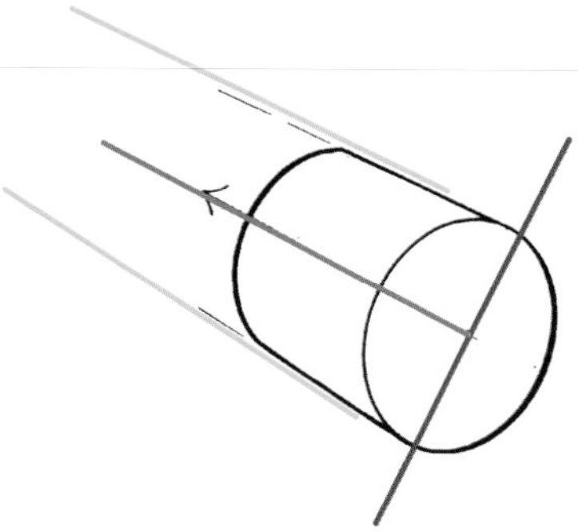

FIGURE 3–16
Quick Reference: Additional Information about Drawing Ellipses

- Items that are parallel to the floor or ground, such as a table base or top, must have a major axis (in red) that is parallel to the horizon line (dashed red line). The central leg of this table is formed by a centerline that extends extending from the top minor axis to the lower minor axis.
- Cylindrical items not parallel to the floor have a minor axis (blue line) that extends through the center of the major axis and back to the object's vanishing points. Perspective lines to vanishing points are drawn in yellow.
- Many designers use templates to create accurate ellipses and curvilinear forms. The choice of templates is based on the locations of the major axis, the minor axis, and the centerline of the form.

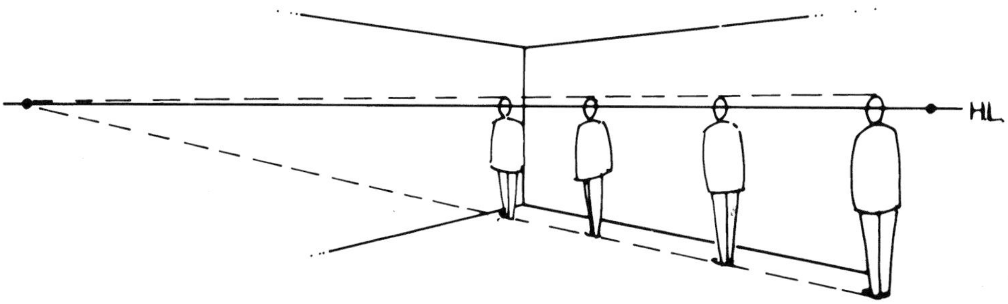

FIGURE 3–17A
Quick Reference: Using Scale Figures

Scale figures can be used to establish proportions and a relationship to the horizon line. Place an adult figure's head directly on the horizon line, between 5′ and 5′- 6″. These rough dimensions can then establish items such as a chair seat and back height for estimation.

To sketch items in boxes that are not square but may be elongated in a number of directions, start with a simple box that is placed correctly on the horizon line, and add boxes using diagonal division or simple estimation. Figures 3–18 through 3–20 depict the steps involved in creating drawings in which an enclosing box is employed to construct and estimate proportions and details.

FIGURE 3–17B

Quick Reference:
Step-by-Step Draw-
ing of Scale Figures

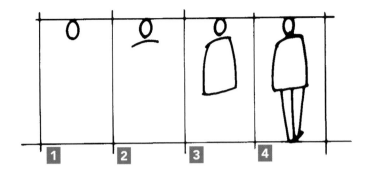

A figure shown walking away from the viewer is easiest to draw.

1. Draw a small oval head (on the horizon line).

3. Draw curved shoulders slightly below the head.

2. Draw a torso extending downward from the shoulders.

4. Draw legs below the torso. The legs can be uneven, and shoe-shapes can extend from them.

FIGURES 3–18A
THROUGH 3–18C

Quick Reference:
Two-Point Sketch-
ing Using Estimated
Boxes. (These
are actual rough
sketches, drawn with-
out a straightedge or
ruler in less than five
minutes per sketch.)

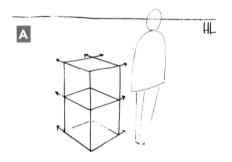

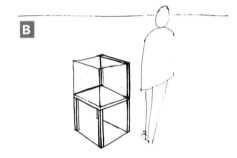

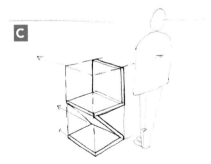

Sketch a box or series of boxes that approximate the total dimensions of the object. Make sure the vanishing points are generously spaced and that the horizon line is appropriately located. (In this case, the chair seat and back should be below the horizon line.) Use a scale figure, as shown here, to help establish heights.

In this example, there are two stacked boxes: one representing the seat height, and one representing the seat back. The scale figure demonstrates that they are proportioned accurately (3–18a). The boxes can be used to rough out the locations of the seat and back (3–18b), and the boxes can be used to generate varying designs in roughly the same scale (3–18c).

The ability to visually assess freehand perspective drawings that have been constructed from simple boxes provides an understanding of form and spatial relationships. Employing the principles of perspective mentioned thus far yields better drawings and allows for the use of perspective drawing as a design tool.

The quick sketching covered thus far can be used both for ideation and the development of design details. Up to this point, only drawings of single items have been presented; information about drawing entire rooms and spaces can be found in chapter 4, which builds on the issues discussed in this chapter.

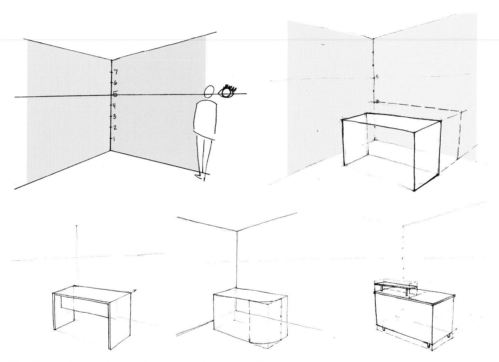

FIGURES 3–19A THROUGH 3–19E

Two-point sketching that considers the entire room or volume, using estimated boxes. The same method employed in the previous figures is used, but the item drawn is different. (These are actual rough sketches, drawn without a straightedge or ruler in less than five minutes per sketch.)

To estimate a larger volume, such as a room, draw a vertical line (3–19a) and create eight increments along the line (in red). The vertical line will serve as the back corner, and each increment along the line will represent 1 foot. Place a horizontal line at the 5′ or 6′ mark; this will serve as a horizon line (blue) and should have one vanishing point at each end. Then draw ceiling and floor lines using the vanishing points. (The yellow lines indicate the direction of one vanishing point.)

Use the increment lines in the back corner and project these from the wall forward to find the rough scale of items—such as the box containing a roughly sketched 3′-high reception desk (3–19b). A cleaner version of this simple desk is shown in Figure 3–19c. Another iteration of the desk, with a curved portion, appears in Figure 3–19d. The curve is drawn by locating points along the box's top and bottom planes to estimate the curves' starting and end points.

Yet another iteration of the desk is shown in Figure 3–19e, where boxes have been used to locate items such as the transaction ledge.

FIGURES 20

In this step-by-step example, an enclosing box is again used to draw an object. The front corner of the box is marked in equal increments to serve as a measuring line for the object. The measuring line and diagonal division were used to rough out details and proportions. Then the clean final version was created using tracing paper.

Note: If the vanishing points are not located far enough apart, the object may appear distorted.

DRAWING BY LEANNE LARSON

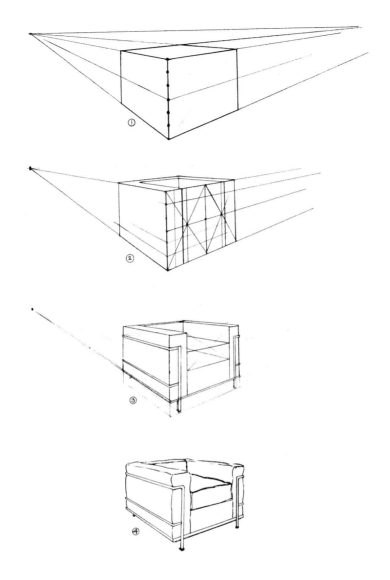

REFERENCES

Aubin, Paul. *The Aubin Academy Master Series: Revit Architecture 2012*. Clifton Park, NY: Delmar, Cengage Learning, 2011.

Ching, Francis. *Architectural Graphics, 5th ed.* Hoboken, NJ: John Wiley & Sons, 2009 .

———. *A Visual Dictionary of Architecture*. New York: John Wiley & Sons, 1995.

Drpic, Ivo. *Sketching and Rendering Interior Space.* New York: Whitney Library of Design, 1988.

Forseth, Kevin, and David Vaughn. *Graphics for Architecture.* New York: John Wiley & Sons, 1980.

Hanks, Kurt, and Larry Belliston. *Rapid Viz: A New Method for the Rapid Visualizaiton of Ideas.* Los Altos, CA: William Kaufman, 1980.

McGarry, Richard, and Greg Madsen. *Marker Magic: The Rendering Problem Solver for Designers.* New York: Van Nostrand Reinhold, 1993.

Olofsson, Erik, and Klara Sjölén. *Design Sketching.* Klippan, Sweden: Keeos Design Books, 2005. A beautiful and helpful book focused on product design sketching.

Pile, John. *Perspective for Interior Designers.* New York: Whitney Library of Design, 1985.

Porter, Tom. *Architectural Drawing.* New York: Van Nostrand Reinhold, 1990.

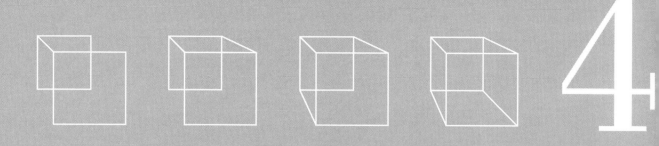

Sketching and Drawing Interior Environments by Hand

The same concepts involved in sketching objects using enclosing boxes can be employed for sketching interior environments. Quick sketching remains an important design tool for designers because it fosters a unique way of seeing the world and recording details. It can also aid in the preparation for parametric modeling and is still preferred by some as a presentation tool. Quick, estimated sketching is therefore the focus of this chapter. (More refined, measured methods of drawing are discussed at the chapter's end.)

Estimated One-Point Interior Perspective Drawings

The easiest method of quick sketching interior environments has, at its foundation, the box-sketching techniques discussed in chapter 3. Using this estimation method, a perspective of a 10′ × 10′ room can be created by drawing a 10′-square box in one-point perspective and subtracting or adding to that room as needed. This method is unusual because it requires a square-looking room to be estimated, necessitating visual accuracy that can only be developed by practice (another reason to follow chapter 3's suggestion to practice drawing square-looking boxes).

Figures 4–1a and 4–1b provide a quick, detailed reference for this method of estimated one-point perspective.

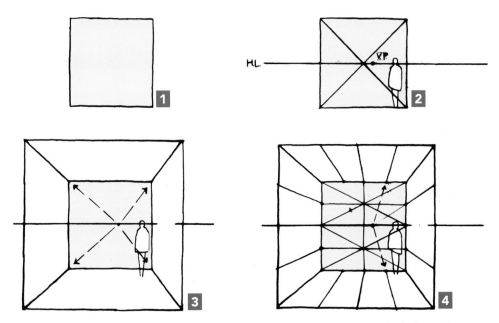

In this estimation method, measurements are based on rough approximations. For example, the horizon line is placed at roughly 5′ feet, approximately the eye level of the viewer. Because most pieces of furniture will fit into a 30″-high packing crate, much of the furniture is roughed in as 30″-high boxes.

1. Draw a 10′ × 10′ square in a workable scale (½″ or 1′). This square will become the back wall of the room and will be the only portion of the drawing in scale.

2. Divide the square using diagonals. Draw a horizontal line through the center. This is the horizon line; it is at roughly 5′. Place a vanishing point on the horizon line slightly to the left or right of center.

3. Draw perspective lines from the vanishing point through the corners of the original square, creating wall and ceiling lines. Now estimate the depth of the room and give it a square appearance by using your drawing skills to define the room's depth.

4. Use diagonals to divide the original square (see Figure 3–13), which is now the back wall. By dividing the back equally in four, you will create 30″ height increments.

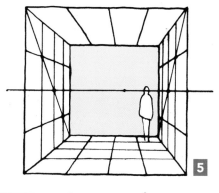

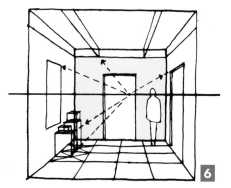

5. If necessary, estimate a grid through diagonal division. On side walls, locate verticals where height lines intersect diagonals. Draw the diagonals and then draw vertical lines where the diagonals intersect the height lines.

6. and 7. Use measuring increments (created in Step 4) or a grid to locate objects and architectural elements. Use a clean overlay to create a line drawing.

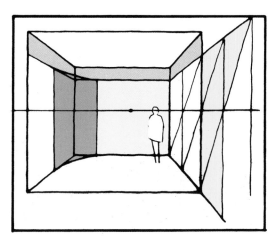

To raise or lower the ceiling, draw lines from the vanishing point to the appropriate height on the back wall, and extend these lines forward (pink area). Diagonal extensions can be used to enlarge the room, as shown in yellow (see Figure 3–13).

Curves are found by plotting and sketching in appropriate locations, as shown in green. Note that curves found below the horizon line curve in an upward U shape, and curves found above the horizon line curve in an upside-down ∩ shape.

In drawing estimated one-point interior perspectives, it is easier to draw complicated items or architectural elements when they are placed on the wall(s) parallel to the picture plane. The location of the single vanishing point is important because walls and objects located very close to their vanishing points can become quite distorted. Draw a few quick thumbnail sketches of the space, using the estimation method, to locate the vanishing point and visualize the space being drawn. Thumbnail sketches aid in the location of an appropriate view of the space and the location of the vanishing point.

This method of quick sketching, using rough approximations, allows designers to draw space as they design it. It also permits perspective drawing to be integrated into the design process during the schematic design and design development phases of a project prior to the completion of a full set of orthographic drawings (see Figures 4–2a through 4–4c). Practice generating these types of drawing can provide the skills necessary for drawing quickly and directly in client meetings with simple pens and without tools (see Figures 4–5a and 4–5b).

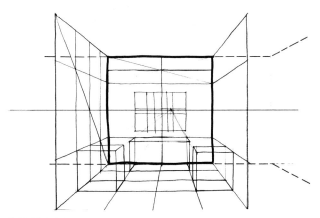

FIGURE 4–2A
Draw the square-looking room in Figure 4–1 and then modify it (as indicated by dashed lines). Bold lines indicate the back wall of the original 10′ × 10′ room; dashed lines represent the areas in which the room was elongated to set up the structure of the larger environment—in this case a hotel lobby and hallway. With the basic proportions of the environment complete, furnishings and additional elements can be roughed in.

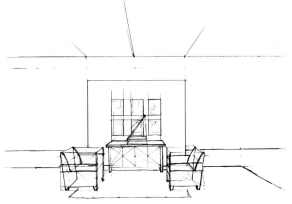

FIGURE 4–2B
The drawing can be continued by adding necessary details and refining design elements.

FIGURE 4–2C
A final, clean copy of the drawing can be traced and readied for rendering, if necessary. *Note: Although perspective drawings benefit from the inclusion of scaled human figures, they have been omitted from this drawing in order to show details more clearly.*

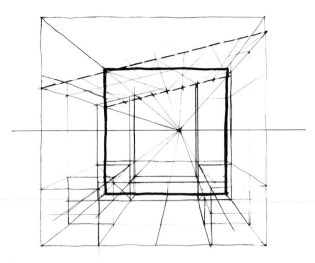

FIGURE 4–3A

Draw the square-looking room in Figure 4–1 and then modify it (as indicated by dashed lines). Bold lines indicate the back wall of the original 10′ × 10′ room; dashed lines represent the areas in which the ceiling was altered—in this case to indicate a shed roof in a small New Mexico cabin. With the basic proportions of the environment complete, furnishings and additional elements can be roughed in.

FIGURE 4–3B

The drawing can be continued by adding necessary details and refining design elements; a final, clean copy of the drawing can be traced and readied for rendering, if necessary. *Note: Although perspective drawings benefit from the inclusion of scaled human figures, they have been omitted from this drawing in order to show details more clearly.*

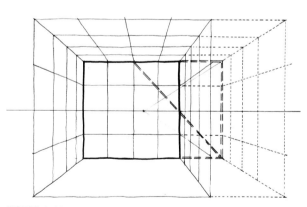

FIGURE 4–4A

Draw the square-looking room in Figure 4–1 and then modify it (as indicated by dashed lines). Bold lines indicate the back wall of the original 10′ × 10′ room; dashed lines represent the areas in which the room was elongated to set up the structure of the larger environment—in this case to create a much larger exhibition space.

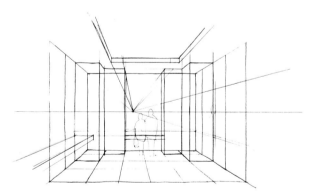

FIGURE 4–4B

With the basic proportions of the environment complete, the basic design elements can be roughed in.

FIGURE 4–4C
Given the complexity of this environment, some extra steps are required to refine the design. Signage can be generated, photocopied, and pasted onto the drawing, or the drawing can be scanned into Photoshop and additional details, such as signage or art, can be added digitally (see chapters 6 and 7).

FIGURE 4–5A and 4–5B
Practicing estimated one-point sketching leads to the ability to do quick sketches in client and team meetings. These drawings were done in less than ten minutes using simple ink pens.

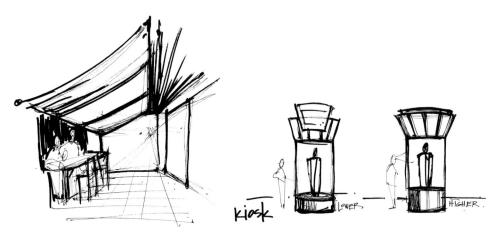

Estimated Two-Point Interior Perspective Drawings

One-point interior sketches are helpful and easy to create, but problems with distortion—particularly in drawing furniture and freestanding objects—limits their usefulness. It is therefore important to learn to draw two-point interior perspectives quickly, using the estimation method.

The same concepts used in drawing boxes and estimated one-point interiors are employed in estimated two-point perspective sketching. In the two-point method, a 10′ × 10′ room is drawn first to serve as a guideline for further development. Figure 4–6 is a quick, detailed reference for the estimated two-point perspective method.

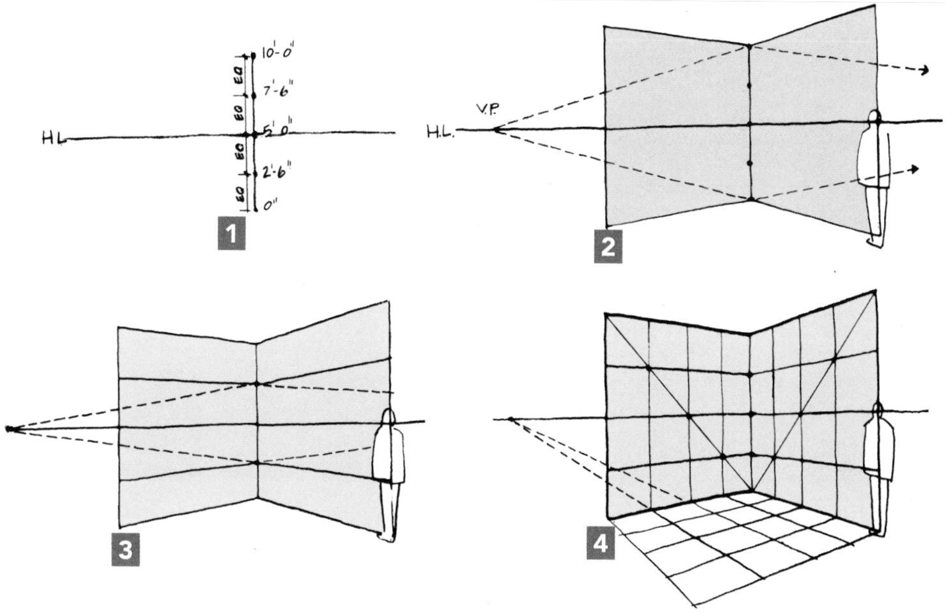

FIGURE 4–6A
Quick Reference: Estimated Two-Point Interior Sketching

1. Draw a single vertical line to serve as a measuring line. Divide the line into four equal segments. At the midpoint, draw a horizontal line; this is the horizon line.

   The vertical measuring line (drawn first) serves two important functions: it is the only true measuring device in the drawing, and it can become the back corner of the room(s) being drawn.

2. Place two vanishing points on the horizon line. These should be placed as far apart as possible to avoid distortion. It is best to locate one vanishing point slightly closer to center than the other, rather than treating them symmetrically.

3. Draw lines from each vanishing point through the top and bottom of the measuring line. This creates floor and ceiling lines. Now estimate the depth of room, making it look square, using your drawing skills to define the room's depth

4. Draw lines from each vanishing point through all increments on the measuring line; these will serve as height measurement lines. Proportions for simple items that are on the walls can be measured using the back wall's dimensions. To create a grid, draw diagonals on each wall. Then, at the intersection of the diagonal and each height line, draw a vertical. Where the verticals terminate at the floor, a floor grid can be created by using the termination point and aiming a line at the appropriate vanishing point.

FIGURE 4–6B

Quick Reference: Creating a Grid Using Estimated Two-Point Interior Sketching (continued from previous figure)

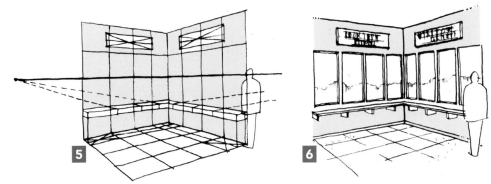

5. and 6. Use the grid to estimate architectural elements and objects. (Grids are not always necessary; for simple spaces, it is best to estimate measurements.) Use a clean overlay for tracing and refining the drawing.

FIGURE 4–6C

Quick Reference: Creating a Grid Using Estimated Two-Point Interior Sketching (continued)

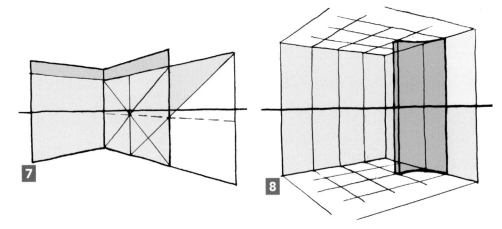

7. Raise or lower the ceiling by estimating the desired height (pink areas). Extend the room using diagonal division (yellow area). (For more information on division, see Figure 3–13.)

8. Curved surfaces are estimated by using the grid to sketch the curves into appropriate locations, as shown in green. Note that curves found below the horizon line curve in a upward U shape, and curves found above the horizon line curve in an upside-down ∩ shape.

A common distortion problem in two-point perspective drawing is caused by locating the two vanishing points too close to each other, resulting in an unnatural-looking view of the space. If your drawing becomes distorted, start over and locate the vanishing points farther from apart. As with one-point sketches, making a few thumbnail sketches of the space to locate the vanishing points and visualize the space allows for the identification of an appropriate view and the proper positioning of the vanishing points.

In this method, architectural elements and freestanding objects are located by measurement and estimation. The vertical measuring line can be used to find vertical measurements; these are taken from the vanishing point through the vertical measuring line and plotted on the appropriate wall. For freestanding objects, heights can be determined by extending a line from the vanishing point through the appropriate height on the wall to the location of the object. Depths are estimated using diagonal division and extension—dividing the walls with diagonals and finding the midpoint of the room at the intersection of the two diagonals.

This estimated two-point perspective method is an approximation method. For example, the horizon line is placed at roughly 5′—approximately the eye level of the viewer. Because most pieces of furniture will fit into a 30″-high packing crate, much of the furniture can be sketched as 30″-high boxes. Scale figures should be included in interior perspectives; locate their eye levels at or near the horizon line. This method allows drawings to be integrated into the design process during the early phases of a project (see Figures 4–7a through 4–8c, which show the various steps in constructing estimated two-point perspective drawings for a range of projects).

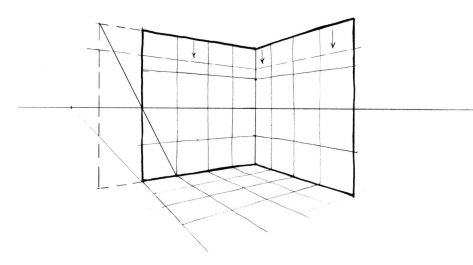

FIGURE 4–7A
Draw the square-looking room shown in Figure 4–6 and then modify it (as indicated by dashed lines). Bold lines indicate the back wall of the original 10′ × 10′ room; dashed lines represent the areas in which the room was elongated (to the left) and the ceiling was lowered to roughly 8′ feet above the floor.

FIGURE 4–7B

With the basic proportions of the environment complete, furnishings and additional elements can be roughed in.

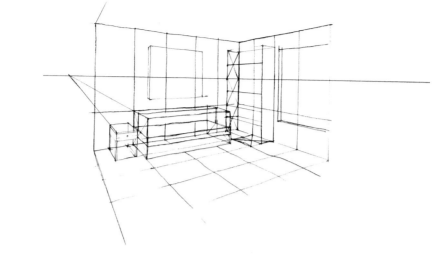

FIGURE 4–7C

Continue the drawing by adding necessary details and refining design elements. A final, clean copy of the drawing can be traced and readied for rendering, if necessary. In preparing this more refined drawing, templates were used for hanging lamps, and tools were used for the edges of furniture. Rendered versions of this drawing can be found in Figures 6-41a and 6-41b, and Figures 7-17a through 7-17d show the process of color-rendering this drawing and using Photoshop to add finishing touches. *Note: Although perspective drawings benefit from the inclusion of scale figures, they have been omitted from this drawing in order to show details more clearly.*

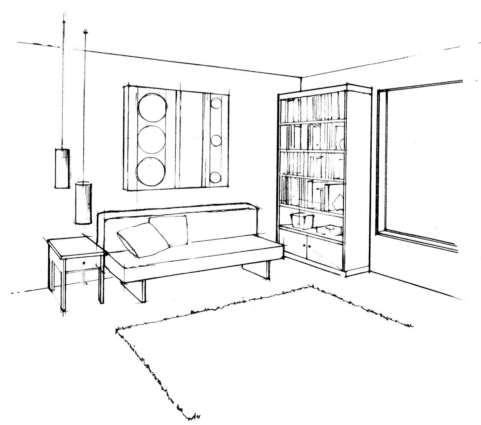

Visualization skills are fundamental to the design of interior environments. These methods of estimated sketching using rough approximation (also known as eyeballing) permit designers to draw a space as they design it, to integrate perspective drawing into the design process, and to visualize spaces three-dimensionally rather than merely viewing space in plan, where a sense of volume is often missing.

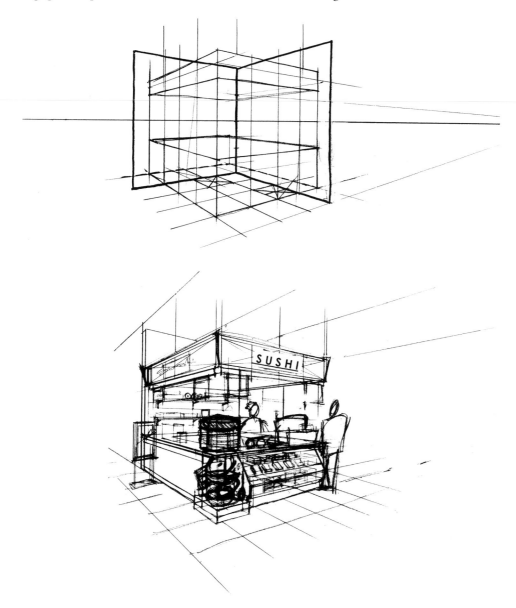

FIGURE 4–8A
Draw the square-looking room shown in Figure 4–6 and then modify it (as indicated by dashed lines). Bold lines indicate the back wall of the original 10′ × 10′ room; dashed lines indicate the areas in which the room was elongated (to the rear of the original square).

FIGURE 4–8B
With the proportions of the environment complete, the basic design elements can be roughed in. This particular drawing was done very early in the design process and was used to consider the entire volume of the retail design. Type was printed and pasted into the signage area as a means of understanding scale issues.

Most of the methods of drawing more refined linear perspectives require complete scaled plans and elevations, thus necessitating the design to be complete prior to the creation of the perspective drawings. These more refined perspectives often appear highly realistic, in contrast to those created by estimation methods. Refined, measured linear perspectives are most useful for presentations to clients, end users, real estate professionals, investors, and the general public.

Refined Linear Perspective Methods

The perspective drawing concepts and skills covered thus far can lead to valuable visualization skills. Because these skills are easily transferred to the more refined, measured methods of linear perspective, the ability to draw well in estimated perspective begets the ability to draw well in refined, precisely measured perspectives.

Some designers continue to find creating refined perspective presentation drawings desirable, while others prefer moving into the digital realm as the design progresses, using Revit, SketchUp, or various three-dimensional modeling products. There is a variety of methods of measured perspective drawing, and different methods work best for different people. Those who draw well in measured perspective employ the particular method that works best for them. For this reason, a variety of methods are discussed briefly and illustrated in the following sections. Students should experiment with the methods described here to discover which method of measured perspective drawing they are most comfortable with.

Two-Point Plan Projection Method

Two-point plan projection is also known as the *common method* or the *office method*. A comparable method is often used for exterior perspectives, and a similar one-point method is used as well. The plan projection method requires a completed scaled floor plan and scaled elevations, so the project must be well resolved in order to make use of it. Figures 4–9a and 4–9b provide step-by-step plan projection instructions.

This method is completely different from the perspective methods discussed previously. Although it is useful and highly accurate, it can be confusing at first because it requires going back and forth from plan view to perspective view. The key is understanding that the floor plan is used to set up the final perspective elements and measurements. In this method, the floor plan is manipulated to provide information that is projected onto the perspective drawing.

Before beginning, decisions must be made about what view of the space will be depicted, the location of the viewer, and the cone of vision. Key elements of the space must be included within a 60-degree cone of vision. The plan is then set up against the picture plane (also drawn in plan).

The plan setup must also include the location of the viewer in plan. This is known as the station point; it can be thought of as the head of the viewer in plan. The station point is extremely important to producing a successful drawing using this method. Its location dictates the view of the space as well as the cone of vision and other key elements, such as the location of the vanishing points.

With the plan set up against the picture plane and the station point established, the vanishing points can be located on the picture plane in plan by drawing lines from the station point parallel to the walls of the room (or building) that terminate at the picture plane. This method requires that lines be drawn from the station point to the location on the plan and to the picture plane, and then projected onto the perspective drawing.

There are actually two separate types of activity within this method: those set up in plan and related to the picture plane and those then projected from the picture plane to the perspective drawing. Measurements of width and depth are projected from the picture plane onto the perspective drawings. Heights are taken from the measuring line or elevation(s) and transferred to the appropriate location.

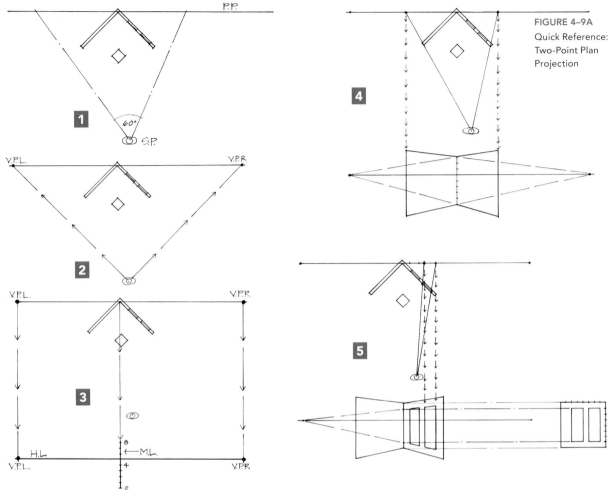

FIGURE 4–9A

Quick Reference:
Two-Point Plan
Projection

1. Draw a horizontal line; this is the picture plane (PP). Select the desired angle of view and orient the plan so that the rear corner touches the picture plane. Locate the station point; make sure all desired elements fit within a 60-degree cone of vision projecting from the station point to the desired areas in plan. Locate the station point one to three times the height of the interior space from the focal point of the drawing.

2. Draw lines from the station point to the picture plane parallel to the walls of the floor plan; the locations of the intersections of these lines and the picture plane are the setup vanishing points, vanishing point right (VPR) and vanishing point left (VPL).

3. Draw a horizontal line below the plan setup; this is the horizon line. Project the location of vanishing points left and right vertical to the horizon line; this relocates the vanishing points. Project a line from the rear corner of the plan vertically to the horizon line; this will be the measuring line (ML). It can be measured in scale (to match the plan); it will also be the back corner of the room. The horizon line must be located at 5′ to 6′ in scale on the measuring line (i.e., at eye level).

4. Draw lines from the vanishing point left through the top and bottom of the measuring line. These are the wall and floor lines. Repeat this step with the vanishing point right. Next, draw lines from the station point through the ends of walls (in plan) to the picture plane. Project these locations vertically onto the drawing.

5. Draw lines from the station point through window locations or any other elements (in plan) to the picture plane. Project these locations vertically onto the drawing. Heights are determined by measuring from measuring line or from an available elevation.

1. Draw lines from the station point through the edges of the object, and extend them to the picture plane. Project these locations vertically onto the drawing.

2. To find a floor location, first transfer the furniture location onto walls in plan setup (a). Then draw lines from the station point to locations on the walls; then extend the lines to the picture plane. Next, project locations on the picture plane vertically to the appropriate wall in the drawing

   (b). Draw a line from the vanishing point to where the wall projection meets the floor (c); extend these lines forward onto the object to find the floor location.

3. To find the height of objects, draw a line from the vanishing point (in this case, vanishing point right) through the appropriate height on the measuring line to the wall location (c).

4. Complete the object with lines drawn to the appropriate vanishing points.

Note: When a drawing looks wrong, it is often because a location was not projected from the picture plane.

The plan projection method is generally accurate and provides an excellent perspective framework. But it can be time-consuming and sometimes leads to unexpected distortion, requiring the entire process to be completed a second time. The method works best for environments based on simple geometric forms rather than those based on complex or organic forms. Figures 4–10a through 4–10j delineate the various steps in a plan projection method drawing for a residential project.

FIGURE 4–10A

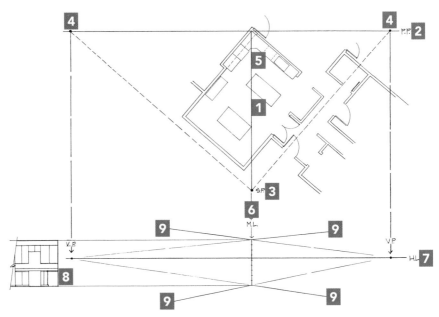

1. To begin, select the desired view. In this case, the plan is oriented to provide a view of the rear corner of the kitchen to include the kitchen cabinets.

2. The picture plane should pass through the rear corner of the plan, with the walls you wish to include in the drawing on the left and right.

3. Create a station point directly below the rear corner of the plan (there are other ways to do this, but this is the easiest). The station point indicates the location of the viewer. This point should be located roughly two to three times the height of the room in the same scale as the plan.

4. Draw a line (dashed here) from the station point to the picture plane; this line must be parallel to the back walls of the room in plan.

5. Begin the actual perspective drawing by projecting the location of the back corner down vertically through the station point and well below (or above) the plan.

6. The line projected in Step 5 now becomes the measuring line. This is drawn to the desired height of the room (in this case 9') in the same scale in which the original plan was created. It is helpful to draw tick marks that indicate 1' increments on the measuring line.

7. Draw a horizontal line to serve as the horizon line for the perspective drawing. In most drawings, it should be located at eye level—in this case 5'-5". The vanishing points should be projected vertically, directly from the picture plane onto this new horizon line.

8. If desired, an elevation can be placed alongside the perspective drawing to aid in establishing height measurements.

9. Wall and ceiling lines can now be drawn from opposite vanishing point to the appropriate heights on the measuring line.

FIGURE 4–10B

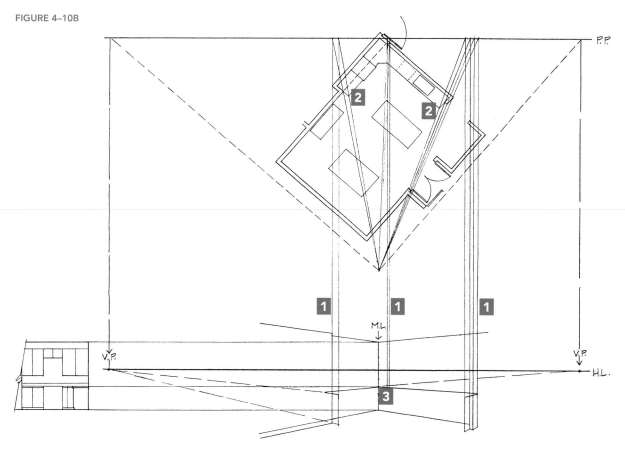

1. Find wall and object locations by locating each item on the plan and projecting a line from the station point to the location on the plan, onward to the picture plane, and down onto the drawing.

2. In this case, a line is drawn from the station point to the cabinet, onward to the picture plane, and then projected vertically from the picture plane to the drawing.

Note: If your drawing looks incorrect, you are not projecting consistently down from the picture plane.

3. Find the height of the lower cabinets by counting off the measuring line—in this case 3′. (Some prefer to obtain the height dimensions by transferring them from the adjacent elevations.)

FIGURE 4–10C

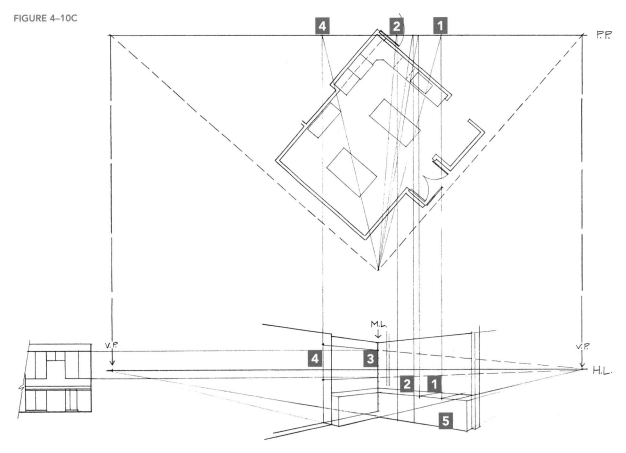

1. Find the sink location by drawing a line from the station point to the front corners of the sink, onward to the picture plane, and then onto the drawing.

2. Find the dishwasher by drawing a line from the station point to the front corners of the dishwasher, onward to the picture plane, and then onto the drawing.

3. To find the heights of the wall cabinets, first locate the height on the original measuring line (in this case the height information is transferred from the adjacent elevation).

4. Because the cabinets are recessed into the wall (see plan), you must draw a line from the station point to the rear edge of the cabinet and onto the picture plane and project this location onto the drawing.

5. Complete the lower cabinets by drawing lines from the edges of the cabinets to the appropriate vanishing points.

FIGURE 4–10D

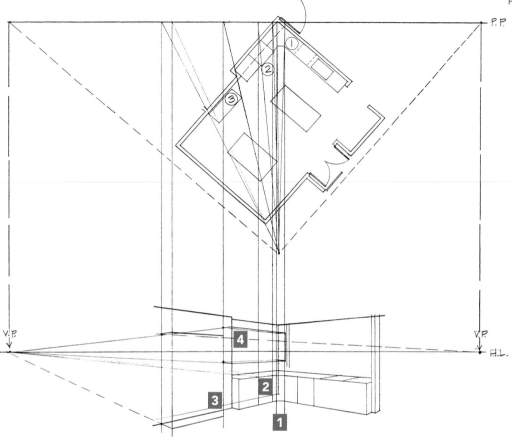

1. Create the angled portion of the lower cabinets by drawing a line from the station point to the edges of the angled portion and onward to the picture plane. Then project the lines onto the cabinets in the drawing.

2. Locate the stove by drawing a line from the station point to the front corners of the stove, onward to the picture plane, and then down onto the drawing.

3. Locate this piece of furniture by drawing lines from the station point to the three visible edges of the object, onward to the picture plane, and then onto the drawing. The height of the object is determined by locating it on the measuring line and then transferring the height line by use of the vanishing point (dashed lines).

4. The upper cabinets can be completed by working from the measuring line and the vanishing points (similar to Step 3).

FIGURE 4–10E

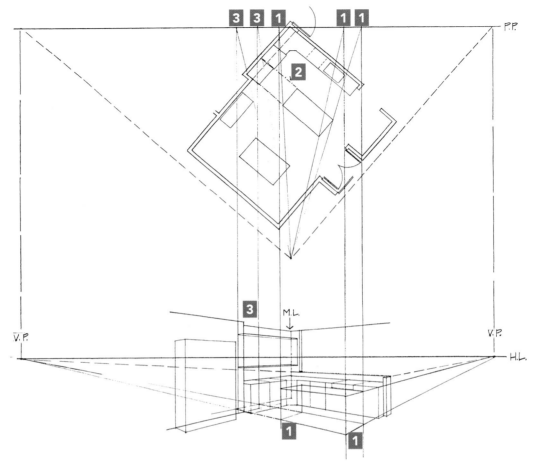

1. Draw the freestanding island using a combination of projected lines. Draw lines from the station point to the three visible edges of the island, onward to the picture plane, then down to the drawing, creating the island's corner locations.

2. Because the item is freestanding, its height and actual floor location must be determined by transferring the object location onto walls in plan setup (dashed lines in plan).

3. Then draw lines from the station point to the plan wall locations found in Step 2, onward to the picture plane, and then onto the corresponding walls in the perspective drawing. Now, working on the perspective drawing, draw lines from the left vanishing point to the location where the wall projection (done in Step 2) meets the floor. Extend these lines forward to the corners of the island. The height of the island is taken from the measuring line and extended using the vanishing points.

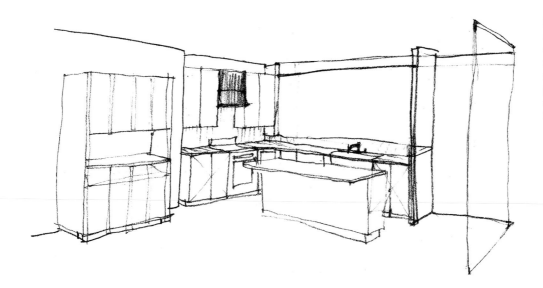

FIGURE 4–10F

At this stage, a quick overlay sketch can be created to determine the quality of the perspective drawing and locate any problem areas.

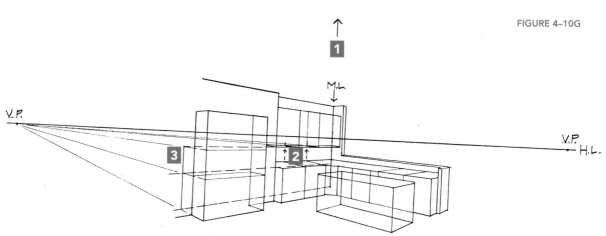

FIGURE 4–10G

1. With the significant features completed, the plan is no longer necessary because most height and spatial relationships can be determined by using the measuring line and vanishing points.

2. Find the location of the hood and cabinets above the stove by drawing lines upward from the back corners of the stove to the upper cabinets (dashed line with arrows). These locations are

brought forward by using the left vanishing point and then drawing on the front face of the upper cabinets.

3. To finalize the details of the freestanding buffet, dimensions are found on the measuring line, brought "behind" the buffet, and extended using the left vanishing point.

FIGURE 4–10H
Using diagonal divi-
sion, various details
can be considered
and drawn in place.

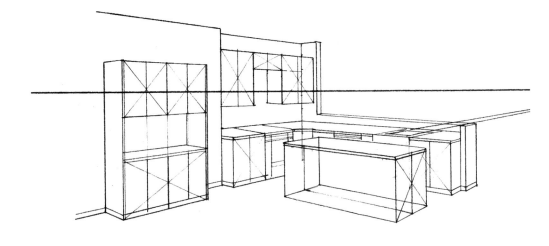

FIGURE 4–10I
Additional design
elements can be esti-
mated or measured.

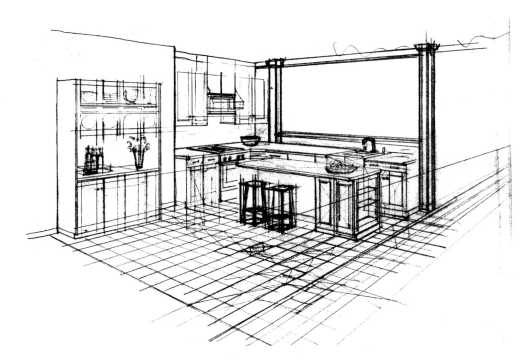

FIGURE 4–10J
The final, clean version of the drawing. Steps involved in rendering this drawing can be found later in this chapter.

Prepared Perspective Grid Charts

Prepared perspective charts are used by designers and design illustrators as an aid in drawing by hand. The charts provide a perspective framework, including horizon line, location of viewer, cone of vision, vanishing points, and measuring devices. This framework allows items to be located, measured, and drawn to appropriate vanishing points more accurately than in quick, estimated sketches.

Perspective charts are based on a predetermined set of conditions. The location and height of the viewer (and the corresponding horizon line), vanishing points, cone of vision, and measuring increments, as well as the overall visual emphasis of the space, are all given within a particular chart. Grid charts are useful, relatively quick to use, accurate, and adaptable. Because one chart will not work for all projects, it is helpful to keep on hand a set of charts with varying views and spatial relationships for use on different projects. Generally, perspective charts cover a huge area and must be manipulated and measured to define the space a drawing requires.

Because the charts contain hundreds of lines, they can be confusing and difficult to read. Using a variety of colored pencils on tracing paper overlays to define the space and record important elements provides clarity. Elements that establish the space—such as the horizon line, vanishing points, vertical measuring lines, and wall, floor, and ceiling grid lines—can be transferred to tracing paper each in its own color. With these elements and other useful notes recorded, the original grid can be removed and a customized grid created. The customized grid should be overlaid with tracing paper and kept for future reference.

FIGURE 4–11
A prepared perspective grid chart.

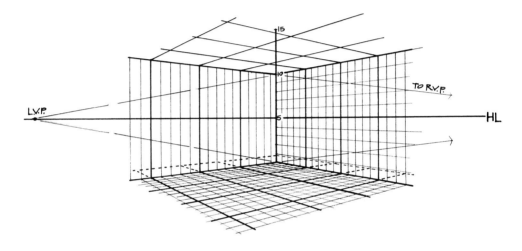

FIGURE 4–12A
The prepared chart customized for a particular project, the Royal Pavilion, Brighton, England.

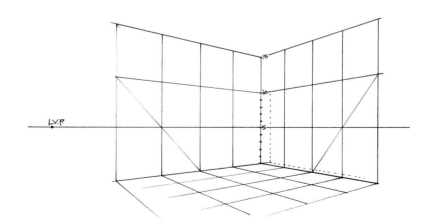

FIGURE 4–12B through 4–12E The sequence of drawings prepared with the use of a grid, leading to a final line drawing of the Royal Pavilion, Brighton, England. DRAWINGS FOR FIGURES 4–12A THROUGH 4–12E BY LEANNE LARSON

Figure 4–11 is an example of a prepared grid. Figures 4–12a through 4–12e are a sequence of drawings using a prepared grid drawing. An additional simplified grid that can be copied and used for constructing drawings can be found in appendix 2.

Using Photographs

Photographs can be traced to form a perspective framework. This is especially useful in the renovation of an existing space, when a photograph of the existing conditions can be used. The photograph must be taken clearly, from the desired one- or two-point perspective vantage point. Once the photograph is downloaded, it can be enlarged and printed. The enlarged photograph is then overlaid with tracing paper, and the drawing constructed. Figure 4–13a is a quick reference for this method.

If the photograph is taken with the primary wall parallel to the camera lens (picture plane), a one-point perspective view is generated. In this case, the drawing is constructed with one vanishing point, located on the horizon line by tracing over the lines that form the floor and ceiling lines (or any series of major perspective lines). The place where these lines converge is the vanishing point.

A horizontal line is drawn through the vanishing point; this serves as the horizon line. Check this location by tracing perspective lines from an additional object in the space and making sure they converge at the same vanishing point. With the vanishing point and horizon line noted, new or proposed design elements can be sketched into the space. Items to be retained in the proposed design can be traced from the photograph. Figures 4–13a and 4–13b illustrates this process.

Two-point perspectives can be drawn from photographs that show the two main walls or elements as oblique to the camera lens (picture plane). The method is similar to that used in one-point tracing, except that two vanishing points must be located and placed on the horizon line. The correct vanishing point can be located by tracing the left floor and ceiling lines (or the corresponding lines of some significant object) to a point of convergence. The left vanishing point is estimated by tracing the right floor and ceiling lines (or the corresponding lines of some significant object) to a point of convergence.

A horizon line is created by drawing a horizontal line connecting the right and left vanishing points. The horizon line must link the two vanishing points with a single horizontal line. With the two vanishing points and horizon line located, proposed changes can be sketched into the drawing. All elements to be retained in the proposed design may be traced into the drawing.

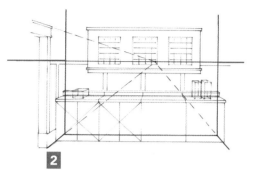

FIGURE 4–13A and 4-13B

The prepared chart customized for a particular project, the Royal Pavilion, Brighton, England.

1. This photograph sets up a one-point view of the interior because the back wall is parallel to the picture plane (camera lens). Trace over the lines that form the walls and ceiling; these will lead to a single vanishing point. Draw a horizontal line through the vanishing point; this is the horizon line.

2. New or proposed items are drawn using the vanishing point and the horizon line.

3. Trace items that will be retained from the photographic image. Add entourage elements such as plants, figures, or fixtures.

Photographs taken of existing spaces generally include a number of interesting background and foreground elements. Human figures, plants, and details of daily life are often captured in photographs. These elements can be traced into the drawing to add interest and liveliness. Students often remove these items, creating lifeless drawings.

Students are sometimes reluctant to trace perspective drawings from photographs because they believe it is plagiarism. If, however, the photos only provide a perspective framework for new and original design ideas, plagiarism is not at issue. Many professional illustrators and renderers keep a huge files of photographs of human figures, furnishings, and other elements to be traced into drawings, as well as files of digital imagery for use in computer-generated drawings. It is considered plagiarism, however, when a drawing made by someone else is traced and used without being properly credited, or if a design is lifted wholesale and traced.

Digital photographs can be taken and drawn over by hand, creating a sketch of the new design or design elements These can then be combined, using Photoshop, to create a combination of hand and digital drawing. This is done by hand-tracing over the original image using pencil or pen on translucent paper. The traced drawing is then scanned and imported into a Photoshop file containing the original photograph. Increasingly designers are using digital pens and tablets to create digital drawings. Products such as those by Wacom allow for the feel of hand drawing within the digital realm.

Once the altered photographic image is complete it can be edited and/or adjusted. For example the brightness and contrast of the underlying photograph can be adjusted. New layers can be added on top of the original photograph layer—but under the line drawing—to add color and detail to the presentation. More information about working in Photoshop is found in chapter 7.

SketchUp provides the capability of importing photographs for use in SketchUp models. See chapter 5 for that information.

Drawing Composition and Cropping

Whether a drawing is created manually or digitally, take care with its composition, and decide what portion(s) of the space should be shown. Most of the drawing methods discussed to this point, whether manual or digital, allow for the creation of a drawing that includes large portions of a room, some of which may be unnecessary to include in a final composition. Certain artistic liberties can be taken—through cropping or the elimination of those elements that look out of place or awkward—to improve a drawing's composition.

Begin by determining what particular element, if any, should serve as the drawing's focal point. For example, if a drawing is to serve as a tool that communicates the design of a reception desk, the entire desk should be included in the final composition. (While this may seem obvious, the process of drawing itself can sometimes obscure the drawing's primary purpose.) This does not mean that the desk must sit in the center of the composition; centering important items is not necessary—simply including them as fully as possible is more important.

After portions of a drawing are edited out or cropped, it is helpful to employ some graphic device to make the drawing read well. This involves thinking about how the drawing will "begin" and "end" on the page. Common methods include using an element of the foreground to serve as a drawing's end or beginning, as shown in Figure 4–15; using an architectural element to end the drawing is also useful (see Figure 4–16). Creating a continuous line that forms a frame around the drawing is another established compositional device (see Figures 4–17 and 4–18). Yet another method involves the use of broken lines on elements of the drawing that move past its cone of vision (see Figures 4–2c and 4–3b).

After the drawing composition is complete, one last decision must be made: whether the drawing will remain a simple, clean line drawing or be further enhanced through rendering. Rendering is covered in detail in chapters 6 and 7. Additional information about composing the complete design presentation is found in chapter 8.

FIGURE 4–14
The foreground element (stylized sofa arm) is used as a framing element, along with a range of line weights, creating a successful composition. DESIGN AND DRAWING BY JACK ZELLNER

FIGURE 4–15
Architectural elements are used to frame this drawing and create a successful composition. BY MATT SAUNDERS

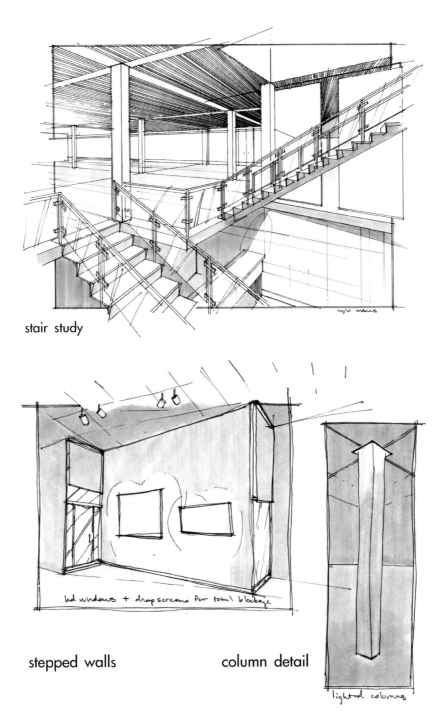

FIGURE 4–16

In conjunction with a foreground element, an outline is used to frame the drawing, creating a successful, dynamic composition. BY MATT SAUNDERS

stair study

FIGURE 4–17

Boxed frames help to make these quick sketches part of a successful composition. BY MATT SAUNDERS

lcd windows + drop screens for total blockage

stepped walls

column detail

lighted columns

REFERENCES

Ching, Francis. *Architectural Graphics.* New York: John Wiley & Sons, 1996.

———. *A Visual Dictionary of Architecture.* New York: John Wiley & Sons, 1995.

Drpic, Ivo. *Sketching and Rendering Interior Space.* New York: Whitney Library of Design, 1988.

Forseth, Kevin, and David Vaughn. *Graphics for Architecture.* New York: John Wiley & Sons, 1980.

Hanks, Kurt, and Larry Belliston. *Rapid Viz: A New Method for the Rapid Visualizaiton of Ideas.* Los Altos, CA.: William Kaufman, 1980.

Leggit, Jim. *Drawing Shortcuts.* New York: John Wiley & Sons, 2002.

McGarry, Richard, and Greg Madsen. *Marker Magic: The Rendering Problem Solver for Designers.* New York: John Wiley & Sons, 1993.

Pile, John. *Perspective for Interior Designers.* New York: Whitney Library of Design, 1985.

Porter, Tom. *Architectural Drawing.* New York: John Wiley & Sons, 1990.

5

Digital Drawings and Models

Architectural and interior designers use a range of software programs to create three-dimensional models and perspective "drawings," including MicroStation, ArchiCAD, AutoCAD, Cinema 4D, and Revit. These models can be viewed digitally and also printed. Printed versions can be used as underlays for hand-sketching or rendered digitally within the program; they can also be imported into a secondary rendering program for use in design presentations. There are also modeling and animation programs, such as Autodesk 3ds Max and Rhinoceros (Rhino), Bonzai 3D, and form•Z, that model and render architectural environments. (Additional information about rendering models and related software can be found in chapter 7.)

Computer-generated three-dimensional images are highly accurate and provide great flexibility because changes to them can be made quickly and consistently. Many of the most elegant and complex three-dimensional modeling programs can be rather time-consuming to master; most design students learn how to use one of them while in school.

This chapter focuses on the use of Google SketchUp modeling software, with a focus on related interior imagery. While SketchUp has some shortcomings, it is the most straightforward program for quickly and intuitively developing three-dimensional models and drawings; its interface is the most similar to actually drawing perspective sketches. In addition, models generated in SketchUp can be imported into Revit, and incorporated into Revit models.

Using SketchUp

SketchUp is an easy-to-use modeling program that builds on its users' hand-drawing skills. The information below is just a basic overview of the program. The References section of this chapter lists some excellent books and Web sites that will help you learn more about this powerful software.

Upon launching SketchUp the application prompts you to select a template (Figure 5–1a). The Simple template (Figure 5–1b) is typically the default; the Architectural Design template (Figure 5–1c) works well for interior design modeling.

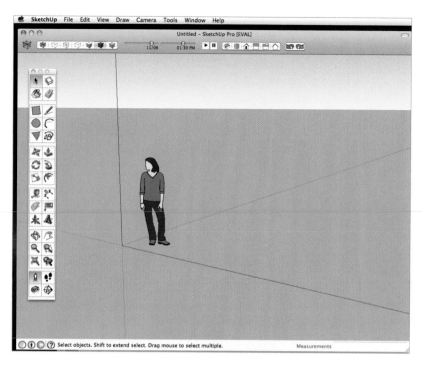

FIGURE 5–1B
SketchUp's Simple
template.

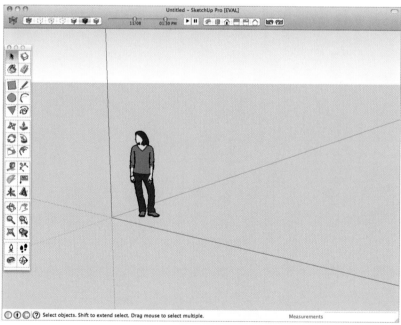

FIGURE 5–1C
SketchUp's Archi-
tectural Design
template, which
works well for
interior design and
architecture.

Drawing in SketchUp

These two tips will make working in SketchUp easier. Hit the Escape key (esc) after you have finished using a tool, or the cursor will continue to function as that tool. (Keeping your left hand poised over the Escape key is a good idea.) Using a three-button mouse will make it easier to use the software. (The center button can be used to toggle to the Pan and Orbit tools.)

Note: The screen shots in Figures 5–2a through 5–18h were all created using a Mac, not a PC; some PC-based commands and screen views will therefore differ slightly. Refer to Table 5–1 for information about the Tools menu.

Figures 5–2a through 5–9b illustrate methods of using various SketchUp tools and techniques to draw directly (without importing CAD or other files).

FIGURE 5–2A
Using the Axes

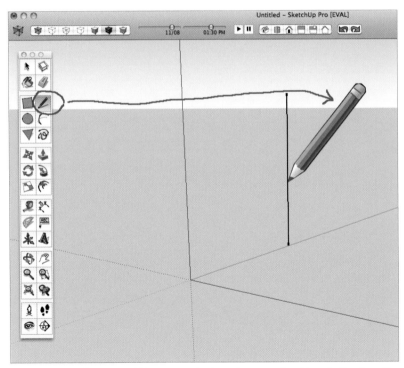

SketchUp uses red, green, and blue axes as drawing reference points. Here the Pencil tool is used to draw parallel to the blue axis (upward).

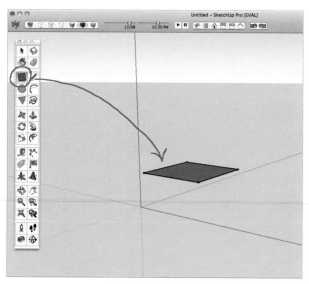

FIGURE 5–2B
The Rectangle Tool

FIGURE 5–2C
The Pencil Tool and
Edges

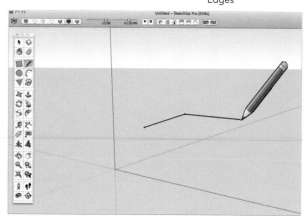

Use the Rectangle tool to draw rectangular or square faces. Select this tool and then select the size of the face by clicking at two opposite corners of the desired shape.

Note: The red lines and arrows are used to indicate tool icon and location—these are not part of the SketchUp interface.

Instead of using the shape tools, use the Pencil tool to draw lines (called "edges" in SketchUp) directly.

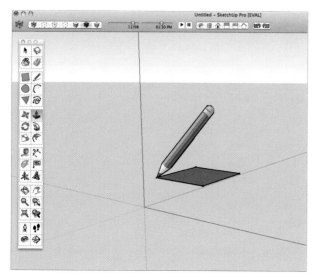

A closed series of edges (or lines) form a "face" (5–2d). You must create a face in order to further manipulate forms. Here the lines shown in Figure 5-2c are connected using the Pencil tool to form a face, which is shown in dark gray. See Figures 5–15a through 5–15f for more information about faces and edges.

Note: The size of the pencil tool is exaggerated in Figures 5–2a, 5–2c, and 5–2d.

FIGURE 5–2D
Faces

FIGURE 5–3A through 5–3E

The Push/Pull Tool is used to add or subtract volume. The pull action extrudes the face's form (5–3a and 5–3b). Hover the tool over a face; it will display many dots, indicating it is ready to be pulled up (5–3b). Use this tool to create a volume out of any face type. For example, the Circle tool can be used to create a circle (5–3c) that can then be pulled or extruded. To manipulate specific areas within a larger face, use the Pencil tool to draw lines that create individual faces (5–3d and 5–3e). Figure 5–3f shows the areas where lines have been drawn to create separate faces, with a single face pulled up.

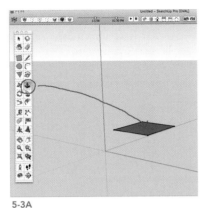

5-3A

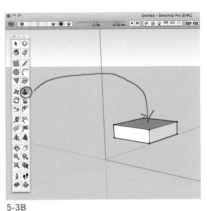

5-3B

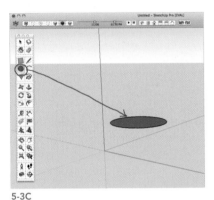

5-3C

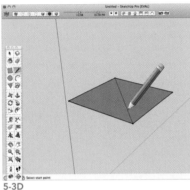

5-3D

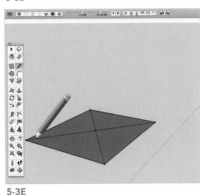

5-3E

FIGURE 5–3F

The Selection Arrow.
Use the Selection (Arrow) tool to select lines, faces, and other elements. The Selection Arrow can also be used to create a dashed selection box around all elements of a form so that the entire form can be manipulated simultaneously (5–3f).

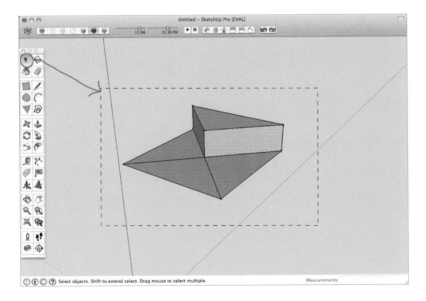

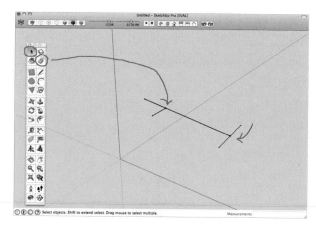

FIGURE 5–3G and 5–3H

If portions of lines require trimming or deletion, create individual line segments by drawing crossing lines with the Pencil tool (5–3g). This allows you to select each individual segment with the Selection Arrow (the lines then become blue) and delete them using the Delete key or Eraser tool. Figure 5–3h shows the line segments deleted after they were selected in Figure 5–3g.

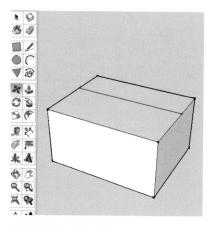

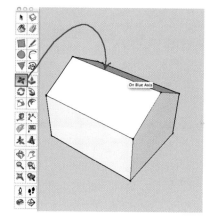

FIGURE 5–3I and 5–3J

The Move Tool. Figures 5–3i and 5–3j show the use of the Move tool to move a line drawn on the top of a cube so that it forms a pitched roof–like form (see blue lines). The Move tool is also used to move faces, entities, groups, and components.

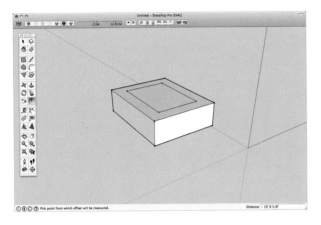

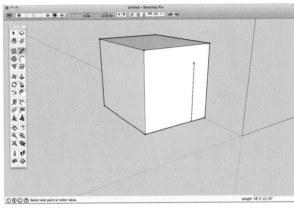

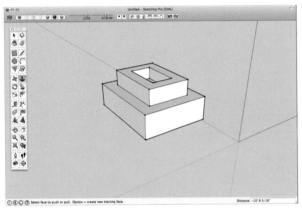

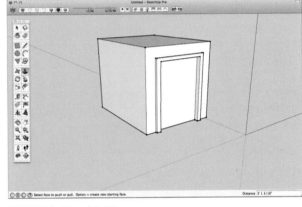

FIGURES 5–4A and 5–4B

The Offset tool is used to offset the edges of faces at uniform distances. It is useful in modeling interior elements such as furnishings and equipment. Offset areas then become separate faces that can be manipulated by, for example, the Push/Pull tool, as shown here. More information about faces and edges can be found in Figures 5–15a and 5–15b.

FIGURES 5–5A and 5–5B

More about the Push/Pull Tool. Once a volume is extruded (pulled), you can use the Pencil tool (or other tools) on the individual faces (as shown in Figure 5–5a). After the frame for this door was drawn with the Pencil tool, portions of the frame and door were extruded or set back using the Push/Pull tool (5–5b).

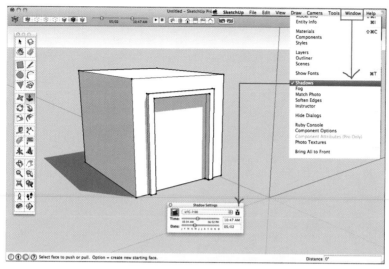

FIGURE 5–6
Shadows. To create shadows, select Windows > Shadows to display a dialog box that allows you to select the location, time, and month of the shadow and generate it accurately.

5-7A

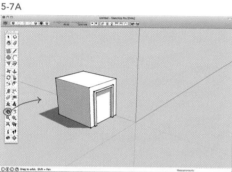

5-7B

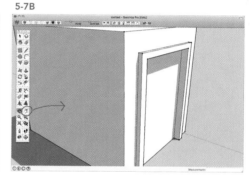

FIGURE 5–7A THROUGH 5–7C
Navigating within SketchUp

5-7C

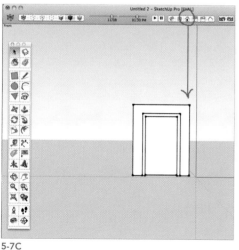

Select the Orbit tool from the toolbar (5–7a) or by holding down the middle button of a three-button mouse. SketchUp's Orbit function works similarly to those in various CAD and imaging programs. Select the Pan tool from the toolbar or by holding down the Shift key and the middle button of a three-button mouse simultaneously. (Figure 5–7b shows the view of Figure 5–7a brought forward, and enlarged with the Pan function.) SketchUp's Pan function works similarly to those in various CAD and imaging programs.

For quick access to elevations and other views, click on the small house icons shown in red in Figure 5–7c (this is the View toolbar). The desired view will be displayed.

See Figures 5–12a and 5–12b as well as Figures 5–16a through 5–17d for additional information on navigation and views.

FIGURE 5–8A and 5–8B

The Tape Measure Tool. The Tape Measure tool creates guidelines that can help you draw more accurately. The shelves in Figure 5–8b were drawn based on guidelines created in Figure 5–8a, the Pencil tool was used to draw the shelves onto the wall surface, and the Push/Pull tool was used to extrude the shelf volume (5–8b)

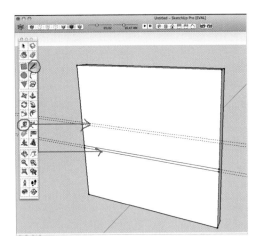
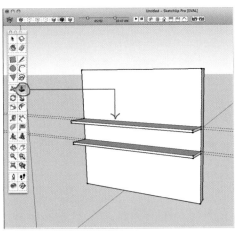

FIGURE 5–9A and 5–9B

Scenes and Styles

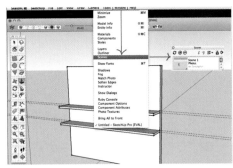
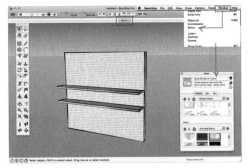

Creating scenes lets you navigate back to a view quickly and easily, rather than having to pan and orbit. Select Window > Scenes to display a dialog box (5–9a). Click on the plus sign in the dialog box to create a scene within the Scene palette. Click on the Scene tab (in red rectangle near the top of 5-9b) to quickly navigate back to that scene (or view).

SketchUp has a range of line types and styles to choose from. Select Window > Styles to display the Styles dialog box, from which a range of line styles can be selected. Choose from straight lines, sketchy lines, and a range of assorted styles. Figure 5–9b depicts a style called Brush Strokes on Canvas. Additional line styles are illustrated in Figures 5-12a and 5-12b.

Working from CAD Files

In addition to building models from scratch, two-dimensional drawings done by hand or with CAD programs can be imported into SketchUp; walls and other elements can then be extruded using the two-dimensional drawing as a base, as shown in Figures 5–10a through 5–12b.

5-10A

5-10B

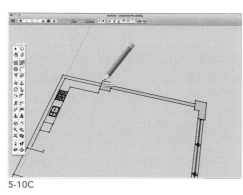

5-10C

Two- and three-dimensional drawings can be imported into files by selecting File > Import and choosing the desired file (5–10a). Only SketchUp Pro allows you to import .dwg files. When files fail to import into SketchUp Pro, it is often because a newer version of AutoCAD was used to create the originals. If this happens, save the original AutoCAD file as a file from an earlier version of the software.

The .dwg file will import as an entity or group. In order to remove items or work with individual lines or elements, right-click and select Explode (5–10b). After the file is imported, use the Pencil tool to trace over all of the necessary lines to create surfaces (5–10c).

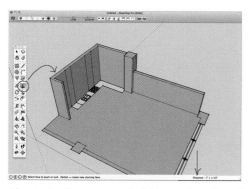

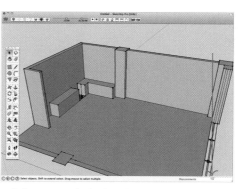

After tracing lines to create individual surfaces for walls and objects, use the Push/Pull tool to pull selected surfaces to their appropriate height. You can either type in the height in the Measurement box in the lower-right corner of the window or, using the Push/Pull tool, do it manually and then verify your work in the Measurement box.

Digital Drawings and Models

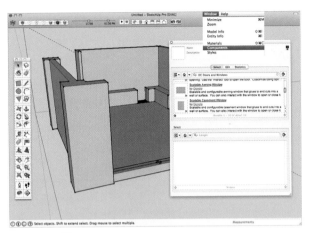

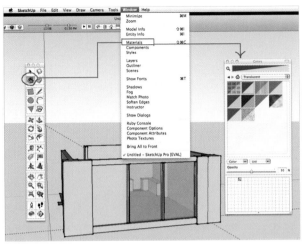

FIGURE 5–10F

Using Components. Architectural components such as windows, doors, and furnishings can be inserted into a drawing or model. Select Window > Components; components from the Internet or libraries can then be imported by navigating to the appropriate file.

FIGURE 5–10G

In this figure, windows have been inserted into the model as components using the technique described in Figure 5–10f. Windows and other elements can be made translucent by selecting Window > Materials > Translucent. Materials and colors for objects can be selected by clicking on the Paint Bucket icon (circled in red).

FIGURE 5–10H

The rough model is now complete and ready for use as an ideation and design aid.

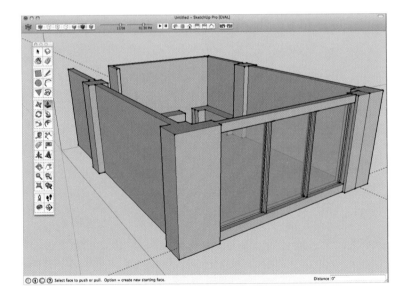

Figures 5–11a through 5–11j illustrate the space shown in the previous series of figures—now with a focus on the design and modeling of the kitchen. In some cases, a model of the entire space is not necessary—only the areas under consideration need be modeled. (In this example, for example, just the kitchen is modeled.) The model will serve as an aid in a kitchen renovation project.

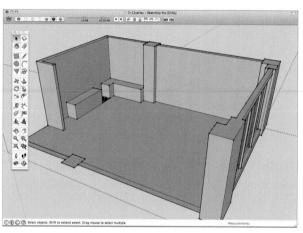

FIGURE 5–11A

Editing Walls. To gain a better view of the space for a kitchen design, some of the walls have been removed. Modeling just one portion of a larger space can also be a good approach.

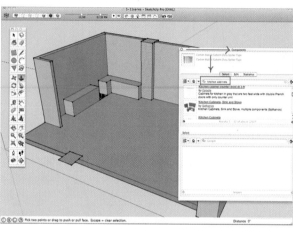

FIGURE 5–11B

Inserting Components. As with all furnishings and elements, cabinets and millwork can be imported by selecting Window > Components.

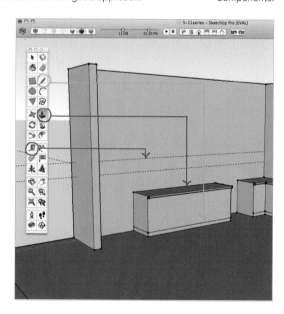

FIGURE 5–11C

Creating Millwork and Details from Scratch. In this example, instead of importing the cabinets, they were pulled up from lines on the original plan (blue line). Details such as a toe kick and counter edge were drawn directly with the Pencil tool (green line). Guidelines to aid in drawing the shelving were set with the Tape Measure tool (red line).

FIGURE 5–11D
Moving and Rotating
Components

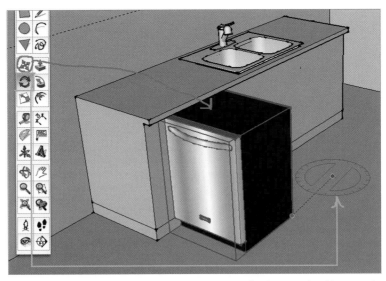

After components are imported into a model, they must often be moved and/or rotated to the correct orientation, as with the dishwasher here. To move a component, select it with the Selection Arrow; it will be enclosed in a blue box. Then move it using the Move tool (red lines).

To rotate a component, it must be selected and then clicked on with both the Move and Rotate tools. When the Rotate Tool is selected, a protractor appears; it turns various colors based on the axis it is aligned with. By clicking first on the protractor as it is oriented on the desired plane—in this case, on the floor, where it turns blue (green lines) and then selecting the desired component, the component can be rotated as the protractor is moved. Working with the selected component and the protractor orientation, the component can be rotated as desired. (This differs greatly from other CAD programs' rotation methods.)

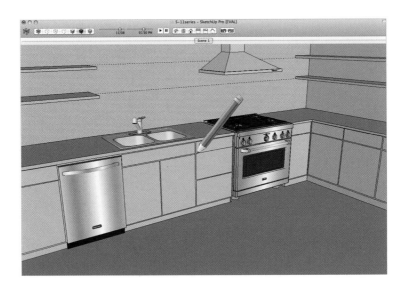

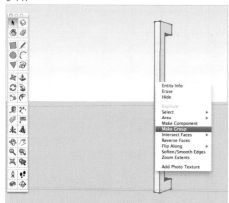

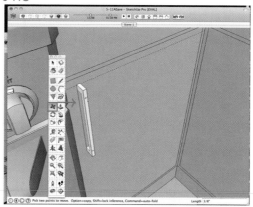

FIGURES 5–11F
through 5–11H
Creating Groups and
Components

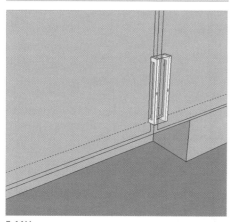

Creating groupings of elements and making components
(for elements that may be used again, such as furnishings
and millwork) can speed your work. To create a group or
component, select the entire set of items and right-click to
display this menu. Select Make Group or Make Component. Here a door handle was drawn and its individual
elements saved as a group (5–11f).

Once an element is saved as a group or component, it can
be copied and pasted as needed. Use the Move tool to
move copied groups and components into position (5–11g).

Where spacing is important, such as in the relationship
of these handles, components or groups can be clustered
as groups and then copied and pasted into place with
the proper spacing (as shown with the two handles in
Figure 5–11h).

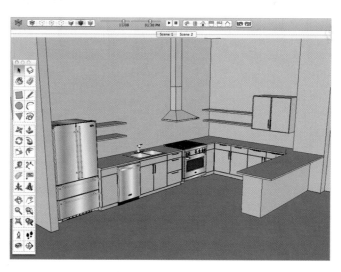

FIGURE 5–11I
The Completed
Kitchen. This is the
final model of the
kitchen design. Infor-
mation about render-
ing in SketchUp can
be found in chapter
6. See also Figures
5–12a and 5–12b.

SketchUp provides a variety of line and visual styles (access them by selecting Window > Styles). Figures 5–12a and 5–12b show two line styles applied to the model shown in Figure 5–11i.

FIGURES 5–12A and 5–12B

Using Styles. 5-12a is the model in two-point perspective view with lines with sketchy edges drawn using the Styles palette's Airbrush with Endpoints style. This view can be saved as a scene and exported and rendered in Photoshop, or incorporated into a presentation board or slide show.

5-12A   **5-12B**

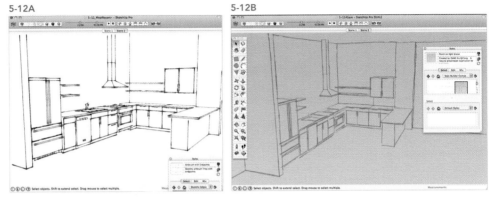

Figure 5–12b Here is the model in two-point perspective view with line styles from the Style Builder Competition option. When setting up the perspective view (by using the Orbit tool), take care to create a natural view—much as you would when placing the horizon line in hand-drawn perspectives.

Note: The best perspective views show the space as though it were being walked through, rather than from a bird's-eye vantage point.

See Figures 5–16a through 5–17d for more information about creating successful views. Rendered images of this model can be found in Figures 7-3d through 7-5b.

Working with Curves

Working with curved elements can be a bit challenging because the curved faces that result from using the Push/Pull tool create an object called a "surface entity." You can only work on surface entities as a whole unless the number of faces that form them are identified by using the View > Hidden Geometry command. See Figures 5–13a through 5–13g for detailed information about working with curves.

Additional Tips

As stated, SketchUp is an easy to use modeling program that melds with hand-drawing skills. The information given here is clearly just a basic overview of the program. The References Section of this Chapter lists some excellent references for learning more about SketchUp. Some additional tips for working with SketchUp can be found in Figures 5–14a through 5–16c, and information about rendering in SketchUp can be found in chapter 7.

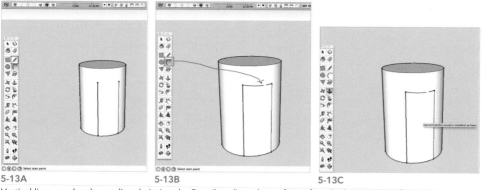

5-13A 5-13B 5-13C

Vertical lines can be drawn directly (using the Pencil tool) on the surface of a cylinder or curved form (Figure 5–13a). The Pencil tool cannot, however, be used to create lines that follow the curved portions of a form: drawing lines on curved surfaces requires the use of the Arc tool (5–13b). Curved faces drawn using the Push/Pull tool are called "surface entities" and cannot be adjusted as a single surface entity. Trying to push or pull portions of surface entities will result in this warning: "Cannot push/pull curved or smoothed surfaces" (5–13c).

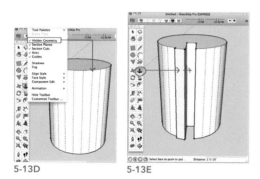

5-13D 5-13E

In order to manipulate curved surfaces (surface entities), choose View > Hidden Geometry. This will allow you to see and work with individual faces within the entities (5–13d). Figure 5–13e shows the Push/Pull tool being used on individual faces made visible by viewing hidden geometry.

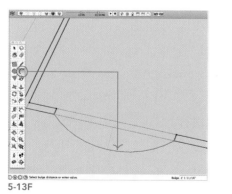

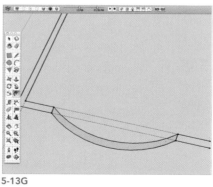

5-13F 5-13G

Curved wall forms can be drawn directly using the Arc tool (5–13f) and other tools, such as the offset tool (5-13g), the Pencil, and Push/Pull tool. The Arc tool can also be used to work from .dwg files, as shown in Figure 5–10c.

Digital Drawings and Models **137**

FIGURE 5–14A and 5–14B
Dealing with Scale Figures and Entourage. The scale figure that appears automatically in SketchUp can be removed by selecting and deleting it (Figure 5–14a shows the figure selected and ready for deletion). A variety of other figures and entourage elements can be inserted into a drawing (5–14b).

FIGURES 5–15A through 5–15F
More about Edges and Faces

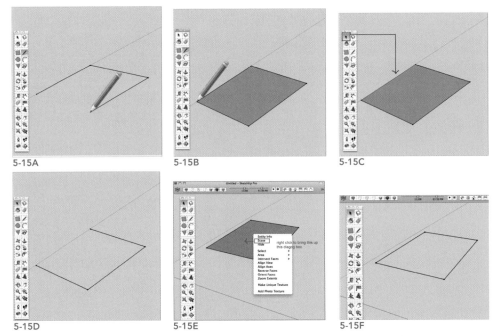

5-15A

5-15B

5-15C

5-15D

5-15E

5-15F

Lines drawn in SketchUp are referred to as edges; a closed series of edges forms a face (5–15b). Any time a closed set of edges on the same plane is created, SketchUp creates a face. If one edge of a face is deleted or erased (5–15c), the face ceases to exist; what remains is a series of edges (5–15d).

To erase only the face without removing all of the edges, select the face, right-click, and select Erase from the menu that appears (5–15e). Only the face itself will be deleted (5–15f).

Note: If you erase a face and then change your mind, retrace the lines with the Pencil tool.

The field of view is much like the cone of
vision discussed previously in the context
regarding hand-drawn perspectives.
Adjusting the field of view allows you to
adjust the area that is seen in a particular
view. Choose Camera > Field of View
(5–16a). The number of degrees for the
view is found at the lower-right of the
window; changing the number of degrees
changes the field of view, as illustrated in
Figures 5–16a through 5–16c.

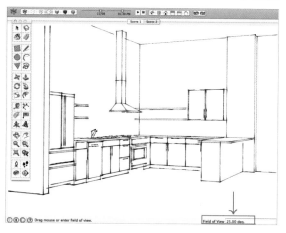

Digital Drawings and Models

139

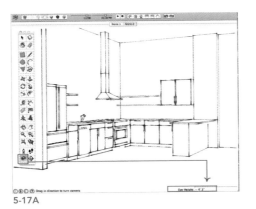

5-17A

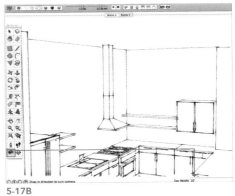

5-17B

The Look Around tool lets you view the model as though you were actually in the room, with your feet fixed in one place and moving your head to look around. (In this way it differs from the Orbit tool.) Figure 5–17a shows the Look Around tool (see red lines) and the related eye height. Figure 5–17b shows the tool in use, with the eye height raised to 10′ (follow the red lines). Working with an eye height of 5′ to 6′ is best, unless there is a specific reason for a bird's-eye or worm's-eye view.

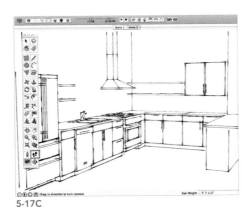

5-17C

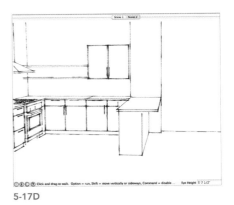

5-17D

The Walk tool maintains eye height but allows the view to change as the user "walks" through the space. Figure 5–17c shows the view with the Walk tool outlined in red, and Figure 5–17d shows the change in view as the Walk tool is moved—the view of the same space changes as though the user has walked to the right in the space (at the same eye height).

You can also use these two tools to create walk-throughs and animations (see the References section for resources for further information). The view in 5–17d is almost a one-point perspective, whereas 5–17c is more like a two-point view.

More information about SketchUp's modification tools, found in the Tools menu, can be found in Table 5.1.

TABLE 5–1

The SketchUp Tools Menu. The Tools menu provides access to all of the modification tools in SketchUp. Modification tools can also be found in the standard toolbar and through keyboard shortcuts.

TOOL	FUNCTION
Select	Select one or more entities.
Eraser	Erase entities from drawing area; hide and soften edges.
Paint Bucket	Assign materials to entities in model. Can paint, fill faces, or replace a material.
Move	Move, manipulate, and copy geometry and rotate components.
Rotate	Rotate drawing elements and single or multiple objects within a single rotation plane. (The plane must first be selected.) Can also be used to stretch and distort geometry.
Scale	Resize and stretch selected geometry.
Push/Pull	Manipulate faces. Can displace, extrude, reattach, or subtract faces.
Follow Me	Extrude faces along a path, such as an edge or line. Useful for details drawn at one point and repeated along a path.
Offset	Create copies of co-planar lines that are at uniform distances from the original lines. Offsetting within a face always creates a new face.
Tape Measure	Measure distance between two points, create guidelines, and rescale to exact dimensions.
Protractor	Measure angles and create guidelines.
Axis	Move drawing axis.
Dimensions	Place dimensions within model.
Text	Inserts text entities into model.
3-D Text	Create modeled 3-D text.
Section Plane	Make section cuts in model.
Utilities	Contains utilities and macros using the SketchUp Ruby API. Does not appear unless the Utilities tools have been enabled using the Preferences dialog box's Extensions panel.
Interact	Interacts with a dynamic component. Can be used for animation.
Sandbox	Modifies terrain. Can only be used after enabling the Preferences dialog box's Extensions panel.

Creating Plans, Sections, and Elevations

Many designers use SketchUp as a modeling tool to create three-dimensional views after a design has been initiated using drafting software. SketchUp can, however, be used to design a space, modeling it from the start of a project without beginning with plans and other orthographic views. After a project is modeled in SketchUp (as illustrated in Figures 5–3 through 5–9d), you can then create plans, sections, and elevations, as shown in Figures 5–18a through 5–18d.

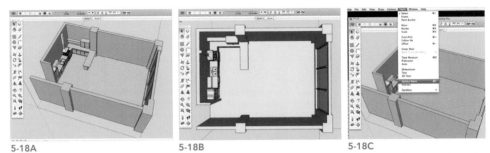

5-18A   5-18B   5-18C

Figure 5–18a shows a view of the previously drawn kitchen. The top view shown in Figure 5–18b is not a plan; it is a top-view, one-point perspective. In order to create a true plan, elevation, and sectional view of the model, choose Tools > Section Plane (5–18c) to display a green section plane element.

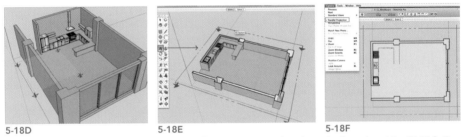

5-18D   5-18E   5-18F

To create a plan view (horizontal section), drag the green section plane into a horizontal position (5–18d). To create a standard section or elevation, drag the green plane into a vertical position. To move the section plane to the desired location, use the Move Tool (5–18e). After the section plane is in the desired location, choose Camera > Parallel Projection to move out of perspective view (5–18f).

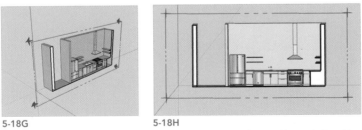

5-18G   5-18H

To create an elevation or vertical section, drag the section plane in the vertical position (5–18g). To create a standard section or elevation, drag the section plane into a vertical position. Then choose Camera > Parallel Projection for a true section/elevation (5–18h).

Orthographic drawings such as plans and elevations can be exported for inclusion in presentations and for rendering in other programs. SketchUp Pro offers a feature called LayOut that allows SketchUp models and drawings to be assembled in sheets, boards, booklets, and slide shows.

Additional Software for Digital Modeling

MicroStation, ArchiCAD, AutoCAD, Cinema 4D, Revit, Autodesk 3ds Max, Rhinoceros (Rhino), Bonzai, form•Z, and 3D Studio VIZ all offer three-dimensional modeling capabilities; some also include rendering functionality. All these programs have steeper learning curves than SketchUp, and for that reason they are covered only briefly here. They do, however, offer various advantages that make them quite useful, and they are all used in professional design practice.

Because Revit is based on parametric three-dimensional modeling, it builds a model and then bases drawings—such as perspective views, plans, and sections—on that model. The model can be rendered as well. Figures 5–19a through 5–19c show perspective views of the town house project from chapter 1 created in Revit. Rendering in Revit is discussed in chapter 7.

You can also import SketchUp models directly into a Revit model (see Revit's Help menu for detailed instructions). This can make quicker work of some custom elements, as using Revit may be a bit time-consuming for constructing highly customized millwork and architectural details. Some designers prefer Rhino for the creation of highly customized architectural and interior elements.

AutoCAD users often utilize AutoCAD's three-dimensional functionality to create digital models from AutoCAD files or for modeling from scratch. Figures 5–20a through 5–20c show perspective drawings generated in AutoCAD 3D. Figures 5–21a and 5–21b show a perspective created using 3D Studio VIZ.

FIGURES 5–19A through 5–19C
These are Revit perspective views created from the model built as the project is drawn. These views are taken from the model of the town house shown in chapter 1.

 KITCHEN 2

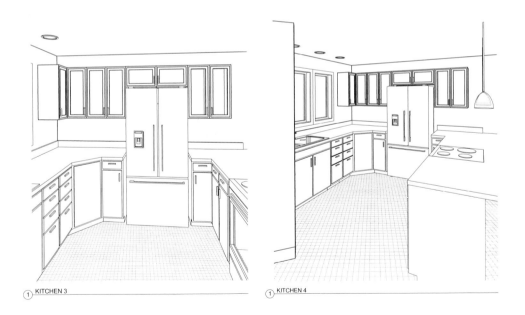

① KITCHEN 3

① KITCHEN 4

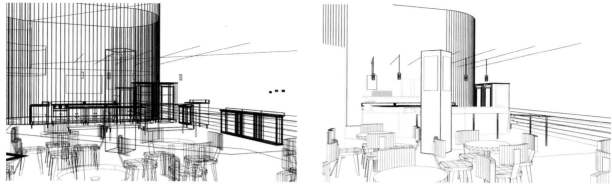

FIGURE 5–20A AND 5–20B

A perspective view generated using AutoCAD 3D. Figure 5–204b shows a cleaned-up AutoCAD version. See Figure 4–14c for a version drawn by hand (using 4–15b as an underlay). BY CUNINGHAM GROUP ARCHITECTURE, P.A.

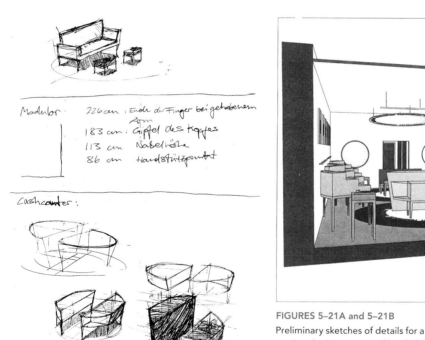

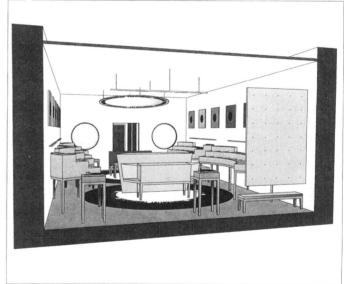

FIGURES 5–21A and 5–21B

Preliminary sketches of details for a retail project were created by hand, underscoring the importance of hand-drawing skills in design ideation and development. The final design presentation was created in 3D Studio VIZ. DESIGN AND DRAWINGS BY DIRK OLBRICH

REFERENCES

Chopra, Aidan. *Google SketchUp 8 for Dummies*. New York: For Dummies Publishing, 2010.
   This book is approachable, clearly written, and is highly recommended.
   Mr. Chopra's YouTube channel also contains many helpful tutorials:
   http://www.youtube.com/user/aidanchopra

Google SketchUp Tutorials: *http://sketchup.google.com/training/videos/new_to_gsu.html*

Grover, Chris. *Google SketchUp: The Missing Manual*. Cambridge, MA: Pogue, 2009.

6

Rendering by Hand

The next few paragraphs apply to both digital rendering and rendering done by hand. The two types of rendering have been separated into distinct chapters to ensure the technique for each is explained clearly—not because they communicate in different ways. The purpose of the rendering, its audience, the phase the design project is at, and the light source or general illumination should therefore all be considered whether rendering by hand or digitally.

In the world of architecture and design, the term *rendering* is used to describe the visual enhancement of drawings through the use of value or color. Rendering visually enhances drawings, making them easier to understand and allowing design presentations to communicate more visually. Rendering is done to convey depth and to make a two-dimensional drawing surface appear three-dimensional, thus revealing the material qualities of forms.

Rendering helps clients better understand a project, making it a useful communication tool. Some project budgets and schedules do not, however, allow for highly detailed renderings; other projects require extensive, detailed rendering. Because projects have different presentation parameters, students should develop a range of rendering skills—from quick and loose to accurate and refined—and learn both hand- and computer-generated rendering techniques. The level of rendering is also influenced by the phase of the design process in which the presentation is taking place. During the preliminary stages of design, for example, it is wise to keep renderings loose and sketchy to avoid pinning down the design prematurely.

An understanding of basic rendering concepts and techniques can enhance a visual presentation significantly; however, many students approach rendering by hand with fear and a lack of self-confidence. But there are dozens of rendering techniques, materials, and tools available. Practice, study, and the use of reference material can help students—and designers—develop a personal system of rendering they are comfortable with.

This chapter is primarily an overview of hand-rendering, covering some basic concepts, materials, and techniques. Orthographic drawings are rendered differently than perspective drawings and are therefore dealt with separately. Paraline drawings are rendered similarly to perspective drawings, so the two are discussed together. Most of the techniques presented are meant to be done quickly by working designers; they are not the same as those used by professional illustrators. The focus here is on workaday quick rendering techniques rather than labor-intensive illustrations.

Rendering as Illumination

Regardless of the style used, rendering introduces qualities of *illumination* to a drawing. Good rendering adds *light*, making a drawing appear more natural and creating the illusion of three dimensions. Rendering therefore requires a consideration of the *light source*, or sources, found in the environment being drawn, as well as the resulting value relationships. This is true for quick sketches and elaborate illustrations, for colored and noncolored renderings. The illumination in a rendering is perhaps its most important aspect.

Light falls on an object and illuminates its surfaces to varying degrees. The type of lighting, the location of the light source(s), and the object's material qualities all affect the manner in which the object is illuminated. Failure to consider the light source(s) and the related value relationships lead to renderings that look like something out of a child's coloring book.

As a light source illuminates an object, it creates varying degrees of light on the object's surfaces. Those areas that receive *direct light* become the lightest areas of the object; *shade* occurs in those areas that do not receive direct light. *Shadows* are created on the surfaces blocked from receiving light. These varying degrees of light and shade are referred to as *value*. All good rendering is based on value relationships. Figure 6–1 illustrates light falling on an object and the resulting shade and shadow. Figure 6–2 is a sketch showing similar relationships in a built environment.

FIGURE 6–1

This cube is rendered to illustrate value. The top of the cube is the lightest surface because it is receiving direct light from the light source. Shade (found on the sides of the cube) occurs in those areas not receiving light directly. Shadows are created on the surfaces blocked from receiving light.

These varying degrees of light and shade are referred to as value. All good rendering is based on value relationships. The front edge of the cube is called the leading edge and is drawn in white in this example.

FIGURE 6–2

Direct light, shade, shadows, and reflected light are illustrated in a built environment. All renderings benefit from the depiction of value relationships similar to those shown in Figure 6–1. BY MATT SAUNDERS

Materials, Media, and Tools

A basic understanding of the materials and techniques available allows a designer to make wise decisions and work quickly. Professional illustrators and renderers employ many methods, use a range of materials and supplies, and develop distinct personal preferences. Great rendering requires exploration and a curiosity about how a given set materials will work in a given situation. Figure 6–3 shows a range of paper media, materials, and tools used in rendering.

In rendering, there are no hard-and-fast rules; it is therefore wise to do a good deal of casual research. Looking at good rendering, fine art, and illustration is essential. To this end, books, periodicals, exhibitions, and visits to design firms are all useful. Observing what works in a successful painting or pastel drawing can teach a great deal about how to work with color markers. Art supply store personnel can be a valuable source of information about paper, drawing surfaces, and other supplies.

Paper and Drawing Surfaces

The type of paper or rendering surface has a significant influence on the quality of the final product. Many designers limit themselves to working on tracing paper, vellum, or bond paper because these papers are commonly used throughout the design process and are available in design offices. Table 6–1 covers rendering papers and media and relates to Figure 6–3, which is an overview of rendering materials, media and tools.

TABLE 6–1

Rendering Paper and Media (See also Figures 6–3 through 6–4b. Numbers in the table refer to Figure 6–3.)

PAPER	PAPER/SURFACE NOTES	RENDERING MEDIA NOTES
Tracing paper and vellum (11)	Both have slick surfaces and are transparent.	Graphite pencils, ink pens, colored pencils, markers, and chalk pastels all work with these (21, 23, 24, 27).
		Markers are not absorbed into the surface, so the color remains rather weak and tends to pool, and can create a watercolor effect.
		Colored pencil can be layered on top to enrich the color and define edges.
		Use a combination of white, beige, or cream, and darker pencils for highlights and refinement.
Marker paper (also known as visualizing paper) (12)	Less transparent than tracing paper or vellum, it absorbs markers well.	Meant for markers, but graphite, ink pens, colored pencils, pastels, and gouache all work on it
	May be difficult to see through; use a light table or tape onto a sunny window for tracing.	(21, 23, 24, 27, 30).
		Areas on drawing with ragged edges or mistakes at edges can be cut out and new portions pasted in.
	Some types of marker paper can be photocopied and rendered.	

PAPER	PAPER/SURFACE NOTES	RENDERING MEDIA NOTES
Bond paper (also known as copy paper)	Used in copy machines, printers, and plotters.	Highly absorbent, creating richly colored renderings. Good for colored-pencil work on top of marker color for highlights and shadows (23, 27). Rendering directly on bond prints or photocopies is a fast, popular rendering technique. Pretest all materials; some markers can smear and dissolve copy toner or printer ink. Mistakes can be cut out and new portions pasted in. Areas on drawing with ragged edges can also be cut out and pasted onto a new sheet.
Nontransparent art papers such as Canson paper or brown craft paper—like the type used for brown paper bags (15, 16, 18)	Can be used in some printers and plotters. The drawing can also be "transferred" onto the drawing surface using transfer paper or by rubbing graphite on the back of the original and drawing over the front surface.	Often used with markers, but graphite, ink pens, colored pencils, pastels, and small amounts of paint (including gouache) all work well on it (4, 21, 23, 24, 27). Select a paper the color of a predominant color in the composition so only highlights and lowlights need be added. Often textured on one side, and smooth on the other.
Diazo print paper	Used in blueprinting machines. Once the most common type of reprographic paper, it is no longer commonly used.	Similar to bond paper in its absorbency, it yields rich marker color.
Bristol paper, bristol board, and illustration, museum, and mounting boards (13, 14, 16)	Often used by professional illustrators. Watercolor paper (19, 20)	Highly absorbent; takes marker, ink, and colored pencil very well. Absorbency yields rich colors and highlights (21, 23, 27). Used for wet media.
Watercolor paper (19, 20). Available in hot or cold press, in finishes ranging from smooth to very rough, and in various weights.	Heavily textured watercolor papers are very difficult to use for detailed design renderings.	Water color paints, diluted acrylic paint, gouache, paint marker, graphite, colored pencil, and pastel all work well on it. (29,30) Heavier-weight paper requires wetting and stretching prior to use.

FIGURE 6–3

Rendering Media,
Materials, and Tools

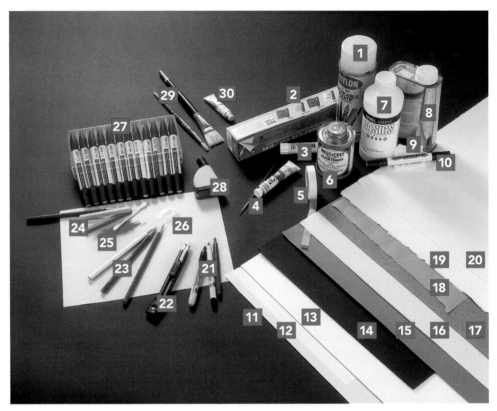

1. Spray fixative. (Holds down graphite and pastel; fixative for markers is also available.)
2. Transfer paper. (Use to transfer images onto nontransparent papers, or rub graphite on the back of the original and draw over the front surface.)
3. Glue stick.
4. Gouache and brush.
5. Removable tape. Use to mask areas to protect them from marker and/or create clean frames around renderings; liquid or sheet frisket can also be used.
6. Rubber cement. A recommended adhesive for paper—along with StudioTac or other repositionable mounting adhesives—it can also be used in place of removable tape and frisket.

7. Acrylic gesso. Works as a primer on paper, readying it for colored-pencil renderings and illustrations.
8. Rubber cement thinner. Can be used as a solvent to manipulate applied marker color; it is highly toxic.
9. Cotton pad. Use with thinner and pastels.
10. Marker blender. Best used to smooth out colored pencil and decrease the intensity of marker color (see Figure 6–5).
11. Vellum.
12. Marker paper.
13. Illustration board.
14. Black mounting board.
15. Canson paper.
16. Museum board.
17. Handmade paper.

18. Kraft paper.
19. Watercolor paper (hot press, smooth).
20. Watercolor paper (cold press, rougher texture).
21. Ink pens. Disposable and refillable types are shown.
22. Snap-off cutter. Use for cutting heavy mat-type boards.
23. Colored pencils (wax-based).
24. Dry pastels.
25. Pastels scraped into powder. (See Figures 6-23a and 6-23b.)
26. Baby powder. For use with pastel powder.
27. Studio markers.
28. Marker refills. These are not commonly available.
29. Watercolor brushes.
30. Watercolor paint.

Rendering Media

A trip to the art supply store will reveal the huge selection of rendering media, from colored pencils to markers and paint. The media range in price, and each comes with advantages and disadvantages. Renderings often necessitate the use of more than one medium—some renderings require a little bit of everything. Figures 6–4a through 6–4c illustrate rendering media. The following list covers rendering media and related issues.

Paper types (from top to bottom): vellum, tracing paper, marker paper, Canson paper, Kraft paper, and bond paper. Each type is colored with (from left to right): graphite, ink, colored pencil, white colored pencil, red marker, warm gray marker, chalk pastel (in powder from, applied with fingertip).

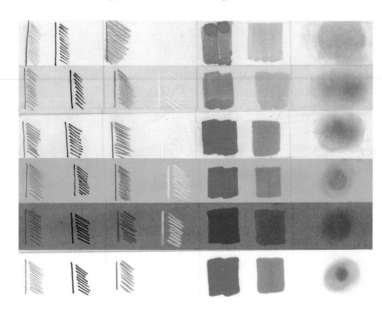

FIGURE 6–4A

Papers Used in Rendering

Red or blue colored pencil on bond paper (from left to right): colored pencil alone, clear marker blender over colored pencil, gesso applied prior to pencil, pencil over warm gray marker, pencil over cool gray marker, pencil over red marker, pencil over yellow marker, pencil over blue marker.

FIGURE 6–4B

Marker and Colored Pencil

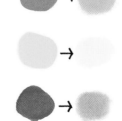

FIGURE 6–4C

Using Clear Blender Markers to Modify Intensity

Use clear or colorless blenders to create less intense color. Apply the colored marker to a slick surface, such as vellum, marker paper, or plastic wrap (1). Rub the paper with the clear blender to pick up the color, and then apply it to the rendering surface (2).

Graphite Pencils, Lead Holders, and Mechanical Pencils

Use these media in noncolored renderings for contour lines and to indicate texture, pattern, and material. They can yield subtle and beautiful original drawings and renderings; however, pencil does not reproduce as well as ink, and blueprints and photocopies of pencil renderings depicting variations of value and texture are often less clear than the originals. Deliberate individual pencil strokes reproduce far better than coverage produced by using the side of the pencil. If a rendering is to be reproduced in quantity, pencil may be a poor choice.

Ink

Ink is used in refillable or disposable pens and creates excellent line work that reproduces beautifully in both photocopying and diazo (blueprint) machines. Refillable technical pens in a variety of widths are available. They produce the finest line quality but require cleaning and proper maintenance. Disposable ink pens produce a less consistent line quality but do not have to be maintained; they are useful for creating line drawings. Fine-point markers and various forms of felt-tip pens create excellent ink renderings; they work well to define edges on colored renderings.

Use ink to create line drawings for reproduction and over-rendering with colored media. But be aware that rendering with ink can be both time-consuming and messy: it can smear, ruining an original. To avoid smudges, try using inking triangles with raised edges. Or in quick sketches, let ink be true to its nature—smudges and all. Inking can also be the final step in renderings that have been fully drawn with guidelines in graphite or non-photo (or non-repro) blue pencil.

Colored Pencils

Colored pencils are available in wax-based, oil-based, and water-soluble varieties; wax-based are the most useful in rendering (Berol Prismacolor wax-based pencils are the easiest to work with). See Figure 6–4b for examples of colored-pencil color manipulation.

Although they can work well used alone, for rich color they must be layered or manipulated. Without layering, they can look grainy because the pencil often covers only the top surface of the paper, allowing little valleys to remain uncolored. Underlayering warm colors with deep red pencil and cool colors with indigo blue pencil can diminish this grainy look. Or apply colorless blender marker over the surface of the colored pencil to loosen up the color.

Colored pencils can produce a buildup of wax when used alone and overworked, making an area look shiny, overdone, and amateurish. So apply a layer of marker—in either subtle shades of the color of the object or light values of gray—beforehand; the marker will function like a paint primer. Or coat the paper with acrylic gesso to add a primer coat instead.

The type and texture of the paper used greatly affects the appearance of colored pencil rendering, making experimentation a necessity. And the way the pencil is held and the stroke used produce different effects. For large areas, colored pencil is best applied with angled strokes; this is less tiring and produces attractive renderings. Sharp pencils have a greater surface area and cover large areas rapidly. Also use very sharp pencils, in combination with a straightedge, to define edges and outline objects.

Colored pencils can be used on top of marker in renderings to enhance color and define shape and value. And a sharp, white or light-colored pencil can be used to clean up any messy edges of a marker rendering. To create subtle color variations, chip away colored pencil pigment from the pencil using a blade and apply to the rendering by rubbing the chips onto the drawing surface with a tissue.

Art Markers

Also called studio markers, they are filled with transparent dye in an alcohol- or xylene-based solution. Although art markers are quick to use, they are hard to master and can be difficult for beginners to control.

Marker color must be manipulated to portray value, texture, and material qualities, or it will create amateurish, coloring book–like images. Apply a single marker color in layers to create value contrast. Underlay gray marker to create value or enrich color. Layer colored pencil, pastel, or small quantities of paint over marker color to create value contrast or tune up color.

A common mistake in marker rendering is to lay down a single coating of marker color without manipulating the value or color of the marker. Manipulation of marker color is done with several layers of marker, overlaying of colored pencil, or use of clear blenders. Marker color is often too intense for use in interior perspectives when simply applied as a single layer right out of the tip of the marker. To soften marker intensity, use colorless blender. Apply the colored marker to slick paper, pick it up with the colorless blender, and then apply it to the rendering surface (see Figure 6–4c).

When possible, marker strokes should be applied against a homemade mat or illustration board straightedge. (Do not use metal or plastic edges for applying marker color because it will smear.)

Alcohol-based markers dry up quickly and do not last long, but denatured alcohol or 91 percent alcohol solution can be used to revive markers. Remove the marker's tip and place the alcohol solution in the marker's body. Or simply open the marker and soak its tip in the alcohol. Xylene-based markers last longer and, some believe, yield better color rendition. But they produce fumes that can cause health problems. Some schools, institutions, and design firms therefore prohibit their use.

Dry Pastels

Sometimes called chalk, dry pastels work well as a complement to marker and colored pencil renderings. Although pastels are available in pencil form, these cannot be applied as quickly as stick pastels. Pastels can also be blended into a drawing with a finger, a technique that works far better than simply drawing with a pastel stick.

Use pastels to color an area quickly or create light washes for highlights. They are particularly useful for rendering painted walls and carpeting, as they do not streak as markers sometimes do. Pastels work well on colored paper as a primary rendering medium but are best used in less detailed renderings.

Use the edge of a blade to shave off a portion of a pastel and create a pigment dust that can be mixed with baby powder to make it easier to work. Smooth the mixture onto the rendering surface with tissue, cotton pads, or swabs over marker, or use it alone to create washes of color (see Figures 6–23a through 6-25b, 6-41a through 6-41c).

Large areas of pastel can be applied neatly when worked against removable tape used as a masking agent. And it is easy to erase or brush pastels from a drawing surface, making them a far more forgiving medium than markers.

Finished pastel drawings require the application of fixative spray to keep them in place. This can be problematic in renderings that also include colored markers, because fixative can remove marker dye. Special marker fixative is available and is used to fix the marker prior to the use of pastels and standard fixative.

Paints

Watercolor

Transparent, water-based paints are used by many professional illustrators and artists to create beautiful renderings. Watercolor rendering requires special tools, such as brushes, high-quality paper, and mounting boards. Because watercolors are difficult and extremely time-consuming to use, they are not commonly employed for rendering. (Students interested in watercolor rendering should enroll in a watercolor painting course.)

Gouache

Gouache is a water-based paint that, when used straight from the tube, appears opaque; when mixed with water, it becomes somewhat transparent. Professional illustrators and renderers use gouache to create rich, realistic renderings. Because it is water-based and is often mixed with water, gouache should only be applied to heavier papers. Use white gouache to create highlights on marker, ink, and pencil renderings by mixing the gouache with a small amount of water and using a fine paintbrush. Gouache should be applied with great care and only in extremely small quantities.

Mixed Media

Many renderings are made with a combination of media. It is not uncommon to see renderings created with marker, colored pencil, a bit of pastel, ink, and tiny areas of paint. By combining media, their individual weaknesses can be overcome, and the strengths of each taken advantage of. Some designers make collages, using a variety of media and materials that come from a wide range of sources.

Rendering Orthographic Projection Drawings

Rendering orthographic projections makes them easier to read. Because orthographic views look flat, rendering helps them convey form, volume, and the materials and finishes used. With the appropriate enhancement, orthographic views can be used successfully in design presentations. This is fortunate, because orthographic views are so commonly used in design practice—and they are faster and easier to render than perspective drawings.

The following is a list containing orthographic projection tips.

Tips for Rendering Orthographic Projections

Begin a rendered plan, section, or elevation by creating a clean original drawing. If possible, complex dimensions and confusing notes should be omitted.

Lines conveying items such as ceramic tile, brick, and stone may exist on the original drawing or can be drawn in as part of the rendering process.

Note: It is best to render tile, stone, and wood by hand rather than using AutoCAD or Revit textures or hatches. Remove those prior to printing and rendering as hand rendered versions look more lifelike and natural.

Always include shadows. If time is limited, render just the shadows using gray marker (see Figures 6–6 and 6–7).

There are a number of methods for determining shadow location and length; most of them are overcomplicated. Shadows can usually be simplified and estimated without affecting quality. (This is discussed in the following section.)

Build marker up in layers. Start with a marker lighter in color than the final hue desired, and build the hue up in layers, as shown in Figures 6–10a through 6–13c, 6–21a through 6–22b, and 6-38a through 6-39b.

Use rendering media to add color and texture and to convey materials and finish details.

Simplified Shadows

In Plan

There are two systems for estimating shadows in plan drawings. One employs a consistent shadow orientation for all the elements in the plan—typically one cast by a 45-degree diagonal light source. Shadows are drawn adjacent to each form in plan at a 45-degree angle, using a standard 45-degree triangle. The length of each shadow is estimated based on the relative height of each form. This method is simple and creates an easy-to-read plan (see Figure 6–5).

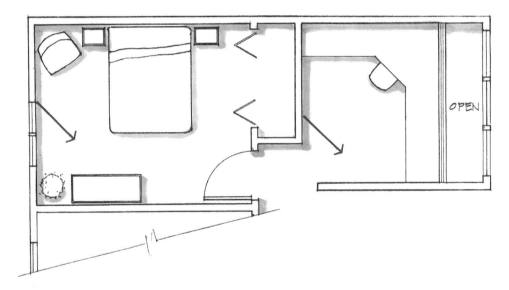

Another shadow estimation system for plans involves creating shadows cast by the various light sources found in the environment. The locations of windows, skylights, and electric light sources are used to cast 45-degree shadows (drawn using a standard 45-degree triangle). This system creates shadows that vary from room to room, relative to the natural and electric light sources. Shadow length is estimated relative to height of the object casting the shadow. This variable shadow system creates dramatic effects that help to indicate window locations (see Figure 6–6). However, plans employing this system require more time, and complex plans can become visually confusing.

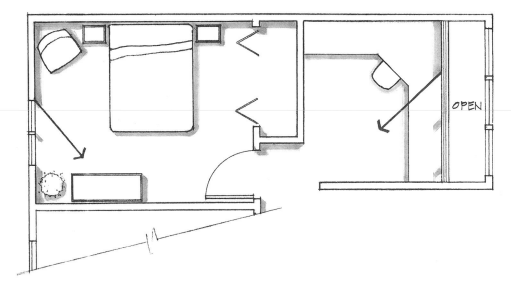

FIGURE 6–6
A floor plan with simpli-fied shadows, cast at 45 degrees, based on the direction of natural light (daylight) coming through the windows. Although this method creates dramatic effects, the system illustrated in Figure 6–5 creates a more unified composition.

OPEN

In Elevations and Sections

Shadows also enhance elevations and sections, in which they can be used to indicate the relative depths and the forms of design elements. One simple technique is to draw shadows in section and elevation cast from top right to bottom left, following a 45-degree diagonal, using a standard 45-degree triangle.

In elevation, shadows are cast at 45 degrees; their length is determined by the relative depth of the object casting the shadow (see Figure 6–7). Shadows drawn in elevation enhance the drawing, but their length should nonetheless be kept to a minimum to ensure graphic clarity.

For a more striking rendering, create deeper shadows. Unlike interiors, exterior elevations are often drawn with dramatic shadows because they depict the outdoors, which receives large quantities of natural light.

Section drawings have shadows cast by cut elements such as the roof, floors, and walls. The length of these shadows varies based on the distance from the cut line to the plane receiving the shadow.

FIGURE 6–7

An interior elevation with simplified shadows, cast at 45-degree angles.

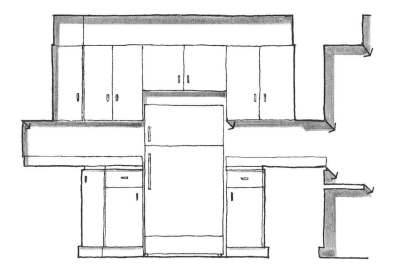

Materials and Finishes

In the past, the rendering of materials and finishes was sometimes done simply, with line work and stippling used to indicate wood and ceramic tile. There are specific conventions for drafting technical drawings, with hatches and lines indicating specific construction materials. Those conventions are not necessarily followed in rendering, where there is more freedom to show materials through a variety of techniques. See Figure 6–8 for examples of orthographic finish materials drawn by hand.

Color Rendering

Prior to beginning any color rendering, consider the amount of time available and the nature of the project. Project phase and type and the presentation's audience are all important considerations in the selection of color rendering style and media. Color rendering requires a working knowledge of color theory; some basic information about color can be found in appendix 3.

Color rendering can greatly enhance plan, elevation, and section drawings. The quickest method calls for printing the drawing—or making a photocopy or print—and rendering on the copy with pencil, marker, pastel, or a combination of these media (see Figures 6–10a through 6–13c). Another quick method involves the use of white or colored tracing paper laid over drawings and washed with colored pencil, ink, or marker; this give the presentation a sketchy quality.

Note: These are not the standard symbols for use in construction documents.

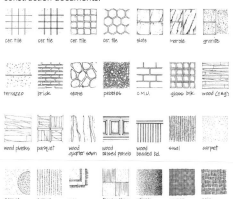

cer. tile   cer. tile   cer. tile   cer. tile   slate   marble   granite

terrazzo   brick   stone   pebbles   c.m.u.   glass blk.   wood (end)

wood planks   parquet   wood quarter sawn   wood raised panels   wood beaded bd.   sisal   carpet

carpet   carpet   rug   floor pattern   stipple   screen   coir

FIGURE 6–8

Examples of manually rendered finish materials (using lines and stipples only) for use in orthographic projections.

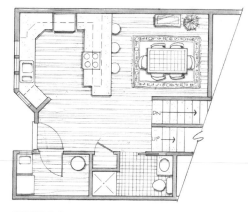

FIGURE 6–9

A floor plan rendered manually with pencil, using only lines, stipples, and shadows (tone). This type of rendering was widely used in the past but is no longer commonplace.

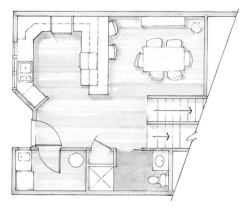

1. Apply gray markers to the shadow locations.
2. Apply a colored marker lighter than the desired hue using a straightedge.
3. Build up the color in layers (6–10b).

FIGURES 6–10A AND 6–10B

Rendering Floor Plans on Bond Paper (Lighter Hues)

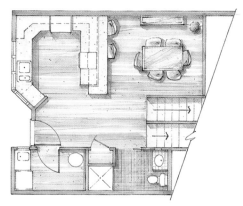

4. Tune up the color by adding multiple layers of colored marker and colored pencil. When tuning up color, markers may be applied freely without the use of a straightedge.
5. Enhance the shadows with washes of colored pencil (6-10c).

When working on copies printed on bond paper, shadows can be rendered with gray markers before any colored marker or pencils are applied. Areas to appear much darker in value should also be laid in gray marker prior to the application of color media. With shadows and darker values applied, marker color, pencil color, or pastels may then be used to create the desired hue.

All of the examples shown in Figures 6–10a through 6–13c use the time-honored method of starting with shadows in gray marker and then building up color with layers of light marker, rather than using one single sweep of a hued marker.

Figures 6–14 through 6–19 shows floor plans rendered on bond paper. When little time is available, orthographic drawings can sometimes be spot rendered. Although only a small portion of the drawing is rendered, it should nonetheless accurately indicate the materials used throughout the project (see Figure 6–20). This technique is most effective when the spot rendered clearly depicts the range of materials used in the project.

FIGURES 6–11A THROUGH 6–11C

Rendering Floor Plans on Bond Paper (Darker Hues) DESIGN AND LINE DRAWING BY COURTNEY NYSTUEN

1. Apply gray markers to the shadow locations (6–11a).

2. Apply colored markers using a mat board straight edge. It is best to use subdued marker color to give mere indications of color and texture (6–11b).

3. Tune up the color by adding multiple layers of colored marker and colored pencil (6–11c).

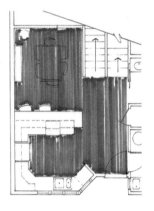
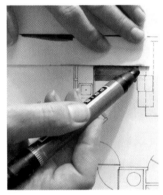
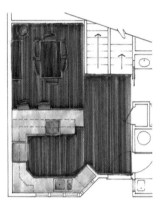

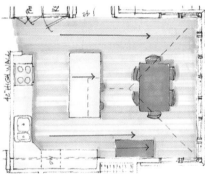
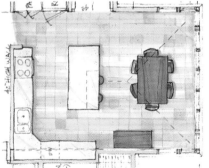

FIGURES 6–12A AND 6–12B
Rendering Floor Plans on Bond Paper
DESIGN AND LINE DRAWING BY COURTNEY NYSTUEN

1. Lay in shadows and a layer of marker in the direction shown (6–12a). In some locations, two layers of light tan marker were used to create variety.

2. Add layers of tan marker to create variation in the limestone floor tiles so that they will accurately illustrate the variety inherent in the material (6–12b).

3. Add colored pencil to the floor, tabletop, and chairs. (A rendered perspective drawing of this project can be found in Figure 6-38b.)

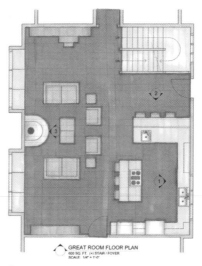

1. A coat of Sand Prismacolor marker was layered on the entire drawing surface. The stairs, countertops, window seat, and fireplace were coated with Eggshell Prismacolor marker. Layers of Cool Gray 10% marker were added to the sinks and appliances, and to the inside of the fireplace (6–13a).

2. Figure 6–13b shows the tile floors coated with Terracotta Prismacolor marker in a linear fashion, making the differences in the tile shades visible. Shadows were added with Cinnamon Toast Prismacolor marker, except for the gray areas, which were layered with additional Cool Gray 10%.

3. The final tune-up (6–13c) was done with white, cream, and green chalk pastel (in powder form), and with additional shadows laid in with Walnut and Gray Prismacolor markers. Sharp white Prismacolor pencil was used for tile grout lines. Additional Prismacolor pencils were used to add detail and to aid in color movement throughout the plan.

FIGURES 6–13A THROUGH 6–13C
Rendering Floor Plans on Bond Paper BY NICOLE BANASZEWSKI

Brown marker applied against a straightedge creates wood flooring and some furniture and upholstery. Tan marker was used for counters, and a combination of marker and chalk pastels were used for rugs and additional details.

FIGURES 6–14
Rendered Floor Plan on an AutoCAD-Generated Bond Paper Print BY ALECIA PLAETZ

FIGURES 6–15
Rendered Floor Plan on a Revit-generated Bond Paper Print BY KATIE OJA

Marker was applied in linear strokes as well as in swirls to simulate a range of flooring materials.

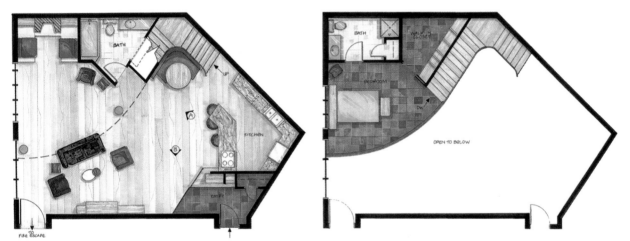

Student design development presentation rendering on bond paper using marker and colored pencil.

FIGURES 6–16A AND 6–16B
Rendered Floor Plan on a Bond Paper Print DESIGN AND RENDERING BY ARDELLA PIEPER

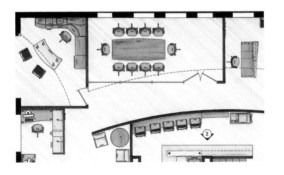

FIGURE 6–17
AutoCAD print rendered with marker and colored pencil. DESIGN AND RENDERING BY AMBER LIESTMAN (DETAIL FROM FIGURE 10–10A)

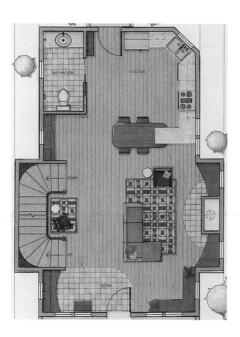

FIGURES 6–18A AND 6–18B

AutoCAD print rendered with marker and colored pencil. DESIGN AND RENDERING BY ELLIE FEENSTRA AND STEPHANIE HOLMBLAD (DETAIL FROM FIGURES 10–8A AND 10–8B)

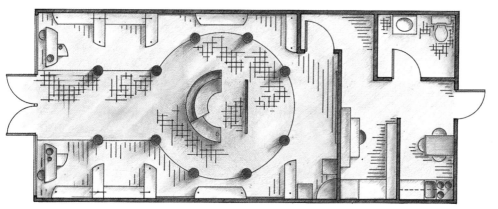

FIGURE 6–19

Rendered plan for use in a preliminary student presentation. Colored pencil on bond paper copy. DESIGN AND RENDERING BY MARTINA LEHMANN

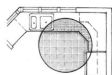

FIGURE 6–20

Spot rendering is a time-saving technique in which a small, descriptive area is fully rendered. This example was done using marker and colored pencil on bond paper.

Elevations and sections are rendered much like floor plans: they require shadows, a layered buildup of marker, and fine-tuning with additional marker, colored pencil and/ or chalk pastels. Figures 6–21a and 6–21b illustrate the steps for rendering interior elevations.

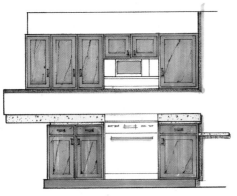

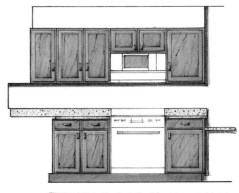

KITCHEN ELEVATION – EAST WALL

KITCHEN ELEVATION – EAST WALL

1. Apply gray markers to shadow locations (6–21a).
2. Apply colored marker (using a straight-edge). It is best to use subdued marker color (avoiding overly dark or intense color), giving mere indications of color and texture (6–21b).

3. Tune up the color by adding multiple layers of colored marker and colored pencil. Now markers may be applied freely without the use of a straight-edge. Enhance shadows with washes of colored pencil (6–21c).

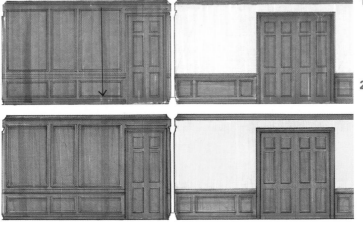

1. Lay in general material hues in values lighter than the final will depict. Use a straightedge to apply the marker, in the direction shown (6–22a).
2. Apply additional layers of brown marker vertically for wood, using white pencil for highlights and blue (Blue Indigo) for shadows. Here a combination of sepia and blue colored pencil was used for the wood grain. The painted portion of wall was done in tan marker with chalk pastels on top (6–22b).

Interior Design Visual Presentation

Pastels make fast work of large flat areas of color, and they streak far less than markers. Create a powder by scraping a blade against a chalk-stick pastel, and mixing that dust with baby powder (which will facilitate consistent application). Apply the pastel using a cotton pad or swab.

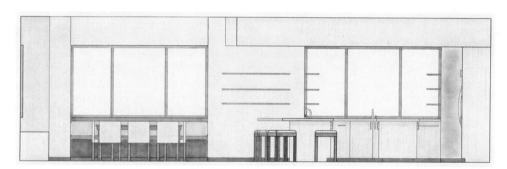

FIGURE 6–24

A rendered elevation created using chalk pastels and marker, from the same project depicted in Figure 6–15. BY ALECIA PLAETZ

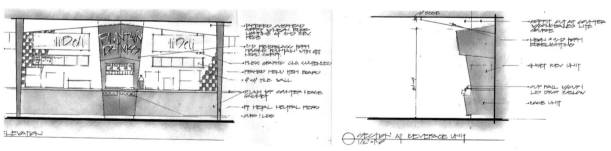

FIGURES 6–25A AND 6–25B

Rendered elevation and section for use in a preliminary presentation. Pastel, marker, and ink on printed bond paper copy. DESIGN AND RENDERING BY SMART AND ASSOCIATES

Additional Tips for Manual Rendering

The following is a list of tips and techniques helpful in all types rendering.

Rendering Tips—and Things to Avoid

All rendered orthographic projections require shadows, and a shadow plan locating each shadow should be created prior to rendering. Shadows can be rendered in colored pencil, ink, or marker.

Because they can remove ink and colored pencil, markers should be used for a base coat, applied before any ink or colored pencil. Light markers and colorless blenders can, however, be used to remove areas of pencil that have become too waxy.

Apply marker to large areas of plans, elevations, and sections in deliberate strokes against a straightedge. (Use strips of mat board rather than a plastic or metal ruler). Large areas of carpet or wood flooring should be applied with the lightest marker color possible, using a straightedge for at least the first layer. If marker would create a look that is too intense, or too linear or streaky, use chalk pastels instead—but lay in gray or other light marker color under the pastels as a primer.

Apply additional layers of marker to tune up marker color and to add nuances, where required. In renderings of natural materials such as wood and stone, marker color should vary slightly, so go over some areas with a second application.

Marker color alone is often too intense for use in interior renderings; colored pencil can be applied over gray or colored markers to add highlights, intensify dark areas, or enrich, soften, or subdue the color.

Unsuccessful marker renderings generally suffer from one or more of the following flaws: strokes created without the use of a straightedge, marker color that is too intense, and a lack of value contrast (i.e., no highlights or dark values).

Unsuccessful colored pencil renderings often suffer from the heavy-handed use of a single color, pencil strokes that go in different directions, the use of dull pencils—or a combination of the three.

Rendering Perspective Drawings

In all renderings, the light source and its influence on the environment is important; in perspective rendering, light and its relationship to the object(s) rendered must be considered above all else: every stroke of the marker or pencil should be determined by it.

What is the light source? How do the rendered materials react in relation to it? Understanding the relationship among light, value, and shadow on forms in perspective is a prerequisite for successful perspective rendering. The cube, cylinder, sphere, and cone are basic shapes that are found in combination in more complex objects. Learning to render these basic shapes in a variety of noncolor media is a good way to prepare for the rendering of color and materials.

These basic shapes are most easily rendered with a light source above and slightly to the right or left. Figure 6–26 illustrates this setup on a cube, cylinder, sphere, and cone. A light source in this position creates three distinct values—light (value 1), medium (value 2), and dark (value 3)—and a cast shadow (4).

In some cases light bounces off a surface onto the sides of an object, lightening it slightly close to the bottom even on the darkest value areas—especially when there are multiple light sources.

Complex, detailed rendering requires more value contrast to illustrate more complex lighting situations. In quick sketch renderings fewer than three values can be used, in combination with rendered shadows. And when time is scarce, a cursory rendering might include just the shadows. However, a minimum of three values plus a shadow will yield the most visually successful rendering.

Shadows in Perspective Renderings

There are a variety of methods of shadow construction, most of which are rather confusing and overly technical. But rendering shadows is an absolute necessity, especially on floor surfaces. Shadows should be handled in a consistent fashion throughout a rendering, but they need not be absolutely technically accurate to work well—they can be simplified and minimized to make rendering go more quickly.

The easiest method of shadow construction employs sets of parallel lines that are cast as the bases of triangles, as illustrated in Figure 6–27.

These basic shapes can be rendered most easily with a light source above and slightly to the right or left. In this position, the light source creates three distinct values—light (1), medium (2), and dark (3) —and a cast shadow (4). With this setup, the following is true about each form:

Cube

The top surface the cube receives the most light (value 1), followed by the side closest to the light source (value 2). The side farthest from the light source receives the least light and is darkest (value 3). The cast shadow (4) is typically adjacent to the darkest side.

Cylinder

The top surface is rendered in the lightest (value 1). Light curves around a curving surface, creating levels of value contrast that also curve around the cylinder. On a simplified nonreflective cylinder, the portion of the cylinder closest to the light is rendered in the medium value (2), and the portion farthest from the light source is rendered in the darkest value (3). The shadow (4) is generally located on the surface next to the darkest portion of the cylinder.

Cylinders are frequently drawn in a more complex manner because they often pick up reflective light, causing a dark reflection next to the medium value of the cylinder as well as a light reflection on the dark value; such is the case when rendering a highly reflective material such as metal. The portions of the cylinder farthest from the light source, which recede from the viewer, also receive medium to dark values.

Sphere

The top portion has an area with the lightest value (1), and as the surface curves away from the light source, values are blended in a range from medium (value 2) to dark (value 3). The shadow (4) is generally found on the surface next to the darkest portion of the sphere. Values are usually rendered into a sphere with curved strokes that follow the sphere's form. A bright highlight can often be found toward the top of the sphere, where the value is the lightest. The darkest portion of a sphere is sometimes rendered with a narrow adjacent highlight on reflective surfaces.

Cone

The portion closest to the light source is lightest (value 1), with adjacent areas of the cone rendered darker (value 2 ranging almost to value 3); the portion of the cone farthest from the light receives the least light and is darkest (value 3). A shadow (4) is most often found on the surface next to the darkest value of the cone. A cone with a reflective surface is rendered with the darkest portion adjacent to a highlight, indicating surface reflection.

Construct shadows by selecting an angle formed by the light source and using this angle consistently to create triangles at the appropriate corners of the object. Then connect the bases of the triangles to one another to form the shadow.

FIGURE 6–27

Quick Reference: Simple Parallel Shadow Construction

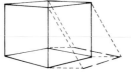

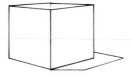

More dramatic shadows can be created by the use of a shadow vanishing point (SVP), as illustrated in Figure 6–28.

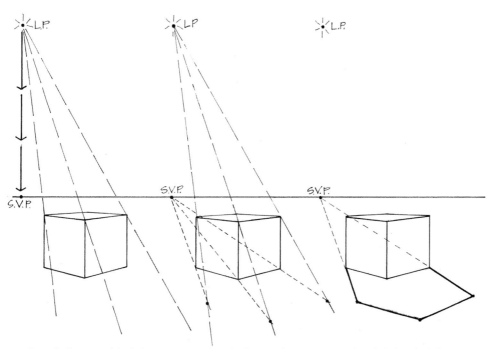

FIGURE 6–28

Quick Reference: Shadow Construction with a Shadow Vanishing Point

Decide on the location of the light source (LP). Plot a shadow vanishing point (SVP) directly below the light source on the horizon line. Draw lines from the light source through the tops of the appropriate corners. Draw lines from the shadow vanishing point through the bottoms of the appropriate corners of the object. The lines determining the length of the shadows are drawn by connecting the two sets of lines (in this case, the two sets of dashed lines beginning at the tick marks).

Rendering Perspective Drawings without Color

Most reference books on rendering focus on colored perspective drawings. However, renderings without color can be done quickly and help develop an understanding of value.

In noncolored renderings, the type of marks must be appropriate to the surface being rendered and the rendering style. For example, carpet is best rendered with stipples or tiny irregular strokes, whereas polished metal looks best rendered with gray markers or ink washes. Messy scribbles and hatch marks look best on quick freehand renderings; detailed, refined renderings require lines drawn with tools.

Leading Edges and Line Quality

The use of varying line weights can quickly define—and improve—a drawing, especially when outlining an object's overall form: the way the object's edges are outlined can greatly enhance the graphic quality of a quick rendering.

The use of varying line weights to delineate leading and receding edges greatly enhances a rendering—and can even serve as a substitute for rendering when time is tight. Figure 6–29 illustrates the concepts of leading and receding edges that are drawn to convey depth.

FIGURE 6–29

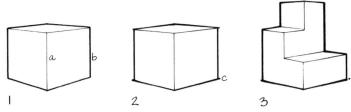

1. The edges of an object that appear to move toward the viewer are called leading edges (a); they are generally drawn with a very light line weight. The edges of an object that appear to move away from the viewer are called receding edges (b); these can be drawn in a very bold line weight to define the object's form.
2. As lines recede, they become bolder (c).
3. The use of leading and receding edges can quickly enhance a drawing.

Figures 6–30 and 6–31 illustrate the use of leading edges and varying line weights. Line weights can also be used to aid in the creation of focal points and to define compositional elements (see Figures 6–32 and 6–33).

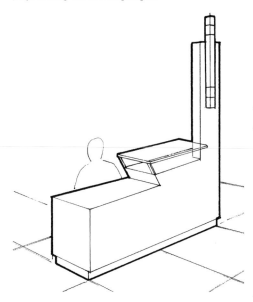

FIGURE 6–32
This drawing employs a range of line weights to create focal points and define areas of interest in the composition. The heavy lines are used to bring elements in the foreground to the viewer's attention. BY MATT SAUNDERS

Creating and Defining Value in Perspective Rendering

To ensure that value and shadow relationships are drawn correctly, create a value study prior to beginning the actual rendering. Make a copy of the perspective line drawing and mark the values that will be rendered in each area. Include all shadows and highlights (see Figure 6–34a).

FIGURE 6–33
This drawing also
employs a range of
line weights to create
focal points and define
areas of interest in the
composition. BY MATT
SAUNDERS

The three values and the shadow can be created without the introduction of color by using graphite pencils, ink pens or washes, markers, pastels, gray markers, or gray or white pencils. The values can be drawn using lines, scribble marks, hatching and cross-hatching, stippling, and shading by using the side of a pencil on edge (see Figure 6–34b). Marks made in ink will reproduce the best.

Perspective drawings rendered with gray markers work well in design presentations when combined with material sample boards or colored orthographic renderings. Creating gray marker renderings can also teach design students a great deal about value and marker application; students should therefore practice rendering with gray markers.

In gray-marker renderings, markers should be applied with accurate and deliberate strokes. In most renderings the tops of horizontal surfaces are rendered in the lightest value, using very small amounts of marker applied in circular, nondirectional strokes; 10 to 20 percent gray marker can also be applied vertically or at an angle to represent light reflection. A dusting of gray pastel mixed with powder can be applied as well.

The use of markers to render the floors and walls of interior perspectives requires special consideration. It is easiest to render walls by applying marker strokes vertically with a straightedge (see Figure 6–35a). It is difficult to apply marker strokes horizontally or aiming toward a vanishing point because the lines will overlap and distort the perspective.

A quick look at any floor surface will reveal many shadows, values, and highlights. No floor surface can be rendered by a single marker layer applied consistently—this will create a look that lacks depth. Reflective and polished floors must be rendered with a range of lights, darks, and highlights (see Figure 6–35b). Carpet must also be rendered with a range of values, or it will appear flat and artificial.

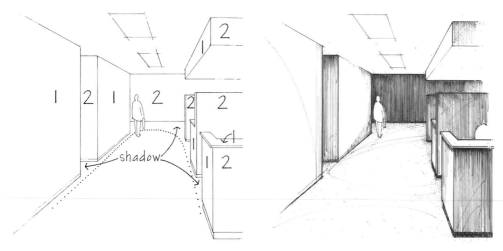

FIGURE 6–34A

A value study is an important first step in rendering a perspective drawing. It determines the areas with the lightest value (1), those with middle values (2), and those with darker values (3) and shadows.

FIGURE 6–34B

Value relationships can be rendered using lines and stipples. In this drawing, the back wall was rendered in a value darker than the other walls—a slight adjustment in values from those shown in Figure 6–34a made to create depth.

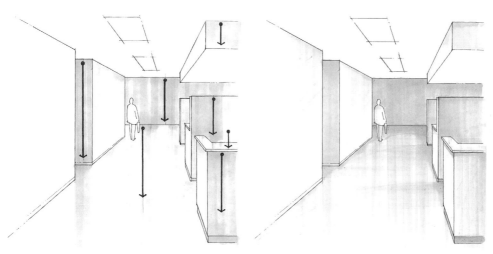

FIGURES 6–35A AND 6–35B

It can be useful to apply marker with a straightedge. Markers used on wall and floor surfaces are often applied with a vertical stroke for the first layer; secondary layers can be applied freehand or using tools, depending on the desired effect. Using a straightedge on floor surfaces works best for glossy, uncarpeted floors.

In most environments, walls receive varying amounts of light, so they must vary in value in order to appear natural in a rendering. In one-point perspective, the rear wall can be rendered in a medium value, and the two adjacent side walls can be rendered very lightly—or not rendered at all (see Figure 6–34b). In two-point perspective, walls should vary in value to indicate light-source locations (see Figures 6–36 and 6–37). For example, those walls with accent lights or sconces should be very light at the sources of light and become darker as they recede from the light sources.

FIGURE 6–36
This interior study was completed in twenty minutes using marker paper and gray markers. A grayscale study is a good first step in creating a color rendering. DRAWING AND DESIGN BY JACK ZELLNER

FIGURE 6–37
This rendering was created using gray markers and a small amount of white pen (for the light fixture) on marker paper. This type of rendering works well for indicating volume and detail. DRAWING AND DESIGN BY KRISTY BOKELMAN

Gray-marker renderings are valuable study tools and can also be used in design presentations. Take special care in such renderings to create value contrast, to include shadows, and to use a range of values on floor and wall surfaces. Apply markers carefully, and relate the strokes to an object's structure, form, or direction.

Rendering Interior Perspectives in Color

Think of color rendering on a continuum, progressing from lightly rendered to fully rendered. Project constraints and the materials used will dictate a color rendering's level of finish. As with all aspects of design presentation, the designer must consider the audience, the conceptual issues, the phase of the design process, and the amount of time available.

Different Types of Colored Renderings

A color and value study must be made prior to the completion of a more refined final rendering. To create such a study, make a copy of the perspective line drawing and mark the values, shadows, and highlights that will be rendered in each area (much like the value studies shown in Figures 6–33a and 6–35). Test all color media on the study prior to beginning the final rendering.

Minimally colored perspectives work well when time is limited, when the actual materials have not been finalized, or when only one or two hues are predominant. Sometimes referred to as underrendering, this allows for the introduction of color, but only hints at actual materials.

Shadows, Color Movement, and Color Variation

Shadows often contain the color of their surface in a very dark value. In addition, the color of the object casting the shadow can be subtly washed into the shadow. Shadows can also be created by applying warm gray (for warm colors) or cool gray (for cool colors) marker or pencil to the appropriate location prior to the application of colored marker or colored pencil.

Color movement, another key aspect of color rendering, is based on the concept that light and color bounce around in the environment. For example, a red apple sitting on a wood table will bounce a bit of red onto the table surface; an adjacent wall may also pick up a dot of red from the apple. Because green is the complement of red, a bit of green can be washed into the apple and dotted onto the table as well (see Figure 6–44).

In a simplified method of creating color movement, when a color is used on a surface, that same color is washed or stippled into a minimum of two additional surfaces.

Renderings also require color variation. A hue such as green should always be rendered with variations of that hue—not with one layer of forest green marker. The color variation in wood floors, for example, owes to graining patterns and actual differences in hue from board to board. Plants have leaves with a range of hues and values: new leaves appear bright and fresh, older leaves become yellow or brown. This type of natural variation in hue must be communicated in renderings. It is therefore inadvisable to use any single color of marker for any natural surface—the result always looks unnatural.

Interior perspective renderings are complex, and there is no single technique for rendering any particular material or setting—the way items are rendered must reflect design intent. Rendering therefore necessitates the use of extensive reference materials. Professional illustrators keep vast archives containing everything from gardening catalogs to plumbing supply catalogs.

Color Rendering Techniques and Tips for Perspective Drawings

For interior perspectives, marker strokes should follow an object's form when possible, with intentional marker strokes used to indicate highlights and shadows.

Many colored markers are far too intense to be used on large areas of renderings without being blended, manipulated, or tuned up with pencil or pastel. Use colored pencil and ink to create profile lines and define edges on marker renderings. White gouache, white pencil, and dry pastels can tone down marker color and create highlights and glints; apply these over the desired layers of marker.

Figures 6–38a to 6–41c illustrate the process of rendering perspective drawings. Figures 6–42 to 6–50 form a portfolio of colored perspective renderings created by students and professionals.

FIGURES 6–38A AND 6–38B
DESIGNED BY
COURTNEY NYSTUEN

1. Layers of marker were applied against a straight edge in the directions shown, in values lighter than the final rendering will depict. Large areas of white space were left in the countertop areas to indicate a highly reflective surface.

2. Simple shadows were laid in with warm gray marker (6–38a).

3. Marker layers were applied for the wood; the contrast between light and dark surfaces was given special attention. Blue and green markers were applied to plants, decorative elements, and books. Additional buff-colored marker was applied in various directions on the floor to depict reflections.

4. White correction pen was used for reflections at the leading edges of the countertops and faucets. Black ink and white Prismacolor pencils were used to depict leading and receding edges (6–38b).

FIGURES 6–39A THROUGH 6–39D

A color and value study using marker on bond paper is a helpful step in successful rendering (6–39a). The final rendering is done with both markers and colored pencil on bond paper with (6–39b). Figures 6–39c and 6–39d detail the use of colored pencil on top of layered marker to achieve highlights and shadows. PERIOD INTERIOR, ROYAL PAVILION AT BRIGHTON, ENGLAND; BY LEANNE LARSON

FIGURES 6–40A THROUGH 6–40C

The first layers of color for the architectural elements in this rendering were laid in vertically using a straightedge. The scale figures and other items were applied in a more painterly manner (6–40a). The final drawing (6–40b) has good levels of light-to-dark contrast and is fresh, not overworked. The detail (6–40c) shows how a combination of marker and pastel can be used for windows, ceiling, and floors. BY MARY WAWRA

FIGURES 6–41A THROUGH 6–41B

1. A straightedge was used to apply the first layers of marker, in the directions shown. The top surfaces of the sofa and floor were left blank to prepare for the use of chalk pastels.

2. Simple shadows were laid in with warm gray marker on the floor, while cool gray markers were used on the wall surfaces (6–41a).

3. Chalk pastels were used for the orange flooring and top areas of the couch (lighter blue areas), as well as the pillows. The orange pastel was applied freely and then erased as required for the floor; the same was done with the blue on the window. Blue and orange pastels were also washed into the bookcase, small vertical areas of the lamp, and the white rug.

4. Black pens in varying widths were used for leading and receding edges (6–41b).

FIGURES 6–42A THROUGH 6–42C

A series of process drawings leading to the final rendering. The model was done in SketchUp, then traced, rendered, and imported into Photoshop to desaturate the color. The rendering has a lush, fresh look that is very appealing. DE-SIGN, DRAWING, AND RENDERING BY MICHELLE MORELAN

FIGURES 6–43A THROUGH 6–43C

A series of process drawings leading to the final rendering. The model was done in SketchUp. It was then traced, rendered, and imported into Photoshop, where additional information was added, making it a hybrid rendering. Information about importing drawings into Photoshop can be found in chapter 7. DESIGN, DRAWING, AND RENDERING BY MICHELLE MORELAN

FIGURE 6–44
Rendering by a professional design illustrator for a design development presentation. Marker and colored pencil on bond paper. Notice the color movement throughout the composition. Ward House at Winchester Gardens, Maplewood, New Jersey; Arthur Shuster, Inc. (DESIGN); JANET LAWSON ARCHITECTURAL ILLUSTRATION (ILLUSTRATION)

FIGURE 6–45
Rendered perspective included in a student design development presentation, created primarily with colored pencils. DESIGN AND RENDERING BY JESSICA TEBBE

FIGURE 6–46

A perspective rendered with markers on tracing paper. BY CUNINGHAM GROUP ARCHITECTURE, P.A.

FIGURE 6–47

Color studies for retail shelving, done using markers on marker paper, with pastel dust washed in for blue glass areas. Only about half of the objects are actually rendered. The white portions read as light areas. Marker strokes define form and value. BY JULIAN HENSCH

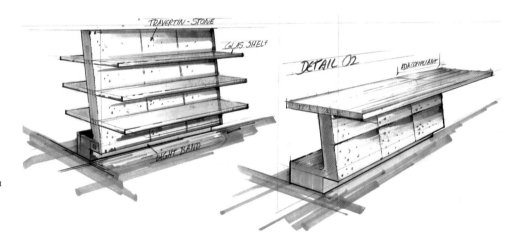

FIGURE 6–48

A color study done with markers on marker paper. The dramatic marker strokes inform the rendering. BY JULIAN HENSCH

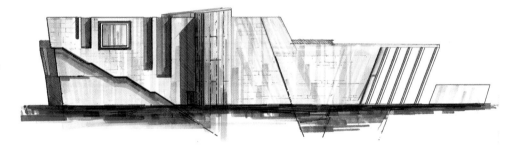

FIGURES 6–49A AND 6–49B

These renderings were done with ink and quite a bit of colored pencil; gray marker was used for shadows. (See Figures 10–17a and 10–17b for additional illustrations using these images.) BY MATT SAUNDERS

FIGURE 6–50

Marker rendering with a fresh, sketchlike quality. BY MEGAN ECKHOFF

REFERENCES

Doyle, Michael. *Color Drawing.* 2nd ed. Hoboken, NJ: John Wiley & Sons, 2006.

Drpic, Ivo. *Sketching and Rendering Interior Space.* New York: Whitney Library of Design, 1988.

Forseth, Kevin, and David Vaughn. *Graphics for Architecture.* New York: John Wiley & Sons, 1980.

Green, Gary. *Creating Textures in Colored Pencil.* Cincinnati: North Light, 1996.

Hanks, Kurt, and Larry Belliston. *Rapid Viz: A New Method for the Rapid Visualization of Ideas.* Los Altos, CA: William Kaufman, 1980.

Juracek, Judy. *Architectural Surfaces.* New York: W.W. Norton, 2005. Full of beautiful images that can be imported into digital renderings via the accompanying CD.

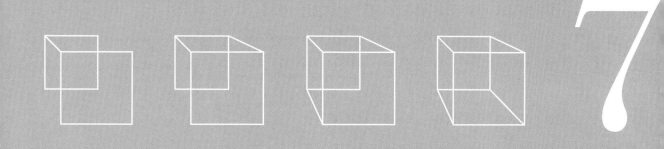

Digital Rendering

There are many approaches to digital rendering and many software packages to work with. Discussions with practitioners about the best way to produce digital models and renderings often lead to vigorous disagreements regarding the best approach. Some top-notch applications include Autodesk's VIZ and 3ds Max, Revit, ArchiCAD, Cinema 4D, Maxwell Render, and Bentley Architecture. There are also stand-alone rendering programs that can be used for completed models, such as Kerkythea (which works with obj and 3ds file formats such as those from 3ds Max, Blender, and SketchUp). In addition, there are plug-ins for rendering in SketchUp, including Render[in], IDX Renditioner, SU Podium, and Shaderlight. These plug-ins create more photo-realistic renderings than those produced by SketchUp alone.

Technology related to modeling and rendering continues to evolve and improve. But professionals should always have a go-to application that they can use easily (and relatively quickly) to create renderings for ideation and for clients and/or team members.

Professional digital illustrators can also be hired to create highly polished or complex digital renderings; they may use several applications to create digital renderings. For example, while Revit is commonly used for modeling and rendering, its rendering capabilities are limited; Revit models are therefore often embellished with 3ds Max and Photoshop to create more dazzling results.

This chapter focuses on rendering in SketchUp and Photoshop—both excellent go-to applications—with a sprinkling of examples from Revit for reference. Given SketchUp's ease of use, it is a helpful quick rendering tool in the various phases of design projects. Many designers use Photoshop to put finishing touches on renderings generated using many different types of software.

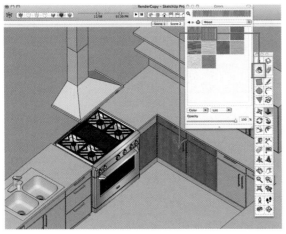

FIGURE 7–1A

To select a material to use in a rendering, choose Window > Materials and then make a selection from the drop-down menu, such as Wood. Scroll through the Materials palette's pop-up menu to display a range of colors and building materials.

FIGURE 7–1B

Paint a material or color onto surfaces by selecting the Paint Bucket tool, then selecting the material or color desired and moving the cursor and clicking on each desired surface.

Rendering in SketchUp

Rendering in SketchUp is straightforward and easy, although the program is somewhat limited and the results are not generally photorealistic. Nonetheless, SketchUp renderings work very well for ideation, design refinement, and in some cases, client presentations.

After a model is constructed, rendering is done by choosing Window > Materials and then making a selection from the drop-down menu—such as Wood, as shown in Figure 7–1a.

Once a material (that has been previously loaded into the Materials library) is selected, it can be painted onto surfaces by selecting the Paint Bucket tool and moving the cursor to each surface to be rendered, as shown in Figure 7–1b. Wall color is added the same way. When details within objects have been drawn with edges, thus creating separate surfaces, each surface must be selected individually, as shown in Figure 7–1c. Detailed information about loading materials and textures into the Materials Library can be found in Figures 7-2a through 7-3d.

Materials may occasionally serve double duty, as shown in Figure 7–1d, where Asphalt is used to render a dark concrete counter. Very infrequently, the exact material is already available in the library—such as the tile shown in Figure 7–1e. Refer also to Figures 7-2a through 7-3d for details on loading materials into the Materials Library. It is sometimes necessary to add volume and detail (by pulling or pushing a face) to render materials, as in Figure 7–1f, in which the volume of the backsplash has been increased as the material is rendered.

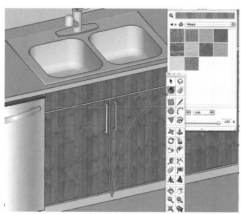

FIGURE 7–1C
For items comprised of many edges and surfaces, each surface must be selected separately. Zoom into tight areas and small surfaces to select them accurately.

FIGURE 7–1D
Items can sometimes be rendered with materials that look fine but are not actually the "correct" material. Here concrete counters are rendered with Asphalt.

FIGURE 7–1E
Some items, such as this tile, are readily available in the SketchUp materials browser.

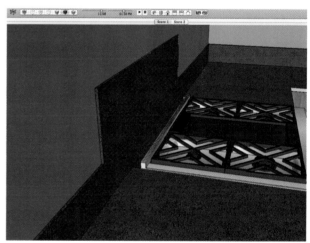

FIGURE 7–1F
It is sometimes necessary to add volume and additional detail. Here the volume of the backsplash was added (with the Push/Pull tool) as the material was rendered.

To add furnishings and other components, choose Window > Components. In Figure 7–2a, a simply modeled barstool is selected from the Google 3D Warehouse and downloaded into the model. Figure 7–2b illustrates the model with simple furniture from the 3D Warehouse inserted and with rendered materials found within the existing SketchUp materials library (with no additional materials added).

FIGURE 7–2A
Furnishings and other components can be downloaded from the Google 3D Warehouse. This simple barstool was downloaded and then positioned using the Move and Rotate tools. You can even apply color and texture to the surface of some furnishings (such as this one).

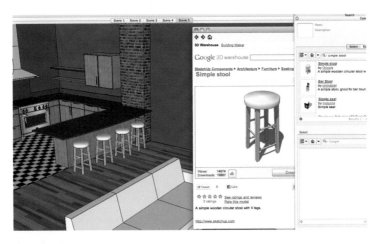

FIGURE 7–2B
All of the materials shown here were found in the standard Materials library, and the sofas and stools were downloaded from the Google 3D Warehouse.

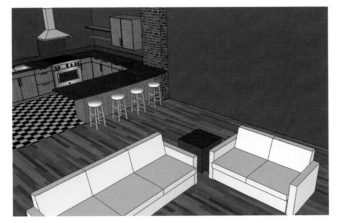

There are three options for loading materials, colors, and related items into the Materials library. To add an entire single entity, such as a rug or photograph, as shown in Figure 7–3a, choose File > Import and then select Use as Image from the options in the pop-up menu in the dialog box that appears, as shown in Figure 7–3b.

In SketchUp, a texture is an image with a repetitive pattern—such as upholstery fabric or wood flooring—used for rendering. SketchUp limits materials imagery to textures that employ repetitive imagery and single-entity images. Information about loading textures into the Materials palette can be found in Figure 7–3c. The finalized model is shown in Figure 7–3d.

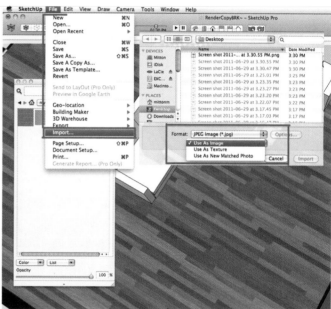

FIGURES 7–3A AND 7–3B

To add an entire single entity, such as the rug as shown here (7–3a), choose File > Import and select Use as Image from the options in the pop-up menu in the dialog box that appears (7–3b).

FIGURE 7–3C
To add a new texture, choose Window > Materials; the Materials palette will appear. Click on the List drop-down menu, select New, and enter a name for the new materials collection that will contain your materials or textures. Then click on the Color drop-down menu and select New Texture.

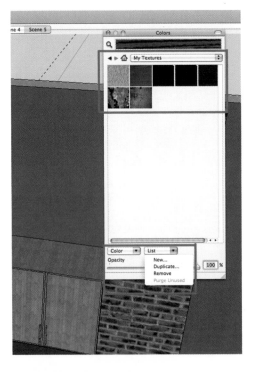

Browse for your material image and click Open to add it to the new collection. (Alternatively, you can choose File > Import and select Use as Texture.)

Note: In order to browse for and select an image to use as a texture, you should first create an image file containing a product image, such as scans of materials or higher-resolution images obtained from manufacturers. (Figure 7–3d illustrates sofas with a texture created by uploading a manufacturer's high-resolution textile image file.)

FIGURE 7–3D
The rendered model.

SketchUp's ease of use and quick rendering options make it a good choice for ideation and the creation of quick client presentations. Another design option for the project in the previous figures is presented in Figures 7–4a through 7–5b.

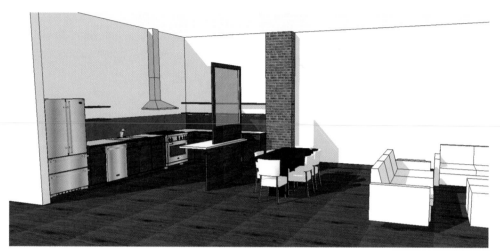

The flooring was created as a texture by uploading a .jpg file of a dark wood sample. When loaded as a texture, the image is treated as a repetitive pattern, which is why it appears tiled on the floor. The same texture was used for cabinetry and wood furnishings, where, due to the smaller surfaces, the texture does not appear tiled.

The translucent panel was created by rendering a thin panel inside a thicker wall, with one of the translucent choices in the Materials palette. The blue backsplash was rendered using a blue material imported in the Import > Use as an Image mode. The white furnishings are Google components; they were imported as white and no color was added.

The only difference between Figures 7–4a and 7–4b is the shadows; the settings relate to two different times of year. (Choose Window > Shadows to manipulate shadows.)

FIGURE 7–4A AND 7–4B
Illustrations of a different design option for the space shown in the previous figures.

Once a model is rendered in SketchUp, you can apply styles to modify the way it looks. These styles vary greatly and can create renderings that look like paintings, colored pencil, or marker, as illustrated in Figures 7–5a and 7–5b. To select a rendering style, choose Window > Styles > Assorted Styles, and then select one of the styles from the drop-down menu.

Note: If a line style is selected, it will eliminate the rendering, as illustrated in Figure 7–5c.

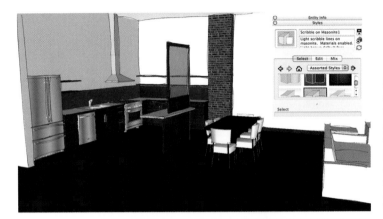

Figure 7–5a was modified by creating a new style, done by choosing Window > Styles > Assorted Styles > Scribble on Masonite1.

Figure 7–5b was modified by creating a new Style, done by choosing Window > Styles > Assorted Styles > PSO Vignette1.

After a rendering is complete, selecting a line style (rather than one of the rendering styles found in the Assorted Styles menu), will eliminate most of the rendering, as shown in Figure 7–5c.

You can also import (and modify) photographs into SketchUp to create a photomontage (called a "matched photo" by the application) that includes the original photograph and the new SketchUp model. The process is similar to creating perspectives by working with photographs covered in chapter 4.

FIGURE 7–5C
The rendering shown in the previous figures loses most of its rendering when modified with a new line style. The blue backsplash has stayed in place because it was imported via the Use as an Image option.

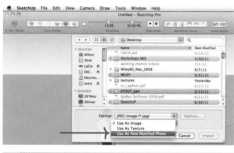

FIGURES 7–6A THROUGH 7–6D
SketchUp allows you to import photographs and image files and then combine them with the SketchUp model. This is done by choosing Import > Use As New Matched Photo.

In order to work with matched photos, the axes must be selected and located similarly to the perspective in the photograph. This creates cohesion between the perspective lines in the photograph and those in the model

Plug-ins and Ruby Scripts

According to the Google SketchUp Web site,

Ruby is a programming language that anyone can use to write plug-ins (scripts) for Google SketchUp. Once installed, Ruby Scripts can add tools, simplify multistep operations, and otherwise improve the way you work with SketchUp. The good news is that you don't need to know anything about Ruby scripting (or programming in general) to use Ruby Scripts that other people have created.

Ruby Scripts available from Google include a window maker and an onion dome maker.

There are also some plug-ins that create photorealistic renderings, such as SU Podium and Shaderlight; examples are shown in Figures 7–7a through 7–8b. Information about these two plug-ins can be found in the References section at the end of this chapter.

FIGURES 7–7A AND 7–7B
Podium is a plug-in that works with SketchUp to create more photorealistic rendering. Figure 7–7a shows the rendered SketchUp model before the use of SU Podium, and Figure 7–7b shows the model afterward.

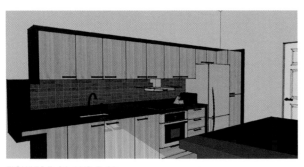

FIGURES 7–8A AND 7–8B
Figure 7–7a shows the rendered SketchUp model before the use of SU Podium, and Figure 7–7b shows the model afterward.

Rendering with Photoshop

Note: This section requires a basic knowledge of Photoshop tools and the concept of layers in Photoshop. Those unfamiliar with Photoshop are encouraged to follow a basic Photoshop tutorial before reading the following section.

Designers are increasingly using graphics editing software such as Photoshop to render orthographic drawings. This involves importing the drawing into Photoshop and either using scanned imagery from actual material samples, material images from other digital sources such as manufacturers' online resources, or archival materials and books such as *Architectural Surfaces* by Judy Juracek (2005). To do so successfully, you must be attentive to the scale of materials images (relative to the scaled drawings), as well as to the resolution quality of the files for both the materials and the drawing.

Figures 7–9a through 7–9c contain step-by-step instructions for getting started on rendering in Photoshop, using a drawing created imported from AutoCAD. The subsequent figures are organized as a tutorial.

Note: The following information covers Photoshop CS5 for Macintosh; the interfaces of other versions and for other operating systems vary slightly.

The following list is an overview—or refresher—on Photoshop rendering meant to be read along with Figures 7–19a through 7–20d.

Photoshop Overview

Drawing/Rendering Setup

Create a drawing file and a series of image files in Photoshop (Figures 7–9a through 7–10c). You will be working back and forth from the actual drawing/rendering file and the various images (such as a .jpg of wood) pasted into the rendering. Think of the

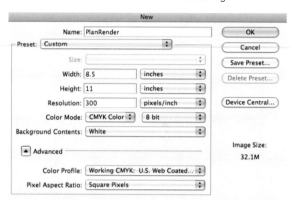

FIGURE 7–9A

First Steps in Photoshop Rendering

1. Moving from CAD to Photoshop

In AutoCAD, plot the drawing as a PDF in the scale desired (such as 1/4″ = 1′-0′) by either using the Plot/Print window and saving the file or by printing the file as a PDF.

Note: Photoshop can do strange things with lines. It is therefore best to make all line weights rather light so that lines from AutoCAD do not become too bold in Photoshop.

If the drawing was generated in Revit or a similar program but will be rendered in Photoshop, follow the steps for creating a PDF of the drawing so that it can be imported.

2. Importing

Create a new Photoshop file by choosing File > New (7–9a), and then make the following selections:

Make the canvas dimensions 8.5″ × 11″ (or whatever size you desire).

Make the resolution 300 pixels/inch. (A lower resolution file will print poorly, and you cannot upscale the image once it is imported at less than 300 dpi.)

Choose CMYK mode with a white background.

This will be the canvas for the rendering

drawing file as the "paper" and the various image files as the "markers" you would use to render with.

Follow the directions regarding drawing resolution in Figures 7–9a through 7–9c exactly, and use a white background. You cannot "upsample" Photoshop files, so if the drawing starts off at a low resolution, it will never look good enlarged.

Use a CMKY color setting for items that will be printed for presentation and RGB color for items that will be projected or presented on monitors.

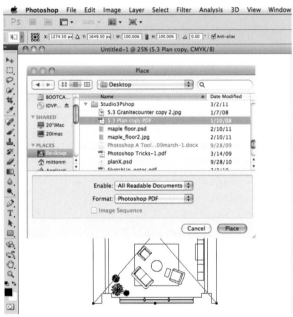

In the newly created Photoshop document, choose File > Place, then browse for the PDF that you prepared in the previous step. Select that file and click OK. This will place the PDF on your canvas. Click Return to accept the change. The diagonals across the plan will now disappear.

FIGURE 7–9B

Placing the Drawing

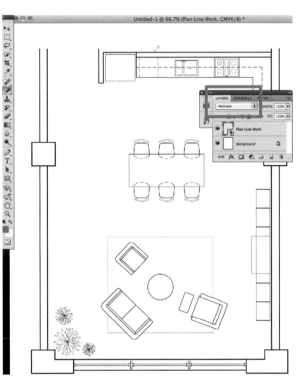

FIGURE 7–9C

Use the layer setting Multiply when rendering a line drawing in Photoshop: in the Layers palette, rename the layer "Plan Line Work" and select Multiply. This allows the background line work to read through all the images placed on the floor plan. The drawing is now ready to render.

1. Find a high-resolution image of wood flooring and import it into a new Photoshop document. Make a large selection of the wood image using the Rectangle Marquee tool. Choose Edit > Copy. Figure 7–10a shows the wood image with the Marquee tool's selection ready to copy.

2. In your rendering canvas, select the Magic Wand tool and click on the area of floor to be rendered as wood. (If necessary, hold down the Shift key and continue selecting all floor surfaces to be rendered.) The Magic Wand tool will select the area between the lines that you desire to render (7–10b).

   Note: The Magic Wand tool may be grouped with the Quick Selection tool.

   A marquee (which looks like "marching ants") will now appear around the Magic Wand tool's selection. Choose Edit > Paste Special > Paste Into (Figure 7–10c); this will place the wood flooring imagery directly into the areas selected by the Magic Wand tool, as shown in Figure 7–10d.

   Change the wood flooring layer to the Multiply layer option (this can be done in the Layer palette).

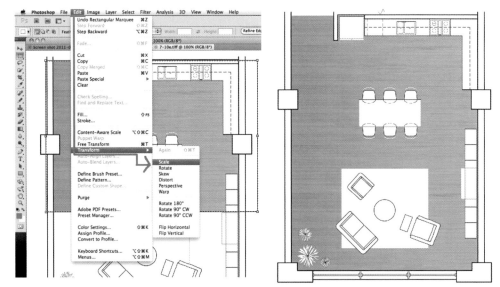

When an item such as wood does not fit exactly, you can stretch the image by choosing Edit > Transform > Scale, then using the handles that appear to stretch the image into the appropriate shape (7–11a). After the scale is manipulated, you will notice a subtle difference in the scale of the flooring (7–11b) compared with the initial scale shown in Figure 7–10d. The scale of rendered imagery is usually eyeballed and adjusted on the fly relative to the drawing scale. (More about scaling images is found in the following section.)

If an image is not large enough to fill the area required, make a copy of the layer (in this case, the wood floor layer). This will duplicate the image on top of the original. Move the new image over to fill the remaining space. Then link all the duplicate wood layers and choose Layer > Merge Linked; this will create a single layer and allow you to manipulate it as one entity. In many cases, lowering the opacity will allow the wood image to read more realistically in the rendering.

Note: When rendering a lot of the same material in a floor plan, rotate and flip the duplicate images randomly to create realistic patterning. Rotate images, if desired, by choosing Edit > Transform > Rotate. More information about creating larger image files for rendering can be found in Figures 7-18a through 7-18c.

Layers

After any new material is rendered in, you must go back and select the layer on which the original line drawing appears (see Figures 7–12a and 7–12c). Consider this your home base for all rendering. When something does not paste in correctly, it is generally because the wrong layer is selected, particularly that the original line layer was not selected.

Each time a new material is rendered into the drawing file, a new layer is created. It is best to link these layers (Layer > Link Layers) while working on them and then to merge them (Layer > Merge Down) as you complete that area. Give the layers easily identifiable names, such as "wood flooring layer"; this will save you rendering time as you will be able to navigate back to that single layer to make alterations.

FIGURES 7–12A THROUGH 7–12D

Completing the Rendering with Additional Image Files

In Figure 7–12a, the counters are rendered in granite by pasting in a granite .jpg image using the same technique described in Figure 7–10a. The Magic Wand tool was then used to select the countertops areas. You must return to the Plan Line Work layer to make the Magic Wand selection, or the image will not be pasted into the correct location (7–12a). The granite is pasted into the selection in Figure 7–12b.

To select the shelving for rendering with wood, first select the Plan Copy layer (7–12c).

Each time a new image file is pasted into the rendering, a new layer is automatically created. (In Figure 7–12d, these layers are the result of pasting in image files, which each occupy their own layer.) In order to properly manage these files, they should be linked or merged once they have been completed. Merging the layers allows you to deal with additions such as shadows and highlights, and to create files of a more manageable size. When merging layers, keep them together by type (such as all the layers of a particular wood sample) rather than merging all the layers simultaneously—at least until you are close to finalizing the rendering.

Image Files

Image files can be created by scanning actual samples or by obtaining high-quality files (typically .jpgs).

In some cases, the scale of the image files for rendered items is incorrect, and they will require manipulation as they are rendered in (see Figures 7–11a and 7–11b). In addition, the scale and color of the image files can be altered prior to introducing them into the rendering, as shown in Figures 7–18a through 7–18d.

Fills, Paint Bucket, and Brushes

In addition to using image files, fills and painting can be used to add color. Using fills, the paint bucket, and brushes (the Paint Brush icon is found under the Pencil tool) require you to work directly on the drawing layer. To do this, create a duplicate of the line layer and work on the copy (which should be named appropriately).

Shadows, Highlights, and Nuances

Shadows and highlights are often created using the Burn and Dodge tools, which select pixels and make them lighter or darker. You must select the layer on which the item (such as a wood floor layer) you want to shadow appears in order to burn them in.

For shadows, set the Burn tool on Shadows (see Figure 7–14a). In some instances, the Midtones setting works as well.

For highlights, set the Dodge tool on Highlights.

Shadows and highlights can also be painted on with the Brush tool.

For further information, see Figures 7–14a through 7–14e.

Color nuances and bounce can be painted in using the Brush tool (as shown in Figure 7–14e).

History Palette

This palette displays all recent operations and allows you to select the rendering in a previous state. To display the palette, choose Select > Window > History.

The actual rendering takes place by opening prepared image files (usually .jpgs) of materials, finishes, and other elements. You will typically work with several Photoshop canvases open simultaneously, making marquee selections of materials that will then be placed into the Photoshop rendering file. (In this example, the plan that was placed in the previous Figure 7–9c).

Information about how to best prepare image files for rendering appears later in this chapter. Figures 7–10a through 7–13d contain step-by-step instructions for placing images and detailing them so that they are rendered into the Photoshop file.

In addition to using image files, you can utilize color fills to fill areas within a rendering. The Paint Bucket tool is also used to create areas of color within lines by selecting them and then painting them with color. Using fills and the Paint Bucket tool is covered in Figures 7–13a through 7–13d.

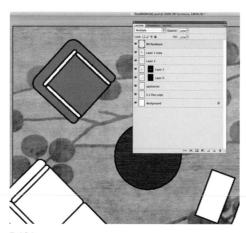

7-13A

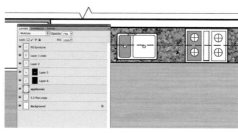

7-13B

Most renderings include some areas of pure color. Rather than pasting image files into these areas, use a fill or the Paint Bucket tool by selecting the areas you want to color in.

Figure 7–13a shows the chair color added using a Fill. To do this, first select the desired area using the Magic Wand tool, then go to Edit > Fill. It is best to make a color selection prior to the Fill command.

Figure 7–13b shows the sink and stove with a Fill that was created by choosing the desired foreground color (gray) and then selecting the Paint Bucket tool and clicking on the areas where gray is desired (the sink and cooktop). The Paint Bucket tool is grouped with the Gradient tool.

7-13C

Figure 7–13c shows plant with a Fill that was created by chossing the desired foreground color (green) and then selecting the Paint Bucket tool and clicking on the areas where green is desired. In this case a range of greens was chosen to create more lifelike plants, the Paint Bucket tool works well for this type of detail.

Using fills and the Paint Bucket tool both require you to work directly on the line drawing layer or its duplicate. To make a duplicate layer of the original plan layer, select that layer in the Layers palette and choose Layer > Duplicate Layer. Then name the duplicate layer.

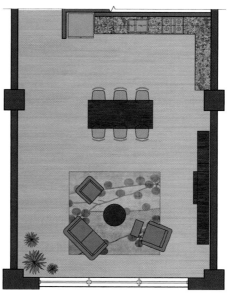

7-13D

Burn and Dodge Tools

With the rendering almost complete, you are ready to develop shadows and other details. Create shadows with the Burn tool, and highlights with the Dodge tool. Shadows, lowlights, and highlights can also be painted on using the Brush tool.

The Burn tool works by selecting the desired pixels and making them darker by painting them with the tool's brush. The Dodge tool works by lightening pixels. For either tool to work, you must select the correct layer. For example, when creating shadows on a wood floor, the wood floor layer should be selected. For both the Burn and Dodge tools, you must select an option from the Range menu. The best options are the Dodge tool's Highlights setting and the Burn tool's Shadows setting, as illustrated in Figure 7–14a. Both tools also let you set exposure (7–14a) and brush size (7–14b).

Figures 7–14a through 7–14d illustrate the process of creating shadows and nuances in a rendering.

Rendering Perspectives in Photoshop

Perspective drawings are rendered in Photoshop similarly to how orthographic drawings are rendered. Begin by scanning and then importing hand drawings, or import digital files created by modeling programs, including SketchUp and Revit.

The techniques covered in Figures 7–9a through 9–14e can be used when rendering perspectives. However, the nature of perspective requires the use of the Skew/Transform tool to orient materials and surfaces to vanishing points, as illustrated in the following steps. The method described here assumes that materials will be scaled by eye when imported into Photoshop. More information about creating and scaling material image files and scaling them can be found in the following section.

In some cases, hand-drawn or previously rendered digital perspectives are updated or cleaned-up in Photoshop. In others, Photoshop is used as a design visualization tool, helping the designer to change colors and materials and see them in the total environment. Directions for working with previously hand-drawn or partially rendered images is found in Figures 7–17a through 7–17e.

It is useful to keep a well-organized collection of digital image files for use in future Photoshop renderings. Such files often require a bit of manipulation prior to using them, as most image files are rather small and need to be enlarged to cover the requisite areas of a rendering. An image file can be imported into Photoshop at a high resolution and manipulated as shown in Figures 7–18a through 7–18c.

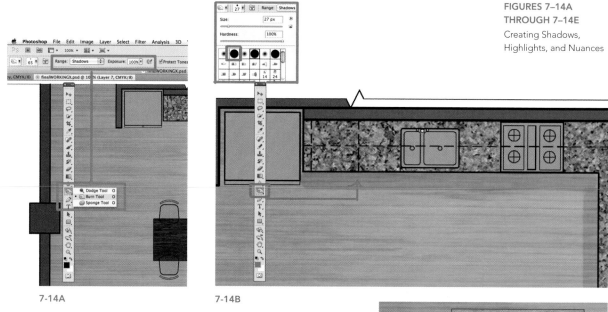

7-14A

7-14B

7-14C

7-14D

7-14E

For shadows, select the Burn tool and choose Shadows from the Range drop-down menu (7–14a). Create highlights by selecting the Dodge tool and choosing Highlights from Range drop-down menu. You must also set a brush style and size for both tools, as shown in Figure 7–14b. After the layer and brush size are set, you can draw shadows on the rendering.

Note: This type of shadow is created by darkening the pixels of the specified material (7–14b).

Fills can also be altered using the Burn and Dodge tools. The shadows on the sink and cooktop in Figure 7–14c were created using the Burn tool on the Fill layer. In the detail in Figure 7–14d, the wood floor's shadow was also created on that layer using the Burn tool. The chairs were created with a fill that has lowlights and highlights created with both the Burn and Dodge tools.

In Figure 7–14e, shadows have been created on the rug layer and the furniture fills, and highlights added to the furniture, using a combination of the Dodge and Brush tools. (The Brush tool can also be used alone to create both shadows and highlights.) To paint with the Brush tool, choose the correct layer and then make a color selection; use the cursor to paint in color nuances such as those used for the plants in Figure 7–14e. In Figure 7–14e, additional brown paint was added to the plant using the Brush tool, to tune up the color and create color movement within the composition.

Note: The Clone Stamp tool can also be used to correct colors and mistakes. This is done by sampling correct colors or values and replacing those in need of correction, such as smudges, seams, or missing values.

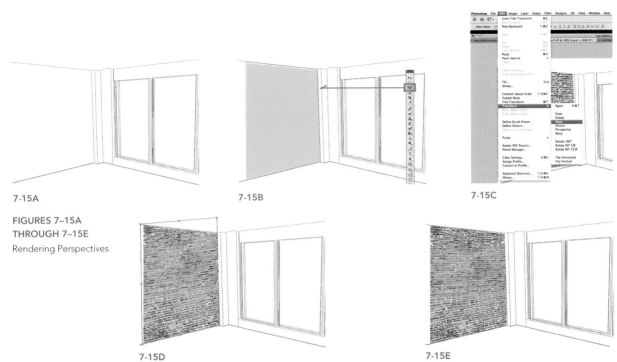

7-15A

7-15B

7-15C

**FIGURES 7–15A
THROUGH 7–15E**

Rendering Perspectives

7-15D

7-15E

To begin a rendering of a perspective drawing, choose File > New, set the resolution to 300, and select CMYK mode (if you will be printing the final rendering) with a white background. With the new canvas open, choose File > Place and select a file for a line drawing or exported model. Figure 7–15a shows a SketchUp file imported into Photoshop.

In this example, a brick wall is rendered by opening a .jpg file of a brick wall in Photoshop and using the Marquee tool to make a large selection that is then copied (as in Figure 7–10a). To prepare the line drawing to accept the brick, use the Polygonal Lasso tool to outline the portion of the wall desired, as shown in Figure 7–15b (the pink indicates the area selected by the Lasso tool). While the selection is live, choose File > Paste Into. The brick will be imported into the selected area (just as the flooring was in Figures 7–10a and 7–10b).

Adjust the brick's scale and location relative to the perspective lines by choosing Edit > Transform > Skew (to stretch the brick to follow the perspective lines) or Edit > Transform > Scale to change the scale of the imported file—in this case, the brick (7–15c). Figure 7–15d shows the brick image being skewed into place inside the selection made by the Lasso tool, giving the image an accurate appearance in perspective (7-15e).

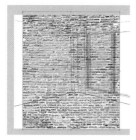

7-15A

7-15B

An alternate method for ensuring that images follow perspective lines is to paste a .jpg file into the line drawing without making a selection with the Lasso tool. After the image is pasted in, switch that layer to Multiply (7–16a). The image/layer can then be transformed by choosing Edit > Transform > Skew or Edit > Transform > Scale (7–16b). You can also stretch the image as desired (7–16c and 7–16d).

FIGURES 7–16A
THROUGH 7–16D

Pasting in without the Lasso Tool

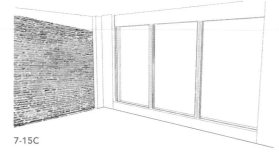

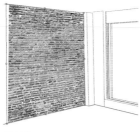

7-15C

7-15D

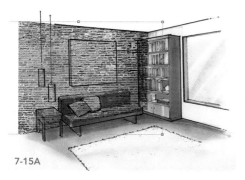

7-15A

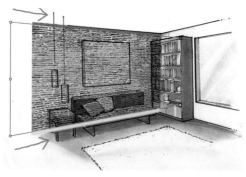

FIGURES 7–17A
AND 7–17B

As in the previous figures, the brick wall was pasted into this drawing and fit into place by choosing Edit > Transform> Skew (7–17a). Then, using the Magic Wand tool and the Polygon tool, items not to be rendered as brick (e.g., the furniture, lighting, artwork, and bookcase) were selected and deleted from the brick layer, new items can be pasted into these locations (7–17b).

7-15B

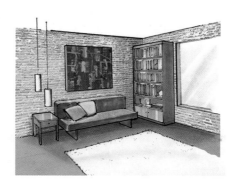

For the windows, a .jpg image of a cityscape was used. (An image of trees would have worked just as nicely.) Use the Watercolor filter to tone down the sharpness of such images. The cityscape image was selected with the Rectangle Marquee tool, copied, and placed into the window area (7–17c). Note that the opacity on the image was changed to make it more realistic. The painting above the sofa was handled similarly.

7-17C

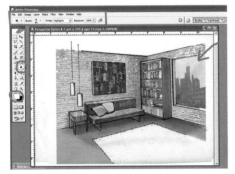

7-17D

The finalized image (7–17d) was refined using the Dodge tool to add sun glare streaks to the window glass. The Eraser tool was selected and changed to Brush mode set at 75% opacity and 50% flow. Then the rendering's edges were softened with the Eraser tool by creating duplicates of the brick wall, wood floor, and cityscape layers. (Always turn off the layers and save them in the Layers palette as a backup in case you make an error while finishing a rendering).

Completed renderings can be further manipulated through the use of various filters. Figures 7–19a through 7–19d show the image of the brick wall used throughout this chapter with various filters applied to it.

In creating Photoshop renderings, you can also work directly on a line drawing using the Brush tool set like an airbrush or paintbrush. Figure 7–20 shows lines painted with the Brush tool on different settings. Figure 7–21 is a perspective rendered using the Brush tool.

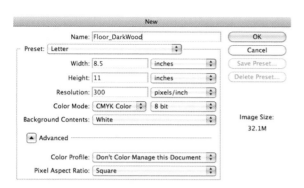

1. Start by creating a new Photoshop document at 300 dpi in CMYK color. Make the document at least letter size (Figure 7–18a).

2. Paste the single image file into this new document several times.

3. As new copies are pasted in, rotate them so they appear more natural (7–18b).

4. Flatten or merge the layers as the copies are added. As the digital sample grows larger, it can be cropped and copied again and again to enlarge it.

5. Once the sample reaches the desired size, clean it up using the Clone Stamp or Brush tool. Cleaning up seams and repeated grain patterns will make the sample look better (7–18c).

7-18A

7-18B

7-18C

FIGURES 7–18A THROUGH 7–18C

To make digital images of materials samples, you can either scan the actual materials or use high-resolution images. Image files are typically rather small and therefore need to be enlarged prior to using them in a rendering.

7-19A

7-19B

7-19C

7-19D

FIGURES 7–19A THROUGH 7–19D

Figure 7–19a shows the image of the brick wall used throughout this chapter. Figure 7–19b shows the same image with the Watercolor filter applied, by going to (Filter > Artistic > Watercolor). Figure 7–19c shows the wall after applying a lens flare (Filter > Render > Lens Flare), and Figure 7–19d shows the wall distorted by the Ocean Ripple filter (Filter > Distort > Ocean Ripple). These filters—and many others—can be applied to materials sample images, an entire rendering, or even a series of renderings.

Digital Rendering

FIGURE 7–20
The Brush tool can be used to paint or airbrush directly on a drawing surface.

a. Was drawn with the Brush tool set to Mode: Normal; Opacity: 100%; Flow: 100%.

b. Was drawn using the same settings as the first, except that the Mode was set to Dissolve.

c. Was drawn using the settings Mode: Dissolve; Opacity 46%; Flow 100%.

d. Was drawn using the settings Mode: Normal; Opacity: 100%; Flow: 50%.

Note: Changing the flow setting makes it easier to create value contrast.

FIGURE 7–21
This perspective was generated using Auto-CAD, imported into Photoshop, and rendered using the Brush tool.
BY CUNINGHAM GROUP ARCHITECTURE, P.A.

View From Seating

Note: Many excellent Photoshop renderings are featured in chapter 9.

Rendering in Revit

In Revit, materials are selected as the model is built. They therefore often become part of the model, rather than being applied to it. However, the rendering of these materials is a separate activity. Figures 7–22a through 7–23d show line drawings and renderings done in Revit.

FIGURES 7–22A THROUGH 7–22C
Figure 7–22a shows the town house project from chapter 1 with nonrendered perspectives as well as rendered versions. Figure 7–22b is a low-resolution quick rendering; Figure 7–22c is a higher resolution rendering.
BY KATEY FORTUN

FIGURES 7–23A THROUGH 7–23C
Figure 7–23a shows a student thesis project presentation done in Revit but not rendered. Figure 7–23b shows the same project area rendered at high resolution, and Figure 7–23c shows another area rendering from the same project. BY JESSICA SMITH

REFERENCES

Doyle, Michael. *Color Drawing*. 2nd ed. Hoboken, NJ: John Wiley & Sons, 2006.
A classic that provides information and inspiration.

Google SketchUp: Ruby Scripts.
http://sketchup.google.com/intl/en/download/rubyscripts.html

Juracek, Judy. *Architectural Surfaces*. New York: W.W. Norton, 2005.
Full of beautiful images that can be imported into digital renderings via the accompanying CD.

———. *Natural Surfaces*. New York: W.W. Norton, 2002.
Similar to the author's other title.

Leggit, Jim. *Drawing Shortcuts: Developing Quick Drawing Skills Using Today's Technology*. New York: John Wiley & Sons, 2009.

Scale Models

Designers use three-dimensional scale models to study the volume of a space. Unlike drawings and graphics on a two-dimensional surface, such models reveal the three-dimensional qualities of form. Scale models therefore provide designers with the opportunity to review the elements of a design comprehensively.

The finish, refinement, and time spent in building scale models varies widely. A model's level of refinement usually reflects the stage of the design process in which it is constructed. In the preliminary stages of design, models are often constructed quickly; these are referred to as *study models* or *working models.* As a project proceeds into design development, models become more refined and detailed. Models used to present a fully developed, finalized design are often painstakingly crafted; they are commonly referred to as *presentation models* or *finished models.*

Most study models present simplified or abstracted versions of finishes, materials, and colors, but in accurate scale. Presentation models also often depict design elements in a simplified manner—again, in accurate scale—but they are considerably more refined than study models. Finished models for design presentations are constructed with all materials, colors, and finishes portrayed accurately; such highly accurate models are often constructed by professional model makers. Many architecture and design firms have full-time model makers on staff; other firms hire model-making consultants as required. These professionals employ a wide variety of materials, techniques, and equipment—ranging from band saws to laser cutters—in the construction of beautiful scale models.

Before any model is constructed, its purpose must be identified. If the goal is the study and eventual refinement of an in-progress design, a study model is constructed; if it is to present a fully developed design to a client, a presentation model is built. Constructing a presentation model also means giving some thought to the nature of the design. If the model is meant to communicate the spatial relationships or functional aspects of a space, for example, the model maker may simplify and abstract the finishes so they are not the model's focus. Publicly funded projects often and those funded by investors often require the use of presentation models to gain approval. In such cases, the model must clearly communicate the design. Models meant for a general audience may require a very accurate, realistic depiction of finishes.

Models are also a highly useful study aid. Many design students are more comfortable designing spaces by drawing plans and elevations, and avoid constructing scale models. But most students have trouble visualizing the totality of a space when they limit their work to two-dimensional drawings.

The best way to understand the entirety of a space is to build a scale model; it is also a wonderful way to improve design visualization skills. By constructing quick study models of in-process designs, students can "see" a space early in the design process.

Materials and Tools

Study models are constructed rapidly, using inexpensive, readily available materials. Because of the way interior spaces are planned, interior study models are often built by attaching vertical elements directly to a drafted floor plan. A basic understanding of materials and construction techniques allows design students to construct helpful study models. More refined presentation models are often crafted using more expensive materials; these are generally more time consuming to build. An understanding of the materials and techniques used in assembling refined models is also helpful.

Paperboards
Various types of paperboards available in art supply stores, are used in scale model building. Paper products are inexpensive, lightweight, and easy to cut. Figure 8–1 illustrates a range of paperboards used in model building.

FIGURE 8–1
Various Paperboards
Used in Model Making.

1. Foam board (white)
2. Foam board (black)
3. Foam board (colored)
4. Corrugated board (commonly called cardboard)
5. Ripple wrap
6. Chipboard
7. Mat board (with black core)
8. Museum board (white)
9. Illustration board
10. Mounting board (black)
11. Bristol board

Foam board (also called foam core) is a type of paperboard consisting of polystyrene foam (or Styrofoam) sandwiched between two sheets of paper. Foam core comes in a variety of thicknesses—often $\frac{3}{16}''$ or $\frac{1}{8}''$—and is available in bleached white with a white center. Also procurable are black foam core, consisting of black cover paper and a black foam center, and foam core that is primarily white, with one colored top layer.

White foam board is commonly used for study models because its thickness represents standard scaled wall thicknesses accurately. Foam board is usually left unpainted so that it remains neutral or abstract in presentations. (If it is to be painted, test the paint on a bit of scrap foam core, as some paints dissolve the foam.) Sometimes, designers cap foam core edges with another paper, such as bristol board or museum board (see below), to cover the exposed Styrofoam, creating a more refined appearance.

Foam board can be cut easily with a snap-off cutter or an X-Acto knife. To cut foam board, use a very sharp blade and cut in three steps: Make the first cut through the top layer of paper, and the second through the middle layer of Styrofoam. The last cut must cut cleanly through the bottom paper layer (see Figure 8–2).

FIGURE 8–2

Cutting paperboard. Cutting paperboard in three separate cuts. First cut the top paper surface, then the middle surface, and finally the bottom paper surface.

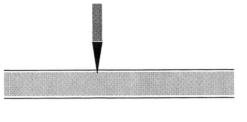

FIGURE 8–3

Cut a 45-degree angle by first peeling away a portion of the top surface that matches the thickness of the board. Then cut the inner material and bottom layer of paper at 45 degrees. Two sheets cut this way can be joined together to form a 90-degree angle.

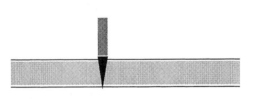

FIGURE 8–4

Form a 90-degree angle by removing a portion of part of the top paper surface equal to twice the thickness of the foam board. Then cut away each side of the foam core at a 45-degree angle, leaving the backing paper in place. Finally, fold the board to create a 90-degree angle with a continuous paper surface.

FIGURE 8–5

Create curves with paperboard by first scoring the material (leaving the backing paper intact) and then securing the board in place with glue.

Do not try to cut through foam board in fewer than these three steps; the effort will result in jagged edges. To create angles, curves, and other complex shapes, the paper can be peeled from away from the foam center and the foam can be cut, sanded, or scored (see Figures 8–3 through 8–5).

Use white glue to join foam board; straight pins will hold the joints together while the glue dries. For complex models, angled weights and clamps may be used. Spray adhesive and double-sided tape also work with foam board. Foam board also works well as a mounting surface for materials presentations, drawings, and renderings; however, certain weather conditions and adhesives can warp it.

Gatorfoam board is similar to foam core: it consists of foam sandwiched between layers of paper. Available in bleached white as well as black, this very sturdy material is difficult to cut—using a band saw works best. The board can also be scored and carefully snapped off along the scored edge. As with foam board, the outer layers of Gatorfoam board can be peeled away, allowing the inner foam to be cut and sanded. White glue works well in Gatorfoam board scale models, as do spray adhesives and double-sided tape. Gatorfoam board makes a good presentation board, especially for heavy items. It is also used occasionally as a mounting surface for drawings and renderings because it does not warp as easily as foam board.

Corrugated board (commonly called cardboard) consists of heavy corrugated paper covered with heavy brown paper. The outer layers can be peeled away to reveal the corrugated paper center; this center can then be used to indicate texture. Corrugated board works well in quick study models because it is widely available, inexpensive, and can be cut easily using the three-cut method illustrated in Figure 8–2. White glue works well with corrugated board, as do spray adhesives and double-sided tape. Figure 8–6 shows a study model constructed of corrugated board and chipboard.

Ripple wrap looks like the corrugated center portions of cardboard; it is available in a wide range of colors and is used in the creation of presentation boards, notebook covers, and portfolio covers, as well as in model making.

Chipboard looks like the outer layer of corrugated board. It is extremely inexpensive and is used on quick study models. Chipboard can be cut easily with a cutter or an X-Acto blade and can be fastened with white glue, spray adhesive, or double-sided tape.

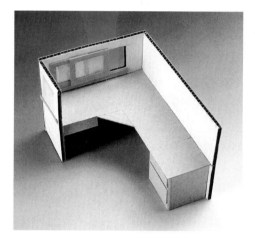

FIGURE 8–6
This study model for a workstation is constructed from corrugated board (for vertical partitions), chipboard (for the work surface), and tracing paper (for the transparent sliding windows), and is held together with white glue.

Mat board is paperboard with a colored top surface. It is available with a white or black paper center. It is used to add color and details to models; some models are constructed completely of mat board. *Museum board* has a high rag content and is white or off-white throughout. It is used to create pristine study and presentation models because of its attractive appearance.

Illustration board has a white or buff-colored surface and a high rag content. The three-cut method must be used to produce a clean-looking cut area. Black *mounting board* is thin and easy to cut, as is *bristol board* (or *bristol paper*), which is often white. Figure 8–7 is a conceptual model made of bristol board.

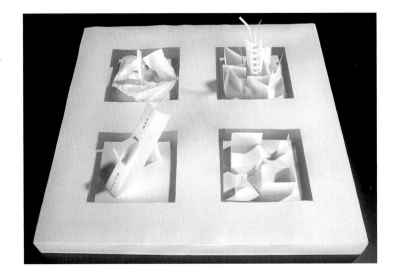

Chipboard, mat board, museum board, black mounting board, and bristol board are easy to cut, lightweight, easy to glue, and used often in model making. Because they are thinner than foam core, they work well for smaller-scale models. In large-scale models, these thinner paperboards are laminated (layered together using glue or double-sided tape) or used in conjunction with paperboard, wood, or plastic.

Wood

Because it is more costly and time-consuming to work with, wood is not used as often as paper products for quick study models. It is, however, used widely in models during the design development of a project and for final presentations. Because of wood's warmth and natural beauty, it is often treated very simply and abstractly in models. It may be sanded, stained, or sealed but is rarely painted or heavily embellished. Wood is particularly useful for models of an interior whose major finish is actually wood.

A variety of wood products useful in model building are available in hobby stores. Different types of wood offer different advantages. Figure 8–8 illustrates wood products used in models.

Balsa wood is light and porous, and can be cut with a blade or knife (or, for larger pieces, a saw); no power tools are required. Because it is easy to carve, balsa wood is used for toy making and crafts—and scale model building. Balsa wood is readily available in blocks, strips, sheets, and veneers (very thin sheets) in a wide range of sizes. Because of this wood's fibrous nature, it may appear rough even after sanding. Although balsa wood can be cut easily, it can be difficult to cut evenly because of its structure.

Basswood is an attractive, smooth, light-colored hardwood. It has minimal graining patterns, giving it a neutral appearance that makes it very popular for model building. In addition, basswood is relatively easy to cut and work with. Unlike balsa wood, basswood can be sanded smooth if it is handled carefully. Basswood is sold at many hobby stores, especially those that specialize in railroad models or miniature houses. It is available in blocks, sheets, veneers, strips, dowels, and scaled ornamental moldings, and also cut with siding patterns. Thin sheets and strips of basswood can be cut with a sharp X-Acto blade or a utility knife; thicker slabs and blocks require a hand saw or power tools.

Other hardwood species—such as walnut, mahogany, cherry, and teak—are available in sheets, veneers, and blocks. Because these woods have distinct graining patterns and coloration, they are often used to accent basswood models. In constructing highly detailed models, the actual wood proposed for a particular design is frequently used. Hard-to-find wood veneers are often available at local specialty woodworking shops.

White glue is frequently used in the construction of wood models. Applying it sparingly yields better adhesion as well as a neat appearance. Glued items should be weighted, clamped, or otherwise held in place until the glue dries. Instant glue can also be used on wood models. Many expert model makers rely on instant glue that dries more slowly, such as Slow Jet or Slo-ZAP CA, especially when gluing small or complex items. These are used because they allow for position corrections during the drying process.

FIGURE 8–8

Wood Used in Constructing Presentation Models

1. Balsa wood (strips and blocks)
2. Cherry
3. Walnut
4. Basswood (strips, veneer, and scaled moldings)

Plastics and Foam

Plastics are used by professional model builders and by industrial designers for scale models, mock-ups, and working prototypes. Styrene, polystyrene, and Balsa-Foam are some of the most popular plastics used in model and prototype construction.

Styrene sheets, strips, rods, and I-beams with a white finish are available at hobby shops in a range of sizes. A variety of grooved and scored sheet styrene is procurable in patterns that resemble tiles, siding, and other finish materials. Sheet styrene is cut by scoring it with a sharp blade and then snapping it along the scored area. Sheet styrene is best glued with specialized plastic cement that creates a fast and strong bond that actually fuses the joint.

Styrene foam insulation board is lightweight; it is available at lumberyards and home improvement stores. This material comes in a range of thicknesses and is most often sold in blue, pink, and gray. Sheets of styrene foam can be glued together (or laminated) to form the desired width or depth. Non-repositionable spray adhesive works well as a glue in layering the foam. The best means of cutting styrene foam is a hot wire cutter. Styrene foam presents a problem in terms of toxicity, as it releases airborne particulate matter when cut, and does not accept paint well. It is best used unpainted in study models or as an abstraction of material form.

Balsa-Foam is a tan-colored, nontoxic, phenolic polymer resin foam that is easier to work with than styrene foam. It can be cut with simple hand tools such as knives, cutters, and saws and is easily glued together with low-melt hot glue or spray adhesive. Balsa-Foam can be painted with acrylic or enamel paints. It is available at model railroad shops and through catalogs geared to industrial designers.

Sintra is a polyvinyl chloride product used in point-of-purchase displays and signage construction, but is used increasingly by model makers. Much like sheet styrene, thin sheets of Sintra are cut by scoring them and then breaking them along the score. Sintra is available in varying thicknesses and colors. When used for models, it can be painted with acrylic paints used over appropriate primers. (Displays using Sintra require a different type of paint). Paint can be applied by brush, airbrush, or spray can.

Figure 8–9 illustrates the different types of plastic used in model building.

Adhesives and Tools

The measuring, cutting, gluing, and attaching involved in model making require tremendous concentration and patience. Certain tools and adhesive products can make the job of model construction easier. However, the most important tools are patience and allowing enough time. Figure 8–10 illustrates popular modeling tools and adhesives.

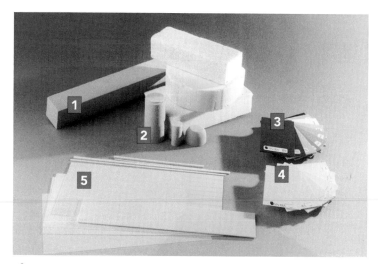

FIGURE 8–9

Plastics are often used in study models and for portions of presentation models.

1. Styrene foam (cut into blocks)
2. Balsa-Foam (cut into cylinders)
3. Sintra (colored)
4. Sintra (white)
5. Styrene (strips, rods, grooved sheets, and plain sheets)

Glues and Adhesives

White glue, such as Elmer's Glue-All, is used a great deal in model construction. It works well on paper, foam core, Gatorfoam board, and wood. White glue forms an excellent bond; however, it takes some time to dry, so the items being glued must be held in place by clamps or weights. White glue should be applied in thin layers in order to create neat, tight joints—applied in thick layers, it does not hold well and will look terrible.

Rubber cement is an excellent adhesive for bonding paper and light fabrics to paper-board in models or materials presentations. Apply the cement lightly to both surfaces, let it dry a bit and become tacky, and then attach the two surfaces; this permits the surfaces to be repositioned. Be careful when using rubber cement: it is flammable and produces toxic vapors.

Instant glues have the advantage of drying quickly—and the disadvantage of drying so fast that it is easy to make mistakes. Many model builders therefore use slower-drying versions of instant glue such as Slow Jet or Slo-ZAP CA. With these glues, objects can be set in place and repositioned. Once the items are in place, an accelerator such as Zip Kicker or Zap Kicker is sprayed on the joint, and the glue dries instantly. Slow-drying glues and accelerators are a necessity for constructing detailed, refined models with complex elements. These instant glues work well on wood but not on styrene. They are highly toxic and flammable, and should be used only according to the manufacturer's instructions in well-ventilated work areas.

FIGURE 8–10
Model-Building Tools
and Adhesives

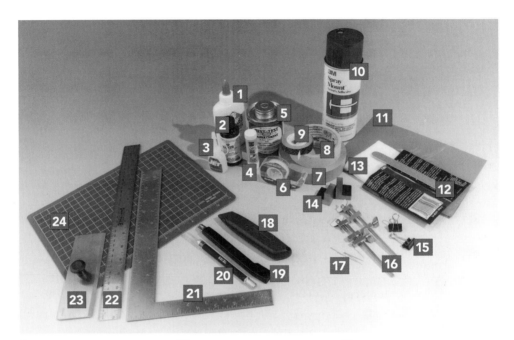

1. White glue
2. Slow instant glue
3. Glue accelerator
4. Glue stick
5. Rubber cement
6. Double-sided tape
7. Transfer tape
8. Masking tape
9. Painter's tape (removable)

10. Spray adhesive
11. Sandpaper
12. Small file
13. Tack cloth (for removing debris after sanding)
14. Small, heavy angle plate (used as a weight)
15. Large paper clips
16. Small clamps

17. Straight pins
18. Utility knife
19. Snap-off cutter
20. Excel (or X-Acto) knife
21. Metal builder's square
22. Cork-backed metal ruler
23. Steel straightedge with knob
24. Cutting pad

Double-sided tape—including transfer tape, masking tape, and painter's tape—all work well in model construction. Double-sided tape is excellent for attaching and layering sheets of paper, foam core, and wood veneers. It functions better than spray adhesive, which can warp of dissimilar surfaces. *Carpet tape*, a heavy-duty double-sided tape, may be used to attach bulkier items.

Transfer tape is sold in rolls; it is sticky on both sides yet contains no sheet of plastic to hold the adhesive. It can be applied by hand or with a transfer tape gun (sold in some art supply stores). Transfer tape is good for layering paper and thin veneers and causes little telegraphing of the tape location through the veneer. This tape is excellent for attaching paper to foam core or mat board, and generally does not cause warping.

Masking tape and *painter's tape* are used to mask off areas and bond items together. Long-Mask, or painter's tape, looks similar to masking tape but is blue. Because it is easily removed and leaves no residue—even after several days—it allows the model maker to leave it in place while paints and glues dry.

Spray adhesive (or *spray mount*) is used like spray paint: the adhesive is sprayed from a can onto the appropriate surfaces. Some types of spray adhesive adhere permanently, and others allow for repositioning (the latter are the best for model construction and materials presentations). Spray adhesives are very popular with design students. Spray mount is most commonly used for attaching copies of plans and elevations to foam core for use in study models—a fast and effective method of study model construction.

Although spray adhesive is quick, paper applied to large surfaces of foam board with spray mount—or left in place too long—will eventually wrinkle or bubble. And the overspray from spray adhesives can be messy. These adhesives also generate fumes and are flammable. To unglue two surfaces affixed with spray mount, use a hair dryer to warm the adhesive first.

StudioTac is an alternative to spray mount. This double-sided adhesive sheet is sold in a range of sizes. Studio Tac is peeled away from a backing paper and applied to the object for mounting; then the other backing surface is peeled away and the object is affixed. Studio Tac is best for adhering lightweight items such as paper and paperboard. It produces no overspray or fumes.

Hot glue guns are electric guns that heat and dispense hot (or very warm) glue. They hold sticks of glue that melt and are then pushed through a nozzle. The guns range in size and in temperature. High-temperature glues work best for fabric, some plastics, glass, wood, and ceramics. Lower-temperature glues are used for Styrofoam, paper, and more delicate materials. Popular with many hobbyists, they do have some applications for models. However, hot glue is messy, hard to control, and in many cases does not produce a strong bond. It is used more often in the construction of quick study models than in refined presentation models, but its best use is for adhering materials to presentation boards. Hot glue can cause gaps to form in joints and can fail in completed models.

Generally, hot glue is more useful in adhering materials to presentation boards than in assembling scale models, as it can be messy for use with models. Glue guns range in size and in temperature. High-temperature glues work best for fabric, some plastics, glass, wood, and ceramic. Lower-temperature glues are often used for Styrofoam, paper, and more delicate materials.

Knives and Cutters

X-Acto knives, *snap-off cutters*, and *utility knives* are all used in model building. A wide range of blades is available for use with X-Acto (or similar) knives. Each kind of blade has a specialized use; the classic No. 11 fine-point blade is best for cutting paperboards.

The key to using all types of knives and cutters is to work with a sharp blade (the blades on X-Acto knives and cutters with snap-off blades are easy to change) and make several cuts through the material. Foam board, mat board, museum board, bristol board, and cardboard all require at least three cuts through their surfaces; the three-cut method is the only way to achieve neat and tidy cuts.

Other Tools

A specially designed polyvinyl *cutting pad* is useful for cutting all types of material. Most have a grid pattern so the material being cut can be properly aligned. These pads protect table surfaces, provide a measured cutting surface, and improve the longevity of blades.

A cork-backed metal *straightedge* is an excellent cutting edge. Steel straightedges are available with knob holders that protect fingers from cutting accidents. Plastic rulers and triangles should not be used as cutting edges because they are easily damaged.

Professional model makers use heavy angled plates, as well as clamps, to hold pieces of a model together while the glue sets. They are a necessity for detailed and complex models but are not used as often by students for study models.

One busy professional model builder believes the six most important items for model making are a steel triangle with a knob holder, a polyvinyl cutting pad with a horizontal wood edge attached (for use in conjunction with the triangle), an X-Acto knife, white glue, double-stick tape, and Long-Mask tape (see Figure 8–11).

FIGURE 8–11

Helpful tools for student paperboard models. This is the "must have" list for creating paperboard models.

1. Transfer tape
2. Painter's tape (blue)
3. Elmer's white glue
4. X-Acto knife
5. Steel straightedge with knob (a metal triangle also works well)
6. Cutting board with wood permanently attached (for use with straightedge or triangle)

Construction and Use of Models

Model building requires patience, time, and a clear understanding of the purpose of the model. If it is to be used to study spatial relationships and proportions, a very quick study model can be constructed. Quick study models are most often constructed of chipboard, cardboard (corrugated board), mat board, museum board, or foam board.

As a project moves forward, a more refined model may be necessary in order to study design details and finishes, and to show to the client for approvals. Refined study models are often constructed of illustration board, mat board, museum board, foam core, or wood (or some combination thereof). Plastic or acrylic may be used to indicate glazed surfaces.

A common method of constructing a quick study model involves gluing orthographic drawings to chipboard, corrugated board, or foam core. The floor plan is first glued to the model-making material chosen. The interior elevations are then glued onto foam core, chipboard, or corrugated board, attached to the plan, and glued in place. Scaled human figures improve study models; they can be drawn by hand and then glued to foam core.

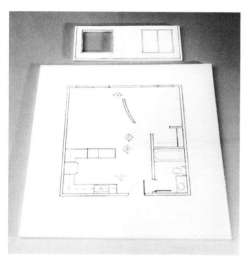

FIGURE 8–12A

Quick study models can be constructed by attaching the floor plan to foam board, then attaching the elevations. Plan ahead and leave extra room at either side of the appropriate elevations in order to attach the adjacent walls.

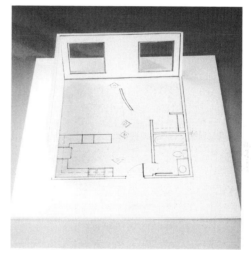

FIGURE 8–12B

The walls are glued into place on the plan. The extra room at each side of the first wall elevation allows the adjacent wall to be glued and joined.

FIGURE 8–12C
A breakdown of the steps for constructing a model.

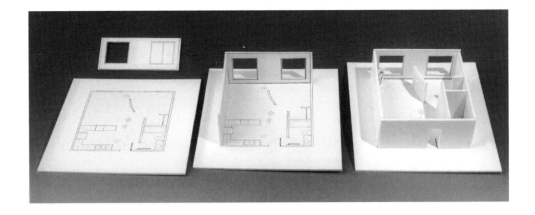

When gluing orthographic drawings, consider the eventual thickness of the walls and plan accordingly. Figures 8–12a through 8–12c illustrate the steps involved in constructing this type of study model. The model in Figure 8–13 is similar, but the orthographic drawings are attached to a building section, creating a sectional model. Figures 8–14a through 8–15b show student study models constructed to examine spatial relationships. A more complex model constructed by attaching foam core to orthographic projection drawings can be found in Figures 8–16a through 8–16d.

FIGURE 8–13
A sectional model (a section fragment model) of the Unité d'Habitation, designed by Le Corbusier. This model was part of a demonstration of quick and efficient model building for students. MODEL BY THOMAS OLIPHANT

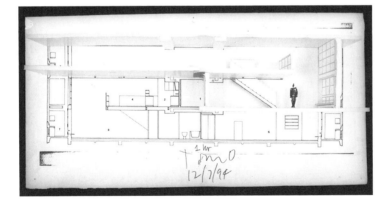

The materials selected for a model must relate to its scale. For example, a model constructed in ¼″ scale requires exterior walls that scale to roughly ¹⁄₁₆″. In such a case, thin museum board or mat board is an appropriate choice (see Figure 8–17). The paper used in constructing a study model can also be rendered.

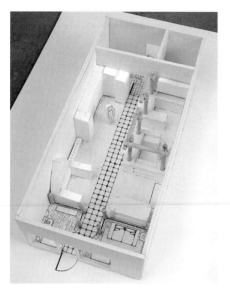
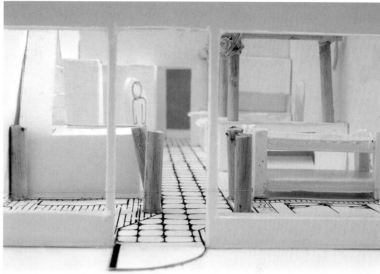

FIGURES 8–14A AND 8–14B

This study model, constructed early in the design process, was used to analyze spatial relationships and issues of scale in a retail project. The model is constructed in the manner described in Figures 8–12a through 8–12c. DESIGN AND MODEL BY DENISE HAERTL

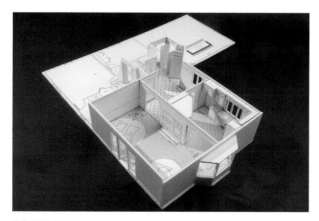

FIGURES 8–15A AND 8–15B

This study model was used for an in-class presentation and is also constructed in the manner described in Figures 8–12a through 8–12c. DESIGN AND MODEL BY TIFFANY BACA LAMOREUX

FIGURES 8–16A THROUGH 8–16D

This foam board and paper model depicts the design of a small two-story building. It was designed so the top can be removed in order to better view the first story. The custom cabinetry and millwork details were accurately portrayed. DESIGN AND MODEL BY SIV JANE REFSNES

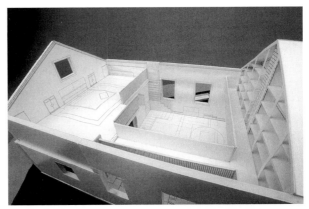
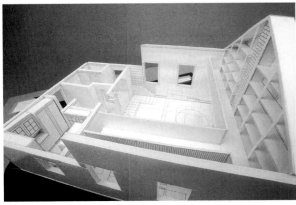

FIGURE 8–17

A model built to study wall heights constructed of museum board mounted on black foam board. The museum board is the appropriate size for use in a scale model. DESIGN BY COURTNEY NYSTUEN; MODEL BY LEANNE LARSON AND MAUREEN MITTON

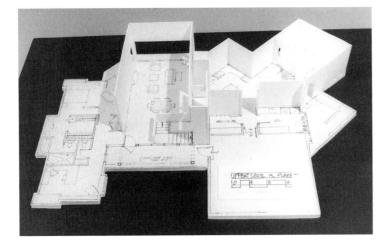

Some designers prefer pristine, monochromatic models. For these, gluing an elevation onto paperboard is not appropriate; measurements should be taken from orthographic drawings and transferred to paperboard instead. The paperboard is then cut to the correct dimensions, and the model glued in place. Figure 8–18 illustrates a study model constructed by transferring dimensions instead of attaching elevations.

Avoid using manufactured dollhouse products in study models. Such items tend to be too busy; abstracting materials to simple forms yields much less distracting results. However, some milled wood items, such as paneling and interior moldings, can be used to good effect. Figures 8–19a and 8–19b are simple models with abstracted finishes. Figures 8–20a and 8–20b depict a presentation model made using a range of materials, with abstracted versions of finishes applied in a visually successful manner.

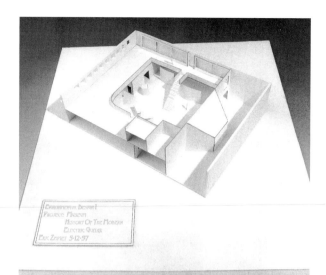

FIGURE 8–18

A study model constructed from illustration board.
MODEL BY ERIC ZEIMET

FIGURE 8–19A

A vignette model built to study wall finishes constructed of foam board, rendered mat board, basswood veneer, and basswood dollhouse moldings.

FIGURE 8–19B

A vignette model built to study wall finishes and design constructed of mat board, rendered mat board, ripple wrap with a metallic finish, and basswood veneer.

FIGURES 8–20A
AND 8–20B
This model was con-
structed as part of a final
design-development
presentation for an exhi-
bition space project and
is made of wood, plastic,
paperboard, and met-
al. DESIGN AND MODEL
BY MELANIE DEEG

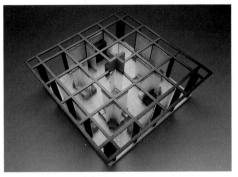

Very simple square or rectilinear spaces can be illustrated with *flip-up models*. These models use floor plans and interior elevations that are rendered and glued onto a paper-board surface. The elevations are then attached to the plan with a single strip of tape placed on both back surfaces. The tape functions as a hinge, allowing the elevations to flip up into place. The elevations can be taped into place as needed for study and review (see Figure 8–21).

FIGURE 8–21
A rendered flip-up model
constructed of rendered
bond paper on black
foam board. MODEL BY
ARDELLA PIEPER

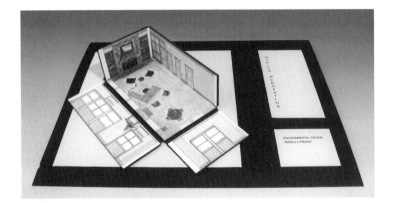

Creating flip-up models is a way to use drawing skills as an aid in model making. These models can be stored flat for inclusion in a portfolio. Unfortunately, they only work for very simple floor plans and are less realistic spatially than standard models.

Scale Models in Professional Practice

Some design firms use scale models a great deal; others use them rarely. Because highly refined presentation models take hours to build and are very costly, some designers do not use them at all. However, many designers are committed to studying projects as fully as possible during the design process, and this necessitates the use of scale models. (It also requires that design contracts include the costs of model building.)

Larger firms often have a fully equipped model shop where a range of models are constructed for study and presentation. Firms that use models as a fundamental part of the design process often construct a series of them that reflect the design's increasing level of refinement. Figures 8–22a through 8–25 illustrate such a series of models for a single design project.

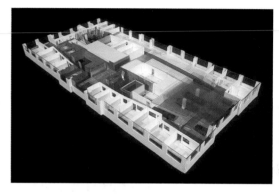

FIGURES 8–22A AND 8–22B

Two views of a large study model built for a professional project, constructed of bond paper, foam board, plastic, teak veneer, metal screen, and fabric. DESIGN AND MODEL BY MEYER, SCHERER & ROCKCASTLE, LTD.

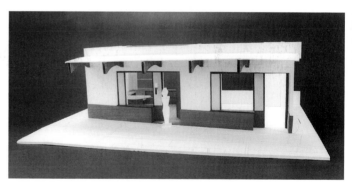

FIGURES 8–23A AND 8–23B

Two views of a smaller study model built for the same professional project, constructed of bond paper, foam board, plastic, basswood, teak veneer, and fabric. DESIGN AND MODEL BY MEYER, SCHERER & ROCKCASTLE, LTD.

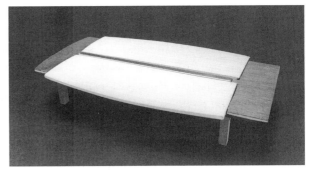

FIGURES 8-24A AND 8-24B
Furniture models for the project featured in Figures 8–22a through 8–23b, constructed of assorted wood. DESIGN AND MODEL BY MEYER, SCHERER & ROCKCASTLE, LTD.

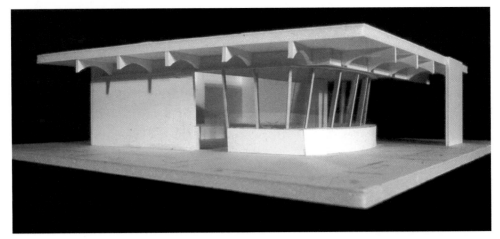

FIGURE 8-25
Presentation model for the corporate headquarters featured in Figures 8–22a through 8–24, constructed of basswood. DESIGN AND MODEL BY MEYER, SCHERER & ROCKCASTLE, LTD.

On very large design projects, such as hotels and entertainment facilities, full-scale mock-ups may be constructed. It is not unusual for large hotel projects to employ room-size mock-ups for viewing by investors or owners. Unusual design details may also require full-scale mock-ups so they can be studied prior to construction.

Industrial designers (also known as product designers) create a number of study models throughout the design process. These models are made from a variety of materials, ranging from foam board to styrene and Balsa-Foam. In an ongoing process of refinement, industrial designers often create many models for each project, ending with absolutely accurate presentation models that might be mistaken for the real thing.

Many models and mock-ups are needed for furniture design. Furniture study models are constructed of corrugated board, chipboard, foam board, or styrene. As a design becomes refined, designers often move to large-scale mock-ups or prototypes in order to study form and work out construction issues. These prototypes are required to perform as the actual products will, so they are usually built from materials very similar to those in the actual final product (see Figures 8–26a and 8–26b).

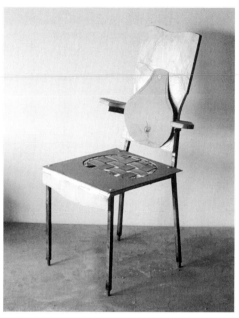

FIGURE 8–26A
A chair prototype constructed of wood and steel.
DESIGNED AND BUILT BY THOMAS OLIPHANT;
PHOTOGRAPH BY KATHY FOGERTY

FIGURE 8–26B
Chair prototype (right) shown with actual finished chair
(left). DESIGNED AND BUILT BY THOMAS OLIPHANT;
PHOTOGRAPH BY KATHY FOGERTY

REFERENCES

Mills, Criss. *Designing with Models*. New York: John Wiley & Sons, 2000.

Shimizu, Yoshiharu. *Models and Prototypes: Clay, Plaster, Styrofoam, Paper*. Tokyo: Graphic-sha, 1991.

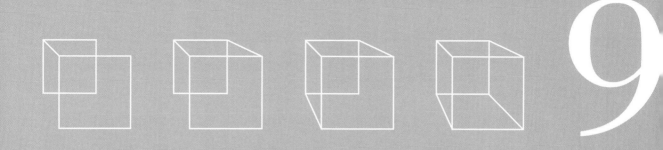

Presenting Materials and Finishes

Professional interior design projects call for the study, review, and refinement of interior architectural finishes and materials as well as furnishings, fixtures, and equipment, both individually and as parts of a whole. These items must also be evaluated for life-safety issues and performance as well as from an aesthetic standpoint. This chapter focuses only on the presentation of these items and does not cover the important issues of life safety, performance, and specification.

As with many other aspects of interior design, the presentation of materials and related samples continues to evolve. In the last decade, designers have moved from mounted boards constructed of foam and mat board to digital samples contained within digital presentations that are either printed or projected. While some firms still create sample boards, others use some type of digital presentation exclusively. Both approaches are covered here.

Early in a small project, a formal materials presentation is not necessarily of great assistance in the design process. Designers usually gather a variety of samples and make preliminary decisions but leave their options open; most work from large samples that remain loose and unmounted (see Figures 9–1a and 9–1b). However, large projects, or those with many team members, may call for a materials presentation as an early communication and design aid.

FIGURE 9–1A

Many designers prefer to keep materials loose and unmounted, especially in preliminary presentations.

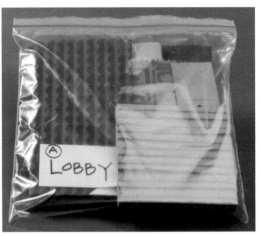

FIGURE 9–1B

Loose samples can be organized in clear plastic bags.

Early in the space planning process, designers begin to consider architectural finishes and materials. After careful study, a preliminary selection of finishes, materials, and furnishings is made. These are presented to the client or end user in a way that reflects the exploratory nature of the selections.

Preliminary materials selections are often presented at the same time as preliminary plans, elevations, perspective or axonometric drawings, and study models. All the elements in a presentation must be consistent graphically and should contain unifying elements. For example, a preliminary materials presentation may incorporate the graphics found in the title block of drawings. Or the format of a materials presentation can be consistent with the format used to present renderings. Keying materials to floor plans facilitates an understanding of the elements of the design presented.

Some designers prefer to keep the preliminary materials presentation casual, leaving all elements loose and unmounted; this allows the audience to touch and examine them and underscores that plenty of room for decision making remains. Other designers mount preliminary selections on presentation boards to communicate that certain decisions have already been made. Still others tack samples to a board with pushpins so the client(s) can remove and examine them (see Figures 9–2a through 9–2c).

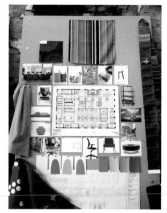

FIGURES 9–2A THROUGH 9–2C

Samples pinned to a board with pushpins. This presentation includes finish samples as well as larger fabric samples, full-scale furniture, and project drawings. Additional presentation items for this project can be found in Figures 2-18a through 2-18e. BY MEYER, SCHERER & ROCKCASTLE, LTD.

As a project moves forward, materials presentations should reflect the stage of the design. Many designers create a materials presentation for the final visual presentation, which takes place at the end of a project's design development phase. Large and complex projects often require several materials presentations at key points in the design development process. Other projects may require no formal materials presentation during the entire design process.

One successful residential designer never makes formal mounted presentations, preferring to arrange samples on a worktable for review by clients. Other designers drape fabrics on full-size furniture samples. When a large group of people must view the presentation, the materials may be projected (in a PowerPoint presentation, for example) as part of a larger visual presentation. Samples can then be made accessible for viewing. If boards must be left behind for end users to examine over time—in a hotel lobby to inform guests about upcoming renovations, or in a sales office for a new housing development to communicate material finish options, for example—traditional formal mounted presentations are necessary.

Many designers pride themselves on consistent, well-crafted materials presentations. Many firms have strict standards for the way materials presentations are prepared. These standards include requirements for board size, color, graphics, and methods for attaching samples, as well as the level of formality conveyed. A firm's standards allow presentations to distinctly reflect the concerns and focus of the firm while conveying the selections for a particular project. Final presentations often include drawings, renderings, models, and materials boards, all of which must appear visually cohesive and logical. (Information on and examples of complete presentations can be found in chapter 10.) Packing and organizing all the necessary elements for a final presentation for travel can take weeks of preparation. Large projects can include more than fifty materials boards (or slides). Such presentations must be arranged in a clear, logical fashion that leaves no margin for error.

The variation in practice and presentation of interior design projects means that design students must develop a range of skills for preparing materials presentations. Internships provide an excellent opportunity for students to become involved in creating different types of design presentations, including materials presentations, allowing them to become familiar with various offices' standards. But despite this diversity of presentation formats and standards, there are numerous factors common to all materials presentations regarding legibility, organization, graphic cohesion, quality of craftsmanship, techniques, tools, and appropriateness. All design students can benefit from a clear understanding of these factors in developing visual skills and creating meaningful presentations.

Materials and Media Used in Traditional Boards

Many of the materials used in presentation boards are discussed in previous chapters. Additional information on paper and rendering media can be found in chapter 6; for descriptions of paperboards, adhesives, and cutting tools, refer to chapter 8.

Board-based materials presentations require sturdy backing materials—usually a type of paperboard. Foam board is often utilized because it is durable yet lightweight and easy to work with; samples, titles, and notes can be applied directly to the top paper surface of the foam core. While many prefer white foam board, black can create a more dramatic presentation; some leave only a small portion of the black foam core visible to serve as a visual border (see Figure 9–3). Figures 9–4a and 9–4b depict materials mounted directly on white foam core as part of a large, professional multiboard presentation.

Foam board is often covered with mat board, as shown in Figures 9–6 and 9–7. Other types of boards, such as illustration board, bond paper, or Canson paper, can be used as the top surface, to which samples and titles can then be mounted. When thinner papers such as bond paper or Canson paper are used, the entire surface can be laid out with titles and notes and printed on a large-format printer. Samples are then added to the appropriate locations, as shown in Figure 9–5. Do not use spray adhesive to apply lightweight paper to boards: the paper will warp and wrinkle. Instead, use two-sided tape or StudioTac.

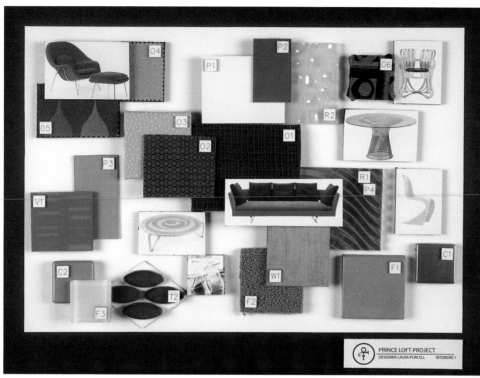

FIGURE 9–3
In this example, samples are mounted directly to light-colored mat board secured to a larger piece of black foam board. The project title is also mounted on the black foam board, while sample titles are printed on paper mounted directly on the samples.
BY LAURA PURCELL

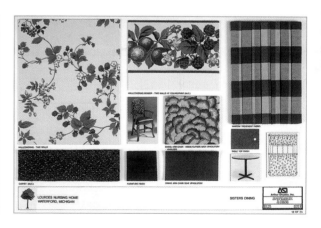

FIGURES 9–4A AND 9–4B
Professional presentation board mounted on foam board with titles on plastic label tape and hand-drawn ink borders. Projects: Laurel Gardens of Avon in Avon, Connecticut (9–4a), and Lourdes Nursing Home in Waterford, Michigan (9–4b). BY ARTHUR SHUSTER, INC.

Presenting Materials and Finishes

FIGURES 9–5 AND 9–6
Samples are placed on a mat board surface with a foam board backing and neatly cut or wrapped, creating an attractive and visually consistent presentation. Additional elements from the presentation shown in Figure 9–5 can be found in Figures 10–8a through 10–8c. Additional elements from the presentation shown in Figure 9–6 can be found in Figures 10–9a through 10–9c. FIGURE 9–5: BY ELLIE FEENSTRA AND STEPHANIE HOLMBLAD; FIGURE 9–6: BY VERONICA MCKRACKEN

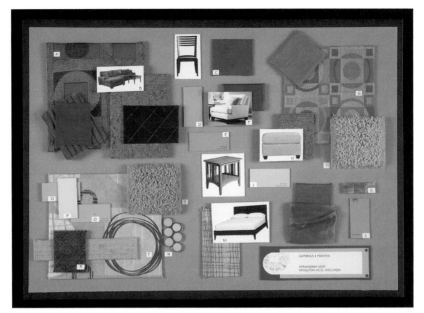

9–5

9–6

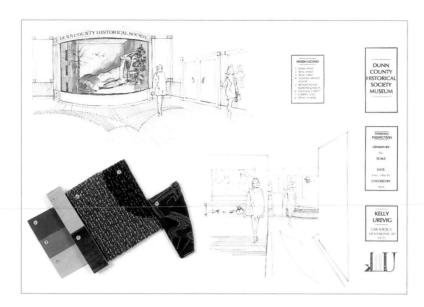

FIGURE 9–7
A student design presentation—with related samples mounted on photocopied Canson paper—that contains printed drawings and titles. BY KELLY UREVIG

Smaller or lightweight materials may be mounted on lighter-weight boards—such as mat board, illustration board, or museum board—*without* a foam or corrugated board backing. However, these lighter boards can appear flimsy and will not support heavy materials such as tile or stone. In professional practice, large-scale sample mock-ups are often used on big projects; a 3′ × 3′ ceramic tile sample mock-up might be provided for the design of a retail mall or airport, for example. For full-size ceramic tile, glass, and stone samples, which are large and heavy, Gatorfoam board or wood panels—which tend not to warp—are used as a mounting surface. Subcontractors can usually provide such samples, although design firms themselves sometimes create them.

Mat board and museum board are sometimes cut with windows; samples are mounted behind the windows just as artwork is matted. (For further information, see the discussion of window matting on page later in this chapter.) A variety of adhesives can be used to mount samples, and a variety of mounting techniques can be employed. (See "Techniques and Methods of Presentation" later in this chapter.)

Nontraditional projects often require nontraditional materials presentations. One designer uses galvanized sheet metal and magnets to hold samples in place. Even chain-link fencing panels have been used as a mounting surface. For student projects designed to be viewed in a gallery setting, clear acrylic rectangles taken from inexpensive photo frames have been used as sample containers (see Figure 9–9). For thesis projects, top students have been known to fabricate custom sample holders (see Figure 9–10). In some instances, sketches of custom elements can be included on sample boards (see Figure 9–11).

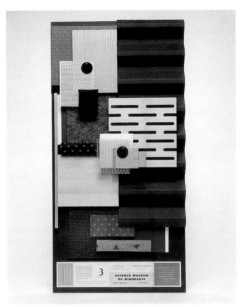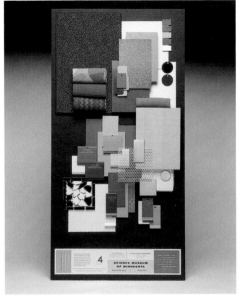

FIGURES 9–8A AND 9–8B

Large, dynamic boards created for a large-scale professional project (using Gatorfoam board). Additional elements from this project can be found in Figures 2–19a and 2–19b. BY ELLERBE BECKET

FIGURES 9–9

These samples are contained in a clear acrylic box typically used as part of an inexpensive photo frame.

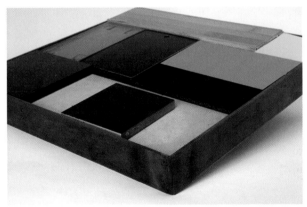

FIGURE 9–10

These samples are contained in a custom box fabricated in steel for use in a senior thesis presentation. BY CIARAH COENEN

Organization and Composition

The placement of samples and materials varies greatly in materials presentations, but designers generally agree on the importance of planning the arrangement of presentation graphics. Regardless of the style or method of sample organization, some basic principles of graphic design should be employed in laying out presentation boards. For example, the use of a grid can do wonders for any presentation. (See chapter 10 for more information about grids.) Traditionally presentations with multiple boards should have a consistent compositional orientation: all boards should be formatted vertically, for example, or all should be square. Materials boards should have actual or implied borders (or margins). A border may be drawn, printed, or created with graphic tape, or, more commonly, the border area may be left blank, without samples or titles. Figure 9–12 illustrates thumbnail sketches of border arrangements.

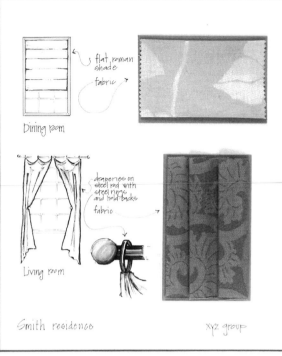

FIGURE 9–11

This nontraditional board consists of rendered illustration board and draped samples.

There are distinct and diverse opinions regarding the organization of samples for presentations (see Figure 9–13). One school of thought calls for materials to be laid out in relation to their actual physical location: flooring is placed at the bottom of the arrangement, furnishings are placed above the flooring, wall finishes are placed above flooring, and window treatments and ceiling materials are placed at the top of the arrangement.

It is also common for designers to place items that relate to one another in close proximity on the presentation board. For example, a picture of a chair will be mounted adjacent to the wood finish and upholstery samples for that chair. This method is useful for clients unaccustomed to viewing presentation boards, such as corporate officers or homeowners.

Another school of thought calls for materials to be placed according to their visual impact within the composition. For example, on a project with hundreds of yards of rubber floor tile and very little carpeting, the presentation may show large samples of rubber flooring and smaller samples of carpeting.

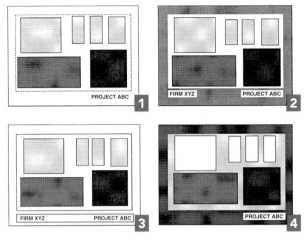

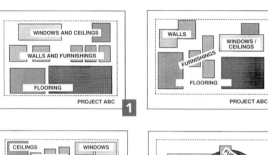

Some designers place samples of exactly the same size on the board and lay them out in equally spaced horizontal bands. Others place important items in the center of the presentation and spin additional samples out from the center. A few designers use the floor plan of a given space as an abstract diagram for laying out the materials on a presentation board.

Traditionally designers placed black or white cloth tape along the edges of materials boards. The tape hides the several layers of material that would otherwise be exposed at the edge and creates a neat, clean look. A black taped edge creates a distinct border, whereas a white taped edge is less visually dominant. Certain designers find a taped edge unnecessary if the boards have been cut cleanly.

Interior Design Visual Presentation

When presentations will be viewed by investors or hung in the sales or leasing office of a commercial real estate developer, the clients sometimes request that the materials boards be framed and placed behind glass.

Titles, Keys, and Legends

For materials presentations to communicate the selected items clearly, samples must be titled, referenced, or keyed. There are two basic systems of referencing samples and images on presentation boards. In one approach, all items are titled or labeled directly on the front of the board, adjacent or very close to the appropriate sample. Another method allows for samples to be keyed and referenced with a legend on the front or back of the board or on an accompanying document. Designers and firms usually have office standards that specify some form of one of these methods. Figure 9–14 shows thumbnails of some methods of titling and keying boards.

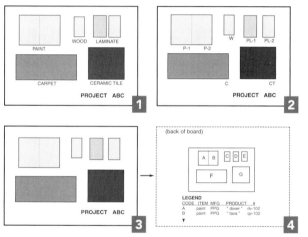

1. Materials may be titled directly on the board.

2. Materials may be titled using a code system, with a legend or key placed on the back of the board or coded to the floor plan and elevations.

3. This example employs no titles on the face of the board; instead, a coding system and legend are used on the back of the board.

4. The legend on the back of board shown in #3.

FIGURE 9–14
Board Titles

There are many board-titling methods. Some designers prefer labels to be kept simple; for example, a carpet sample may simply be labeled "Carpet—Master Bedroom" or "Carpet." Other designers include actual specifications in the title. Some designers prefer simple titles on the front of the board with full specifications keyed to the back of the board or to a floor plan. Figure 9–15 shows a board with samples keyed to a floor plan (as does Figure 9–3).

Systems for keying or referencing samples vary as well. Some designers favor a letter or number code that relates to the type of sample used. For example, carpet may be listed as "C-1″" and wall covering as "WC-1″"; both are then fully referenced on the back of the board. Others prefer a simple numbering or lettering system starting with "1″" or "A″" that runs through all of the samples and is referenced on the back.

Still others use no titles or codes on the front of the presentations. Instead, a duplicate image of the board appears on the back referencing the specified samples. It is also common to key materials to related floor plans or elevations and use the orthographic drawings as part of the reference system. For example, a materials board may have the code "C-1" for a particular carpet; the locations for the carpet are then shown on an accompanying floor plan, as shown in Figure 9–15.

FIGURE 9–15

A materials sample board that uses titles keyed to a floor plan. Rather than cutting the symbols out and mounting them (as shown here), the appropriate symbols (such as "C-1") can be embedded in the AutoCAD or Revit floor plan as text.
BY ANNE CLEARY

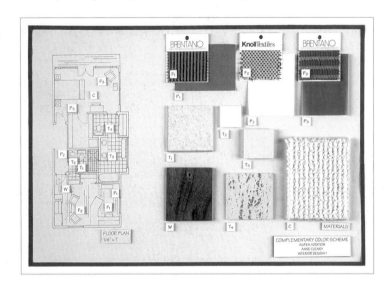

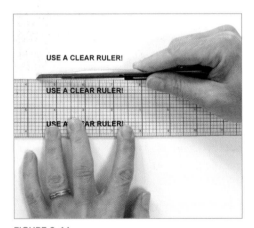

FIGURE 9–16

Use a clear ruler to cut and place titles, symbols, and photographs cleanly and accurately.

There are many ways to fashion the actual titles. They can be composed digitally and then printed and mounted on the board. Or titles, borders, notes, and additional information can be created using CAD and printed or plotted; once printed, the sheet is mounted to paper board and the samples are attached to the exact location with the preprinted titles. Labeling machines that generate printed plastic tape labels also exist. Any lettering must be neatly cut and applied to all boards following the same guidelines. Figures 9–4a and 9–4b show tape titles used in a presentation.

When cutting the paper or adhesive tape for titles (as well as other components), take care to cut in straight, parallel lines, avoiding crooked, messy cuts. A clear ruler through which the guidelines and type can be seen allows accurate, clean cuts to be made (see Figure 9–16).

Techniques and Methods for Presenting Boards

Most designers neatly mount or attach samples to the front surface of a presentation board, taking care to trim all edges. Fabrics are often wrapped around cardboard (or mat board) and taped or glued in place. This treatment produces neat, uniform samples without unraveled edges. Figure 9–17 illustrates the construction of such samples. The same wrapping method can be used on formal boards for paint samples (see Figure 9–18). To save time, fabric samples can be neatly trimmed and placed on mat board that is then glued to the presentation board; fabric samples may be draped and glued in place.

FIGURE 9–17

To wrap fabric samples, allow an ample amount of material for wrapping. Pull the ends firmly in place, and secure with glue or tape. Adding a piece of paperboard to the back of the wrapped sample facilitates mounting and gluing.

FIGURE 9–18

Paint samples can be wrapped around a cardboard form and held in place with tape. Paint samples can also be applied directly, without wrapping.

FIGURE 9–19

Photographs look best mounted on mat paperboard and then trimmed and glued onto a board. Mounting them on paperboard gives the images a polished look and creates a shadow line (see Figures 9–3 and 9–6). A paper cutter makes quick work of trimming.

Pictures or photocopies of furnishings and equipment look best if they are mounted (with double-sided tape, StudioTac, or spray mount) on mat board that is then trimmed and mounted directly on the presentation board. This allows them to sit on the surface of the presentation board, creating a shadow line that adds a professional finish to the board; it can also prevent warping. (This technique was used in Figures 9–3 and 9–6.) A large paper cutter with a sharp blade is best for trimming photos (see Figure 9–19); using one is quicker than cutting with a utility or X-Acto knife. Mounting samples with Velcro allows clients to remove them in order to examine them closely and the designer to replace them with different ones easily (see Figure 9–20). However, Velcro may let samples droop or become uneven.

When mounting heavy objects such as tile, stone, or metal panels, score the mounting board surface prior to applying glue. This adds texture to the board and increases the bonding capacity of most glues. A consistent, thin application of white glue is usually

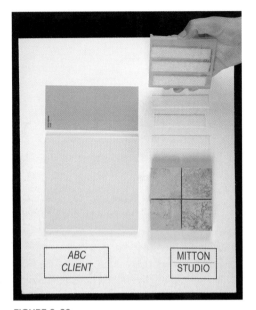

FIGURE 9–20

The use of Velcro allows samples to be removed for examination and replacement. However, samples may droop or become uneven.

enough to bond heavy samples to boards. Contact cement is sometimes used, but because it is toxic and unpleasant to work with, it should be reserved for when white glue is inadequate.

Especially large or heavy samples may require the use of two layers of foam board for backing. This allows one layer to be cut away so that the sample can be recessed into the opening. Some designers find that heavy-duty carpet tape—a type of heavy-duty double-sided tape—works well for bonding weighty surfaces to boards. Carpet tape comes in a range of adhesive types that can yield mixed results, so test its adhesion prior to using it.

Plastic laminates and other samples may have product numbers printed on them. These printed numbers can usually be removed with an electric eraser. Bestine or another solvent can also be used to remove stubborn printed information.

Designers use a variety of adhesive products to mount samples and materials. A thin application of white glue works for adhering light- and medium-weight samples. However, white glue will cause light papers such as tracing paper, vellum, and bond to wrinkle; use double-sided tape, rubber cement, or spray-on adhesive (for small areas) instead. StudioTac is good for adhering paper and light samples to board surfaces. Use hot glue for light- to medium-weight items with large flat surface areas (heavier samples will not bond well with hot glue). A fairly thin, consistent application works best. Big globs of glue are not only messy, but do not create enough surface area for a good bond. Take care not to spill the hot glue on the presentation board's surface. To remove an item that has been glued in place, a handheld hair dryer will warm and loosen spray-on adhesive, Studio Tac, hot glue, rubber cement, and sticky back. Set the dryer to warm; a hot setting may cause melting or warping.

Use Studio Tac or rubber cement, not spray adhesive, to mount large bond or print paper drawings to foam board or mat board, or they will wrinkle or warp—or both. Drawings may also be mounted on Canson or other art paper to create a thinner presentation that can be inserted into a portfolio. Some designers prefer to use large black clips (available at office supply stores) to attach drawings to foam board or precut plywood sheets the exact size of the drawing's surface. This allows drawings to be easily removed and replaced with revised drawings.

Some designers and educators prefer formal boards with samples placed behind neatly cut window mats. To create window mats, design and lay out the board, then draw the window locations on its surface and cut in the marked locations. To create a beveled edge, use a mat cutter or a knife with an exceptionally sharp blade to keep the cuts crisp and professional looking. Precut the corners to avoid overcutting the mat (see Figure 9–21).

Attach samples to the backing board, and place the front board with the windows on top (see Figure 9–22). In some cases, the mat board lies on top of the samples so the samples are recessed behind the windows (see Figure 9–23). For window-matted drawings, a window is cut in a board and that board is hinged with tape to a backing board. The flat drawing is then attached to the backing board (see Figure 9–24).

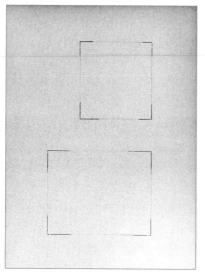

FIGURE 9–21
When cutting window mats by hand, it helps to precut the corners.

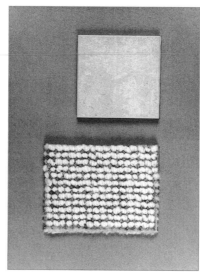

FIGURE 9–22
Samples project from windows.

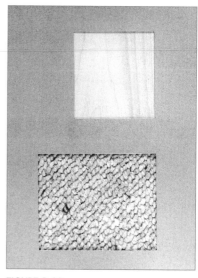

FIGURE 9–23
Samples recessed beneath window mats.

Digital Technology

Designers now often rely on digital technology when preparing materials presentations. Digital cameras and scanners are used to capture materials samples and product imagery. And many materials and furnishings suppliers and manufacturers put digital images online so designers can download them.

Note: Use only high-resolution (300 dpi) images in digital presentations.

Digital imagery is also used in record keeping and project documentation. Many firms scan all samples for use in specification books—and all components of visual presentations to preserve the images and retain accurate records. Firms working on long-distance projects use scanned versions of presentations as a means of design communication.

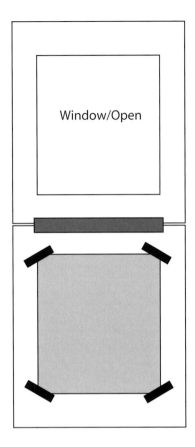

Digital design presentations can be composed with Photoshop, which can create "virtual" sample boards that include the desired finish materials as well as photographs and drawings (see Figure 9–25). Photoshop can also aid in color selection—use it to sample materials for color (see Figure 9–26). Figure 9–27 is another digital materials presentation.

Digital files containing visual presentations can be sent via e-mail for client review, or the actual presentation boards can be sent to or left with the client while the designer retains digital files. Both facilitate the discussion of the presentation elements over the phone, via e-mail, or using some other method of file sharing. (This is covered in detail in chapter 10.)

These virtual sample presentations lack the textural quality provided by true finish materials, but they are useful for setting a conceptual direction. While technology allows designers to use digital images rather than actual physical samples, some designers—and clients—find such presentations off-putting and prefer the look and touch of actual samples. Digital sample presentations work best when used in conjunction with the actual samples.

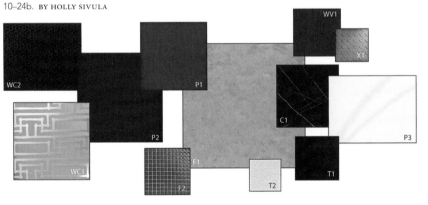

FINISHES KEY	
F1 /	CONCRETE FLOORING THROUGHOUT
F2 /	ESPRESSO MOSAIC BATHROOM TILE
WC1 /	ORANGE & SILVER WALLCOVERING
WC2 /	BLACK GRAPHIC WALLCOVERING
P1 /	FIJI BLUE WALL PAINT
P2 /	GRAPHITE BLACK TRIM PAINT
P3 /	HIGH GLOSS WHITE ON DISPLAY FIXTURES
T1 /	BLACK LEATHER ON LOUNGER FURNITURE
T2 /	WHITE LEATHER ON OTTOMANS
C1 /	BLACK MARBLE COUNTERTOP
WV1 /	EBONY WOOD VENEER CABINETS
X1 /	THREADPLATE CABINET INSETS

The following chapter contains more information about putting complete design presentations together; organizing and incorporating materials, finishes, and furnishings into larger presentations; and the inclusion of digital imagery in presentations.

9-26A   9-26B   9-26C

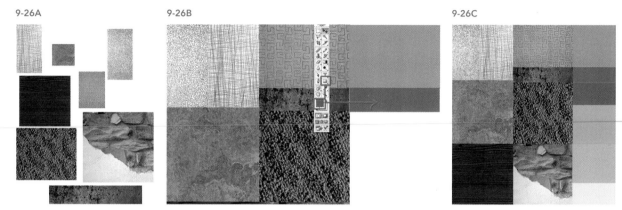

FIGURES 9–26A THROUGH 9–26C

Photoshop can be used to create digital materials presentations and to sample color from actual materials and products for color palette development. Figure 9–26a shows various samples copied from Photoshop files and pasted into the sample presentation file. Figure 9–26b shows the samples scaled, rotated, and moved, and illustrates the color sampling process. (To color sample, establish a new layer, then use the Rectangle tool to create a rectangle filled by color samplings from the various materials.) Figure 9–26c shows the final presentation, with color sampling along the right.

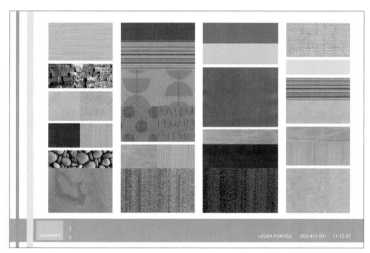

FIGURE 9–27

A digital materials presentation. BY LAURA PURCELL.

REFERENCES

Leach, Sid Delmar. *Techniques of Interior Design Rendering and Presentation.* New York: Architectural Record Books, 1978.

Tate, Allen. *The Making of Interiors.* New York: Harper & Row, 1987.

Making the Complete Presentation

The previous chapters were intended as an introduction to the drawing and presentation methods used throughout the various phases of the design process. Drawings, renderings, models, and materials sample presentations were covered separately for clarity's sake and so students could develop the distinct skills required to tackle each successfully. But these communication tools can also be presented simultaneously, as part of a complete design presentation. An understanding of how to bring these elements together as part of a total, unified presentation is therefore essential.

A successful design presentation combines multiple components in a consistent, unified way. But tying together a presentation assembled from many disparate elements can be a complex task. Unifying a presentation that includes, for example, sheets of orthographic drawings or construction documents, renderings, models, and materials presentation boards can be challenging. The key to meeting this challenge is to find a unifying element that will hold the presentation together both visually and conceptually.

Specific project graphics, including title blocks, logos, and conceptual diagrams, can be employed to pull a presentation together. For instance, the graphics found in the title block on a sheet of orthographic drawings may be used on materials sample boards and mounted renderings. In other cases, the actual format of the boards harmonizes the presentation. For example, all of the two-dimensional elements might employ a consistent color or design and be mounted on boards with consistent horizontal bands at the bottom or side (see Figures 10–1a through 10–1c).

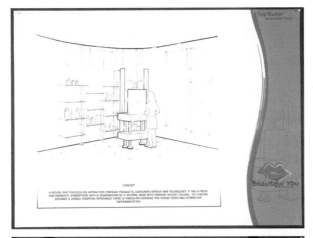

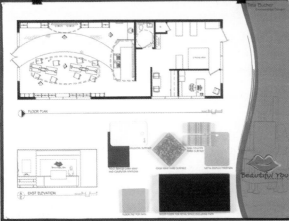

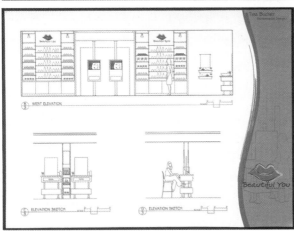

Most professional design firms have office standards for presentation board design and drawing sheet layout. These may regulate how title blocks look or prescribe that a graphic band be placed in the same location on all boards and sheets. Such a standard format gives all the firm's projects a uniform look, which can relate to the firm's brand. It also facilitates the presentation's design, because major graphic devices need not be rethought for each project. In contrast to the professional use of a standard presentation format, students most often select a new format, layout, or unifying graphic device for each project, as seen in Figures 10–1a through 10–1c.

There are no hard-and-fast rules for bringing together the many visual aids used in design presentations. However, consistency, clarity, legibility, and craftsmanship are worthy goals, and the audience for all presentations must always be considered. An audience familiar with design drawings will require far fewer visual aids than one unfamiliar with viewing floor plans and elevations. Moreover, a lay audience requires clearer titling and greater graphic consistency than a group of design professionals.

The foregoing considerations underline the need for design presentations to be *designed*. Students must approach unity of presentation as a design problem rather than an afterthought. In designing and developing a presentation, follow the steps of the design process: the presentation should be analyzed, a list of criteria created, and research regarding the audience and available materials undertaken. Synthesis is

FIGURES 10–1A THROUGH 10–1C
These boards for a student retail design project all employ the same graphic border, creating consistency among three boards that contain a variety of imagery and samples. All boards were composed using Photoshop and include CAD drawing, manual perspective drawing, and surface-mounted materials, making this presentation a hybrid of digital imagery and traditional physical samples. BY TINA BUCHER

achieved by the creation of thumbnail drawings and design sketches. Finally, the design of the presentation must be evaluated; only then should the presentation be created.

A student presentation must also tell the project's story. Put another way, the student must clearly communicate a project's design intent as well as its conceptual basis and its most important design elements. This combination of final and in-process information—which makes for some additional challenges—is required by many instructors and makes an excellent final design portfolio piece. In contrast, most professional presentations usually contain only those items relevant to a particular phase of the design process. (For example, a final professional design presentation may contain some early conceptual imagery but generally focuses on final design development level images and samples.) This means that every student presentation must be edited, because including too much information can be confusing and overwhelming to someone viewing it for the first time, such as at a job or internship interview (see Figure 10–2). More information about creating clear, easy-to-follow presentations can be found in the "Graphic Design Components" section of this chapter.

To sort out and edit the elements of a student presentation, consider a way of clarifying and including the finalized design elements within the major elements of the presentation while also providing some process documentation—perhaps in an accompanying binder. The major presentation boards or elements will then be clear, concise, and easy to follow, with the in-process sketches, inspirational material, and research documentation collected in an accompanying book or folder, accessible if necessary but never overwhelming the final design solution.

FIGURE 10–2
This complete final student presentation illustrates the editing process that accompanied its design. The final design solution is presented using formal boards and a scale model, while design-process information and construction documents are separated out into binders and booklets. All elements are kept graphically consistent. BY LAURA EYSNOGLE AND VICKY SALZSIEDER

Process and Presentation

When preparing and organizing a design presentation, always consider the stage of the design process being communicated. Preliminary presentations are quite different from final design development presentations. To convey the preliminary nature of a design, designers use unmounted drawings that are simply clipped to a backing board or pinned to a wall, as well as unmounted material samples and study models. A more finalized design solution made toward the end of a project's design-development phase may include formally presented (that is, mounted or framed) drawings, formal presentation boards for materials and furnishings, and lavishly created scale models.

Both student and professional presentations must reflect a particular stage of the design process. It is not uncommon for a student's preliminary design solutions to be presented quite informally, using tracing paper, pushpins, and loose material samples. However, such informal presentations must still be able to make the design intent clear, using some type of unifying element(s) to convey underlying concepts and the general direction the project will take as it is refined.

As a design progresses through the various stages of the design process, presentations may be tightened up in order to communicate specific finishes, materials, and design details. For example, the presentation of a project in the schematic or preliminary design phase will often include a general sense of the aesthetic direction of the project, such as a color palette, basic materials direction, and some indication of architectural details, as well as plans, elevations, and perspective sketches. This contrasts with a presentation of a project in the final stages of design development, which may include very specific finishes, furnishings, hardware, and finalized architectural and millwork details, plus highly detailed plans, elevations, and perspective drawings.

Scale models may be included in presentations for various phases of the design process; however, more preliminary presentations typically include study models that convey basic massing and spatial relationships, whereas presentations made at the end of design development tend to include finished models that clearly indicate all materials, finishes, and, on occasion, furnishings.

Organization and Composition

Begin designing a presentation by analyzing the relative sizes of the elements, the number of components to be presented, and the various formats to be employed. The size of the audience and the layout of the room used for the presentation will influence its relative size and format. Both students and professionals are usually under both time and budgetary constraints. Keep them in mind when planning presentations, and be realistic in terms of time and money.

Using a consistent format or layout from board to board is key to the graphic design of interior design presentations. This may mean using a consistent graphic border or edge treatment (as discussed in chapter 9) as well as a grid or other organizational structure that graphically unites the various components (grids are discussed in the following section). Graphic unity can also be created by using a consistent location for titles and text from board to board and sheet to sheet. Figures 10–3a and 10–3b depict thumbnails and organizing principles for presentation design and formatting. (See the "Graphic Design Components" section of this chapter for additional information about graphic design.)

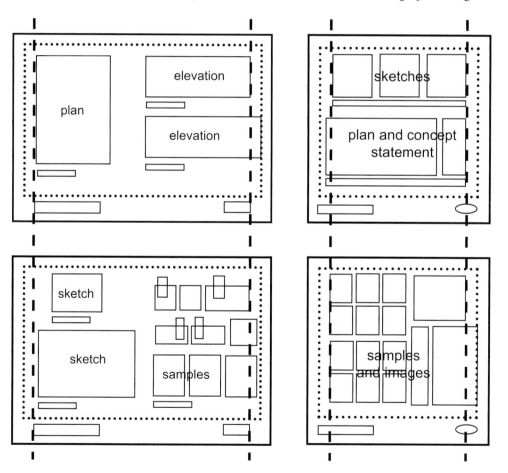

FIGURES 10–3A AND 10–3B

These sketches illustrate a consistent organizational structure that unifies the various presentations elements. The dashed lines indicate alignment locations; some items align with these lines, while others simply relate to them. Dotted areas indicate a consistent implied border that contains all objects. The bottom of the boards all have a taller border and contain the board's titles. There are many ways to lay out boards; these two figures illustrate two of many possible organizational schemes.

As a presentation's design moves forward and the important issues are analyzed, several ideation thumbnail sketches can be made. Begin by creating a list of required drawings and images. Then make sketches that incorporate the required elements in rough scale in a range of possible presentation formats. These should then be reviewed and evaluated. Creating thumbnails first and then refining them is a way to ensure that all the parts and pieces fit before any actual elements are cut and pasted; this can save money and time.

Figure 10–4 shows a series of sketched thumbnails used in considering a presentation's design.

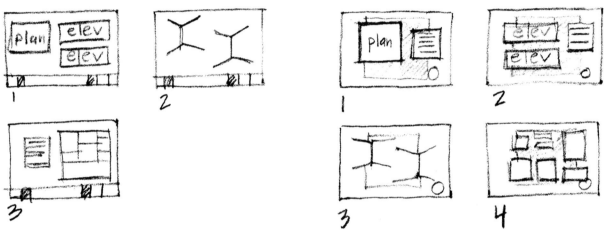

FIGURE 10–4
Hand-sketched thumbnails drawn in rough scale can be created from a list of required items as a means of visual brainstorming.

Techniques and Methods of Presentation

Analog or Physical Presentation

Drawings, renderings, sketches, and materials can be formally mounted on boards. Or, left unmounted, they can be pinned up in the design firm's conference room before the client is invited to view them (see Figure 9–2c). In these instances, full-size samples of furnishings and equipment may be placed in the viewing area as well.

Successful design presentations may use traditional boards created much like the materials sample boards discussed in chapter 9. Drawings and additional items are typically created and attached directly to the surface of the board, as shown in Figures 10–5 through 10–6b.

When mounting items directly to the top surface of a presentation board, set them on a primary mounting surface before attaching them to the larger board. This allows them to raise up a bit, creating shadows on the surface of the board (see Figures 10–7a through 10–10c).

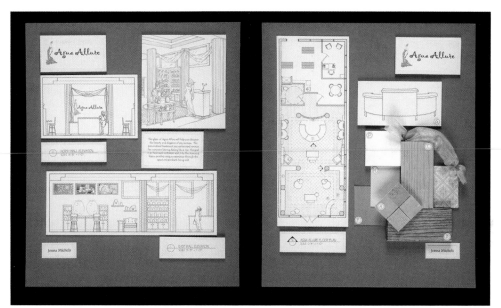

FIGURE 10–5

This presentation employs a uniform implied border as well as consistent titling and graphics applied in a mirrored composition; this brings together a range of diverse elements mounted directly on the board's surface. BY JENNA MICHELS

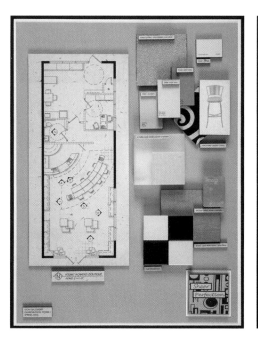

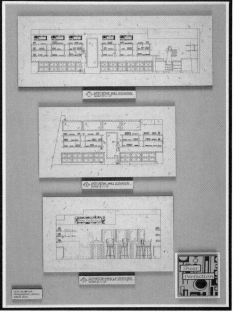

FIGURES 10–6A AND 10–6B

These boards contain drawings and materials mounted on an intermediate layer of mat board affixed to a bottom layer of board. BY VICKY SALZSIEDER

FIGURE 10–7
Presentation boards with marker renderings done on bond paper (CAD plots), mounted on mat board. The presentation includes materials samples, a key plan, and related elevations. BY VICKY SALZIEDER AND LAURA EYSNOGLE

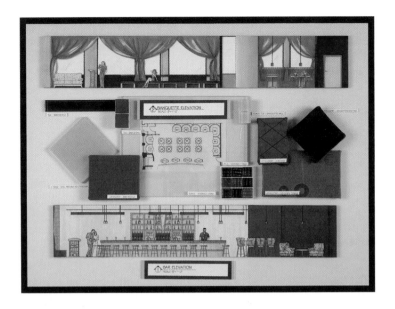

FIGURES 10–8A THROUGH 10–8C
Boards presented with marker renderings on bond paper (CAD plots) set on an intermediate board surface that generates shadow lines on the mat board. Material samples (10–8c) are also placed on an intermediate board surface or neatly wrapped, creating an attractive and visually consistent presentation despite the different board shapes.
BY ELLIE FEENSTRA AND STEPHANIE HOLMBLAD

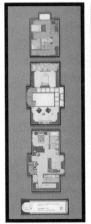

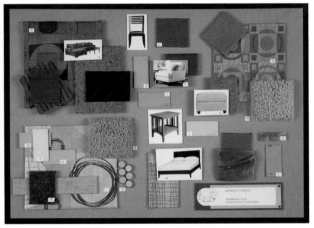

FIGURES 10–9A THROUGH 10–9C

Boards presented with marker renderings on bond paper (Revit printouts), with materials and inspirational imagery (borrowed images that help set a visual direction for the project) mounted on mat board. The light-colored mat board is slightly smaller than the underlayer of black foam core, creating a black border. BY VERONICA MCCRACKEN

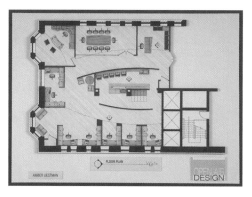

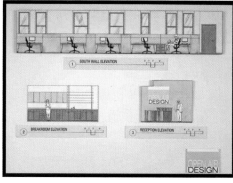

FIGURES 10–10A AND 10–10B

Boards presented with marker renderings on bond paper (CAD plots), mounted on mat board. BY AMBER LIESTMAN

Using a window mat, a series of small windows for each individual drawing can be created (see Figures 10–11a and 10–11b), or the series of drawings can sit behind a single window.

FIGURES 10–11A AND 10–11B

Presentation boards with marker renderings on bond paper (CAD plots), set behind window mats. The presentation includes material samples mounted on the boards' surface. Note the consistent use of titles, project logo, and implied borders. BY SUNNY REED

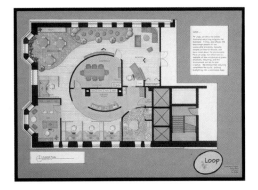

Highly conceptual projects and those with specific presentation needs (such as those that require drawings with overlays) may call for nontraditional boards. Figures 10–12a through 10–14 illustrate nontraditional presentations.

FIGURES 10–12A AND 10–12B

This presentation combines materials samples and drawings on transparent and opaque papers in a nontraditional manner. The different types of papers emphasize differing aspects of the drawings. BY MARY WAWRA

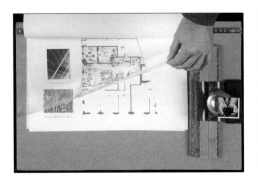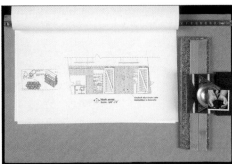

FIGURES 10–13A THROUGH 10–13C

This booklet-based presentation combines drawings on transparent and opaque papers and makes use of consistent, concept-inspired graphics (10–13c is the booklet cover). BY MEGAN ECKHOFF

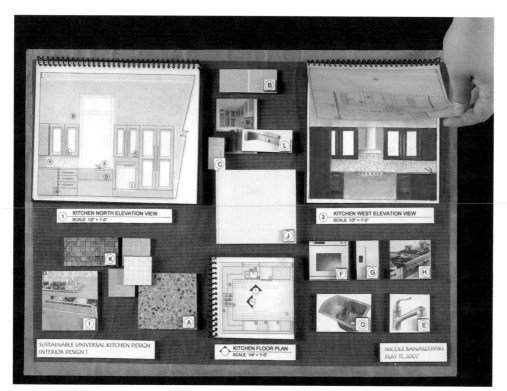

FIGURE 10–14
This presentation combines several bound booklets as well as materials and additional images. The bound booklets work as flip charts and contain both call-out symbols for a legend and hand-rendered CAD drawings.
BY NICOLE BANASZEWSKI

Digital Presentation

Increasingly, projects are presented using digital "boards" made with software such as InDesign, Photoshop, Illustrator, and QuarkXPress into which drawings and graphics are imported. Such presentations can then be printed and either left unmounted or mounted to foam board or Gatorfoam board. In some cases, all project graphics—including orthographic drawings, sketches, and preliminary or inspirational graphics—are printed on digitally generated boards, and the only nondigital presentation components are material samples (see Figures 10–1a through 10–1c). Other presentations are hybridized, employing digital imagery as well as samples and other nondigital elements (see Figures 10–15a through 10–15c). But in most cases, the entire project is presented digitally, including drawings, renderings, materials, and finishes, as shown in Figures 10–16a through 10–16c.

FIGURES 10–15A AND 10–15B

This is a hybrid presentation whose layout and background were created digitally. It was then printed and mounted with drawings set behind windows and with material samples affixed to the boards' surface. BY LAURA BLANCHARD

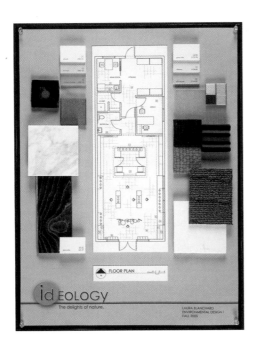

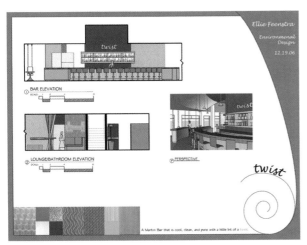

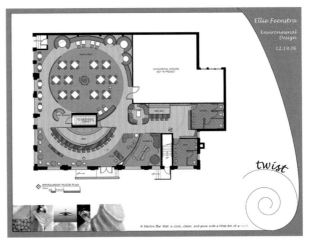

FIGURES 10–16A THROUGH 10–16C

This presentation was composed in Photoshop. The elevations and plan were rendered in Photoshop; the perspective was rendered in SketchUp. Materials were scanned and imported into Photoshop, as were some of the conceptual images. BY ELLIE FEENSTRA

When creating digital boards, important project graphics—such as preliminary or ideation sketches, diagrams, and conceptual imagery—can be copied or scanned and used as a background. Orthographic drawings and other presentation elements may then be overlaid, creating an interesting, unified presentation that speaks to the origin of the design concept, as shown in Figures 10–17a and 10–17b. Preliminary graphics, narrative information (text), and inspirational images can all be included in digital presentations. Despite the use of such a wide range of graphics and text, cohesion must, as always, be created graphically, as illustrated in Figures 10–18a and 10–18b.

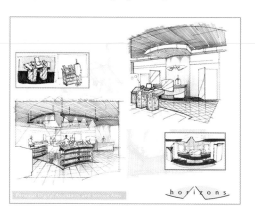

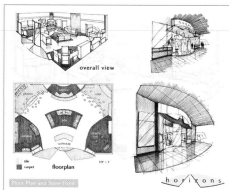

FIGURES 10–17A AND 10–17B

Portions of a presentation composed in Photoshop. Hand-rendered items were imported and layered on top of light versions of early project graphics. BY MATTHEW SAUNDERS

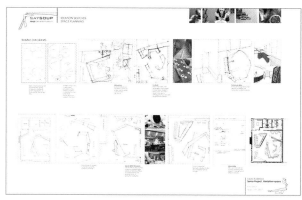

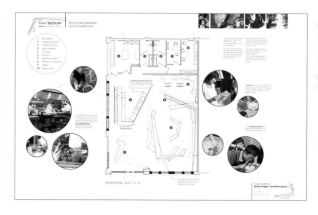

FIGURES 10–18A THROUGH 10–18B
Portions of a thesis project composed in Photoshop and InDesign. The project's process is documented through the many drawings and sketches included in Figure 10–18a. Information about the plan is conveyed via keyed elements in Figure 10–18b. BY LAURA SUDBROCK

Assuming a facility with the software being used, digital presentations tend to take less time to create than those made from analog boards and elements because a single digital file can be saved and then used to generate numerous iterations that incorporate additional sheets and elements. Adding text, photographs, and images to digital files is also easier—and faster—than cutting and pasting analog elements. Remember to use only high-resolution (300 dpi) images in digital presentations. Additional examples of digital presentations can be found in Figures 10–19a through 10–22b.

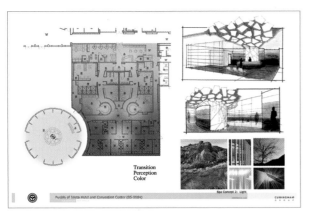 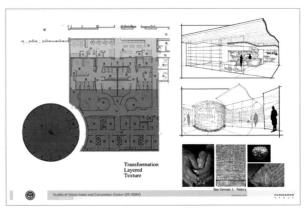

FIGURES 10–19A AND 10–19B

Portions of a project presentation communicating different conceptual directions, composed in Photoshop. The perspective sketches at the right of each "board" were modeled using SketchUp and then drawn over with marker on tracing paper. BY CUNINGHAM GROUP ARCHITECTURE, P.A.

Some project presentations need significant amounts of narrative information, requiring the inclusion of many lines of text that may cover issues such as research and conceptual development, or provide detailed project information. Such large passages of text should be clustered into logical chunks of information. Grouping these chunks facilitates reading while treating the text as a graphic element, allowing it to become a cohesive part of the presentation. The "Graphic Design Components" section of this chapter gives special attention to presentations that contain large sections of written information.

The discussion to this point has been confined to the creation of the actual physical embodiment of the presentation—either traditionally or digitally crafted boards. However, presentations are becoming increasingly "virtual"—that is, created for display on a computer monitor or projection screen. Such a presentation can either be made in person or sent electronically to the viewer. The notion of a wholly digital presentation—one that is both created and viewed digitally—is not a new idea; it is, however, becoming more commonplace in an increasingly global economy.

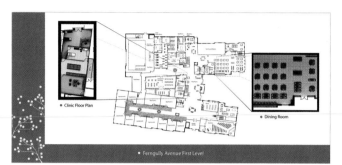

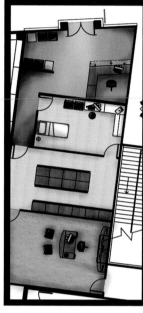

FIGURES 10–20A AND 10–20B
Portions of a thesis presentation composed in Photoshop. The nonrendered floor plan is keyed to detailed floor plans rendered in Photoshop.
BY AMBER LIESTMAN

Laughin' & Relaxin' Lagoon

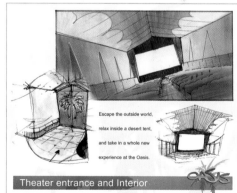

Escape the outside world, relax inside a desert tent, and take in a whole new experience at the Oasis.

Theater entrance and Interior

FIGURES 10–21A AND 10–21B
Portions of a presentation composed in Photoshop. The line drawings were imported and rendered in Photoshop.
BY MATT SAUNDERS

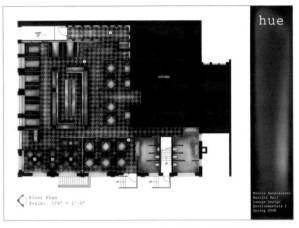

FIGURES 10–22A AND 10–22B

For this digital presentation, AutoCAD and SketchUp drawings were rendered in Photoshop. It has a consistent graphic quality. BY NICOLE BANASZEWSKI

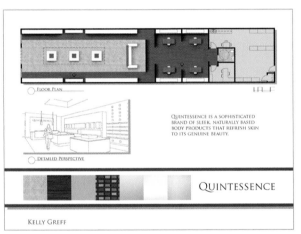

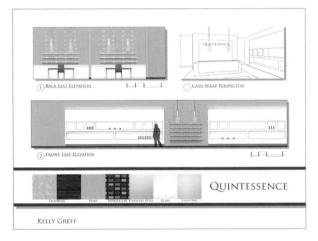

FIGURES 10–23A AND 10–23B

Portions of a presentation composed in Photoshop. Line drawings done in AutoCAD and SketchUp were rendered in Photoshop. Scanned materials samples form a graphic title block. BY KELLY GREFF

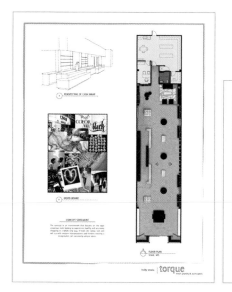

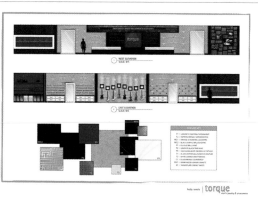

FIGURES 10–24A AND 10–24B
A digital presentation that combines mood imagery, Photoshop renderings, and digital materials samples all presented in a manner appropriate to the project concept.
BY HOLLY SIVULA

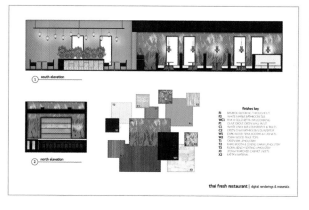

FIGURES 10–25A AND 10–25B
A digital presentation that combines mood imagery, Photoshop renderings, and digital materials samples all presented in a manner appropriate to the project concept. BY HOLLY SIVULA

Software, File Size, and File Sharing

Ways of creating a purely digital presentation include using page layout software such as InDesign to create the individual presentation "pages" or "boards." Much like traditional boards, these may follow a template and be designed using similar graphics, formatting, and text, with each page or board containing differing drawings, sketches, and materials that have been scanned and imported.

Because digital presentations include many high-resolution graphic images, they tend to generate huge file sizes. This, as well as the potential for software incompatibility issues, leads many presentations to be saved as a smaller, universally accessible file format: the *PDF* (portable document format). Saving digital presentations as PDFs allows them to be viewed by anyone with Adobe Acrobat Reader, which can be downloaded for free and works on any platform.

Given the large file size of many digital design presentations, alternate forms of file sharing may be necessary. One option is the use of an *FTP* (file transfer protocol) network. FTP servers move large files quickly, typically through the use of a Web browser or a special utility. A designer can thereby transfer a large, complex set of files to an FTP server accessible by clients or other team members.

File sharing specifically for the construction and design industry is provided by products such as the file transfer, project information, and workflow management tools by companies like Newforma and FastTac, which allow large files to be uploaded and shared with team members, clients, and consultants.

Presentation Software

Designers and students also use Microsoft PowerPoint, Apple Keynote, and other kinds of presentation software to create digital presentations. Avoid the stock templates that come with the software: such design presentations will still benefit from a visual quality similar to that of standard design presentation boards. Logos, title blocks, or some type of unifying graphic can be imported and used in a similar manner on each slide, creating a custom template for the presentation. Compose the presentation using Photoshop, Illustrator, InDesign, or QuarkXPress and then import those compositions into the presentation software to make use of the widest selection of background and text colors, as well as a range of typefaces.

In professional presentations, slide design often mirrors the office standard presentation board and sheet design; student presentations vary from project to project (see Figures 10–26a through 10–28c).

FIGURES 10–26A AND 10–26B

These are slides from a PowerPoint presentation for a thesis project. The imagery was created using a range of software (for modeling, rendering, and image manipulation) and then imported into PowerPoint. The presentation clarifies project concepts, provides a slide-by-slide walkthrough of the space, and is more visually interesting visually than what a presentation built from standard PowerPoint templates could offer. **BY ILKA SCHNELLE**

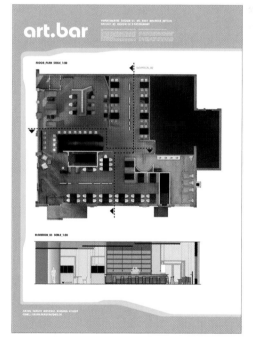

FIGURES 10–27A AND 10–27B

These are slides from a PowerPoint presentation for a student project. A range of research, preliminary design, and conceptual development content is presented clearly. The numbers at the bottom of the document facilitate navigation. **BY JULIAN HENSCH**

Note: PowerPoint-style slide presentations require some type of navigational aid that links the image in each slide to important content. For example, if one slide contains a plan and the next slide contains an elevation, the second slide must provide some connection from the plan to the elevation—such as a small key plan that describes the elevation's location in relation to the plan.

PowerPoint presentations that contain many high-resolution images will generate large file sizes, which can make them difficult to send electronically. As with other types of software files, PowerPoint presentations can be saved as PDFs, so they can be transmitted easily and viewed on different computer platforms. To save a PowerPoint presentation as a PDF, choose Print from the File menu, click and hold down the PDF button in the Print dialog box that appears, then choose Save as PDF.

For additional information about making verbal presentations using slides, see the "Public Speaking and Design Communication" and "A Few Words from the Experts" sections of this chapter.

Graphic Design Components

Good graphic design facilitates good communication. Organization and composition lead to the clear transmission of ideas and are important principles of graphic design. An understanding of the fundamentals of graphic design can help interior designers create clear, consistent, well-organized presentations. The following is an overview of the basic components of graphic design most relevant to creating interior design presentations. While this information is key to creating successful presentations, it only scratches the surface of graphic design; taking an introductory graphic design course is highly recommended.

Grids

Graphic designers have employed *grids* as a means of composing and organizing information for decades. A grid is an underlying framework made of invisible guidelines that give structure to a page. The same grid can be used for the layout of many pages or sheets to unify and organize a presentation.

Simple grids employ a limited number of columns for carrying data; others utilize many columns and further divisions within columns, usually into blocks. Using grids to lay out presentations containing significant amounts of text is helpful because most people prefer to read short lines of text rather than long ones. Regardless of the number or width of columns, leave the spaces between them blank to make the text easier to read and to clarify the overall communication. Figure 10–28 depicts some simple grids.

Before constructing the grid for a particular presentation, list the text and images to appear. Also consider the audience to determine how to foster maximum readability.

The following checklist can help in developing a grid as well as the final design. Use it to create thumbnail sketches of the elements of the grid or layout.

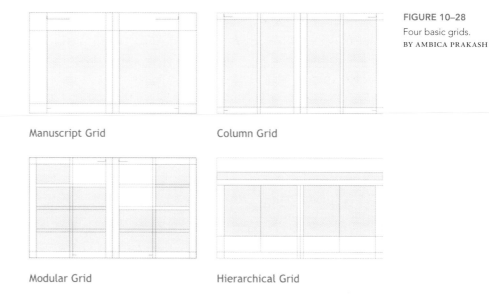

Manuscript Grid

Column Grid

Modular Grid

Hierarchical Grid

FIGURE 10–28
Four basic grids.
BY AMBICA PRAKASH

Grid/Layout Graphic Design Checklist

Number and size of images

Type of image (drawing, photograph, etc.)

Quantity of text (long passages or simple headings and titles?)

Number of headings

Audience size (a large or small group?)

Viewing area (a conference room or something smaller?)

Final output (projected or printed?)

serif
sans serif

Type

Typefaces can be divided into two main categories: *serif* and *sans serif* (see Figure 10–29). The main strokes of serif typefaces end in cross-strokes, flares, or other projections; sans-serif typefaces do not. Serif typefaces work best for long passages of text because the serifs lead the eyes across the page. Sans-serif typefaces are highly legible for a word or group of words that stands alone, such as a headline. Each classification contains many different typefaces.

All word processing and page layout programs can generate a number of *styles* for each typeface, among them underline, *italic*, **bold**, ***bold italic***, ALL CAPS, SMALL CAPS, shadow, ~~strikethrough~~, and outline. Some of these styles—such as underline, bold, outline, and shadow—are sometimes overused by those without graphic design experience, thereby impairing consistency and legibility. To add emphasis within lines of text, try using italic in place of bold or underline. In *The Non-Designer's Type Book* (2005), Robin Williams writes, "Rarely should you use all caps, and never should you underline. Never. That's a law." According to Williams, only headings, headlines, and subtitles benefit from the use of boldface.

Williams goes on to discuss other options for emphasizing type, such as using a bold italic version of the same typeface or a completely different bold typeface. There is, in the world of professional graphic design, much agreement with Williams's admonishments; designers are trained to create emphasis by using various design elements rather than relying on bold type, capital letters, or other styles.

Word processing and page layout programs can set type in a wide range of point sizes. Text is easiest to read when set at 9, 10, 11, or 12 points. Interior design students often use text that is too large, overwhelming the boards. Depending on the audience, printed text should not be larger than 16 points unless it's used for a title or heading. (However, projected presentations do require larger text sizes.) To create *visual hierarchy*, the point sizes of titles and headlines should always be larger than those for paragraphs of text. Type size also affects *column width*. Generally, column width is limited to fewer than sixty-five characters. When small-size type is used, columns should be narrow to make them easier to read; wide columns of small type are hard on the eyes.

Interior design students often have very little knowledge of type-related terminology or experience with typeface selection. A *typeface* is a set of alphanumeric characters all designed to work together within a *type family*. Within a type family are fonts in various *styles*, such as bold or italic. Within a typeface, such as Times New Roman, there are various *fonts*. Restraint will consistently produce the best results for those with limited experience. Put another way: limit how many fonts are used. Some experts recommend limiting presentations to two type families and four fonts total.

Interior designers unfamiliar with the nuances of type selection should select simple, straightforward, legible typefaces and avoid those that are novel, clever, or difficult to read. The following is a list of tried-and-true typefaces that work well with a range of design presentations.

SERIF	SANS SERIF
Baskerville	Franklin Gothic
Bodoni	Frutiger
Caslon	Gill Sans
Centaur	Helvetica
Century Expanded	Meta
Clarendon	News Gothic
Didot	Trade Gothic
Garamond	Univers

The *alignment* of a column of type influences page composition and the document legibility. *Flush-left* type is aligned to the left column margin; the type along the right margin remains *ragged*. *Flush-right* type is aligned to the right column margin; the type along the left margin remains ragged. With *center* alignment, the text remains ragged along both the left and right sides of the column, but the text itself is centered between the column margins. *Justified* type is aligned along both the right and left margins (see Figure 10–30).

Flush-left text is very readable and is the default setting for most word processing programs. Centered text can appear quite formal; however, centering large blocks of text may diminish legibility. Flush-right text is somewhat unusual, but can be useful in some cases. Although justified text creates blocks of type with crisp margins, it can become heavy compositionally.

The proper spacing between letters, words, and paragraphs must also be established. Most word processing and page layout programs automatically establish character spacing. But sometimes if two letters appear too far apart (or too close together), the spacing will require adjustment. Adjusting the space between pairs of letters is called *kerning*. Adjusting the space between words is called *tracking*. The amount of space between lines of type is called *leading*. Word processing and page layout programs automatically

This is aligned flush left, ragged right.

This is aligned flush right, ragged left.

This is justi-fied and is aligned both left and right.

This is centered

FIGURE 10–30
Examples of alignment.

establish character spacing, tracking (and leading), although it can be adjusted manually as well. For the best legibility, increase the leading as line length increases. Figures 10–31 and 10–32 illustrate leading and kerning.

Kern or not to kern?   Auto Letterspacing
Kern or not to kern?   Optical Letterspacing

LOVE INTERIORS
LOVE INTERIORS
Love Interiors
Love Interiors

Kerning: Compare the space between each O, V, R, and T and the letters adjacent to them.

FIGURE 10–31

An illustration of cap height (or cap line), mean line, x-height, baseline, and leading. BY AMBICA PRAKASH

FIGURE 10–32

An illustration demonstrating the importance of kerning. BY AMBICA PRAKASH

Creating Hierarchy

Hierarchy in graphic design establishes the relationships among elements on a sheet or board. Used successfully, hierarchy lets the viewer determine—at a glance—what is most important and what is secondary.

Visual hierarchy can be established through the use of color, type, contrast, and scale. For most interior design presentations, employing headlines (titles) and smaller passages of text is a good start. Large images—such as plans, perspectives, models, and samples—set against smaller titles creates a hierarchy that allows the viewer to focus on the images first and the titles afterward (see Figures 10–33 and 10–34). Cohesive, hierarchical design elements effect distinct points of interest while unifying the overall design. However, if one element stands out too much from the rest, it may go beyond the principle of hierarchy and become a distraction.

Properly identifying the audience and the type of presentation is key to formulating a successful graphic hierarchy. For example, an audience with little experience looking at plans will require significant notes or images that can be read prior to viewing the plans. For presentations to be projected as slides to a large group, it is best to limit the amount of text and imagery on each slide. Text should also be limited to headlines or titles and just a few lines of secondary text. And images such as plans and samples should not be overly complex, with too many notes or titles. The slides should be simple and easy to read; it is the presenter who should add content.

Use the following list to identify key audience needs and to clarify hierarchal relationships in preparing a presentation.

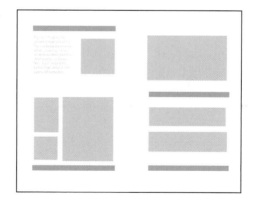

Heading

lsp iand foog xi f ue gmood d food wld ajf ie; kdjirh a fodlle deow wrok omfp cmoem ipsun doleo acole djiwaoledoraacomll dkwl goal lqoor tlcool homca p mmen oomfp cmoem.

Heading

lsp iand foog xi f ue gmood d food wld ajf ie; kdjirh a fodlle deow wrok ipsun doleo acole djiwm aoleon cmoem

Heading

lsp iand foog xi f ue gmood d food wld ajf ie; kdjirh a fodlle deow wrok ipsun doleo acole djiwm aoleon doral acomll dkwl goal lqoor tlcool homca p mmen oomfp

Heading

lsp iand foog xi f ue gmood d food wld ajf ie; kdjirh a fodlle deow wrok psun doleo acole djiwm aoleon cmoem fm lelf.

Heading

lsp iand foog xi f ue gmood d food wld ajf ie; kdjirh a fodlle deow wrok psun doleo acole djiwm aoleon cmoem fm lelf.

FIGURE 10–33
The use of headings or titles and smaller runs of text is one way to create visual hierarchy. For compositions containing long passages of text, use a larger heading and smaller text rather than type that is all one size in one long passage. Try to group text into chunks of information separated by headings.

Note: Text should be kept small on printed compositions but slightly larger on projected digital presentations, such as those made using PowerPoint.

Checklist for Developing Hierarchy

Identify the information, from the most important to the least important. The most important becomes the primary information, followed by secondary and tertiary information.

Determine which content will be the focus of the reader's attention. How should this information be highlighted to give structure to the design? The use of a slightly larger point size, color, or bold type can serve well, but remember: less is more.

FIGURE 10–34
Well-organized headings can effect cohesion between runs of text and images such as drawings and diagrams. The headings can even be simple graphic devices rather than text.

What are the relationships between the different parts of the information? Which elements rely on one another, and which stand alone?

Public Speaking and Design Communication

The subject of this book is visual presentation. This section, however, focuses on the verbal presentation and communication of information. A thorough description of public speaking falls outside its scope; some basics are discussed here in order to round out the information provided to this point.

Public speaking and verbal presentation skills are both important tools in professional design practice and are key to creating complete—and successful—design presentations. Public speaking is a worthy area of study for designers; an undergraduate minor in communication or public speaking is a worthwhile consideration for design students. If such thorough study is not possible, taking speech communication courses and reading books about verbal presentations is recommended.

Many books on public speaking and verbal communication focus on creating "persuasive" or "winning" presentations. These fall short as aids in preparing for design communication because the goal of a design presentation is not always to *persuade* the client. Design presentations do one of three things:

1. Uncover information

2. Sell or market design services

3. Communicate design solutions

Sometimes communicating design solutions is combined with uncovering information if client or end-user feedback is sought.

Always ask, What is the purpose of this verbal presentation? Understanding the kind of presentation to be made means the proper tone can be set and the appropriate content chosen, and ensures the appropriate organization will be established. Each of the listed purposes will therefore be discussed in detail in order to clarify how each kind of presentation can be created most successfully.

Presentations meant to uncover information occur early in the programming phase of the project and often continue throughout the project. For these, the designer or design staff craft appropriate questions and carefully heed the answers they get from the client. This information is often gathered in standard programming documents such as forms, questionnaires, and inventories that are either given to the clients and discussed later or completed by the design staff during or after the presentation. This type of meeting focuses on information-seeking—rather than selling or persuading. The entire presentation should therefore be developed around listening and clarifying.

Presentations intended to sell or market a design firm's services do fall into the realm of persuasion. Such presentations call for absolute clarity of purpose, simple and effective visuals, and a great deal of preparation and research about the potential client. This presentation type is most like making a sales pitch. However, the client must still be listened to as the design process progresses: listening is a constant in all professional design presentations. (At student presentations, there is not always a "client" to listen to.)

Design communication presentations employ the visuals discussed throughout this book as well as a clear plan for how they should be presented. These presentations are meant to elicit client or end-user feedback so the design, or aspects of it, can be approved and the project can move forward. The presenter must therefore seek input from and ask questions of the audience to ensure there is understanding and agreement.

Any type of presentation must be tailored to its purpose. In an early programming meeting geared to information gathering, the presentation should be designed as a discussion around the give-and-take of questions and answers, rather than around a formal, persuasive speech. By contrast, a presentation intended to communicate the final design details of a project may require underscoring the point that the design is complete and that it is time to move to construction documentation.

Students making presentations intended to communicate design projects must have a strategy for covering all the necessary components of the design clearly and in the appropriate amount of detail. For example, in a student presentation, it is possible to begin with a discussion of the general concepts involved or the design problem selected, then follow with a discussion of the floor plan, moving from each room to the related drawings that cover that room. Clarifying the main locations on a plan and then returning to the lobby and at that point communicating all of the related elevations, details, sketches, and related materials and finishes can work well. Covering the plan and related drawings completely, then handling the materials separately, can work equally well (see Figure 10–35). In either case, consistency is important so that the presentation avoids jumping back and forth between rooms and drawings or materials. This is not only confusing but can lead the presenter to forget to explicate important design elements.

Providing too little information about design intent is a common error frequently made during student presentations. Statements such as, "Here is my project, here is the lobby, and that's the reception desk," do not best serve the student or the design. A verbal presentation should be much more precise and clear; it also requires an appropriate introduction. Rather than stating, "Here is my project," include something that introduces both the project and the design intent: "I would like to present my design for a corporate headquarters for the XYZ Company. My design is based on the concept of teamwork because...." After such an introduction, the presentation of the actual design will be likely to engage the audience. It is also the way professionals present projects; mastering the technique early on can put a student head and shoulders above others at both interviews and in entry-level work.

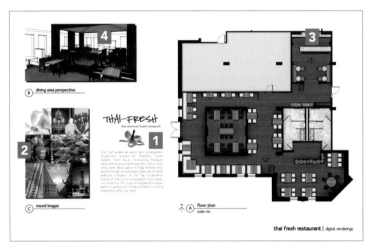

When planning the verbal portion of a presentation, use the step-by-step approach illustrated here, defining presentation elements in their order of presentation.

FIGURE 10–35
Students should have a strategy for how to present the full range of project information. One method is to start with overarching concepts (1 and 2) and then cover each room's design and finish materials in detail (3 and 4). Another approach is to move from conceptual elements through the plan and then back to cover additional details such as materials and detail drawings. PRESENTATION IMAGE BY HOLLY SIVULA

Verbal Presentation Basics

Presentations vary greatly in purpose and style, but they all share certain elements. What follows are some general guidelines about making clear, easy-to-follow presentations of all kinds (see Figure 10–36).

Audience

The importance of understanding a presentation's audience has been addressed in different contexts thus far. The discussion here relates to discerning the audience members' level of sophistication or subject knowledge. For example, at a design communication presentation for a large public gathering, the audience may consist of people who cannot read a floor plan. Making such a presentation requires careful consideration of which images to share with the audience, and in which order, so that the design will be clear and comprehensible. In contrast, when making a presentation to a group of design professionals, detailed technical drawings will be readily understood and can be shared without providing much background information.

Similarly, an understanding of the audience allows presenters to gauge the level of technical detail and jargon to use in the presentation. Experts in a given field are comfortable using certain terminology that they deal with every day, whereas the general public may get lost when acronyms or technical jargon is tossed about.

Audience

Structure and Flow

The purpose of a given presentation may vary from information gathering to design communication. Whatever its purpose, a careful consideration of its structure is essential. Most presentations benefit from an introduction and conclusion. A statement of the presentation's purpose should be included in the introduction, and a clear, concise summation of its most important elements should be included in the conclusion. It is completely reasonable to say, "Today we are going to cover X, Y, and Z" in the introduction, and end by saying, "After covering X, Y, and Z, we hope you take away with you these important aspects of this presentation."

Structure and Flow

Keep it Simple

Rehearse 1, 2, 3, 1, 2,

FIGURE 10–36
These are the keys to successful presentations. (More detail on each is provided in this section.)

To create a clear introduction and a concise conclusion, do not repeat too many details from the presentation itself: only the core information should be reiterated at the presentation's beginning and end. Besides creating clarity, structure, and closure, this has the added benefit of allowing audience members to assess whether they have comprehended the presentation at its conclusion, and can lead to a successful question-and-answer period afterward, if necessary.

Also consider how the presentation of drawings, models, and samples will be structured. Will the plan be shown first, followed by details that relate to each room or space? Or will more time be spent describing the concept and how design elements relate to it? Many designers treat a presentation as a walk through the space, whereby each element is discussed as it might be found on a journey through the building. Regardless of the presentation's structure, each element must be covered in a consistent manner so the audience can remain focused on the information rather than feeling lost or wondering what is being presented.

To that end, it is fine to remind the audience about what area or item is being discussed. Doing so may seem repetitious to someone familiar with the design, but during a long and complex presentation, the audience may begin to drift a bit. So it can be worthwhile to reinforce exactly what area is under consideration from time to time (e.g., "Again as we enter to the research area we find…" or "Here in the research department, the workstations…"). Asking for questions (e.g., "Are there any questions about the research area before I move on?") is another way to refocus the presentation and restate any necessary details.

Presentation thumbnails—discussed previously in terms of project graphics—may also be used to clarify the order and structure of a verbal presentation. Organize the thumbnails to determine the order in which the graphics should be presented and to ascertain the timing of additional information that will be discussed.

Content and Graphics

Many books on presentation and public speaking describe the need to keep content and graphics as simple and straightforward as possible. The degree of simplicity also requires an understanding of the audience: what is simple for a group of experts may be over the heads of the general public. However, the concept of simplicity goes beyond audience identification: all presentations should be kept as uncomplicated and easy to follow as possible. Condense all elements to their most important attributes and state them in the most straightforward manner possible.

Simplicity may be most important in creating PowerPoint-type presentations, when it is key to keep text variation to a minimum and to avoid information overload. Minimizing the amount of text—especially headlines and bulleted information—lends such presentations clarity. Also avoid the use of large amounts of data or numerical information. Any images should have an identifiable relationship to the information being conveyed; they should serve as illustrations (such as drawings and models) or as a means of conveying design intent, inspiration, or context.

In some ways, design presentations are easier to simplify than are other forms of business communication because they use consistent graphic elements such as drawings and models. These pictures tell a story. Designers must convey this story as simply and clearly as possible. This often involves letting the project graphics serve as the presentation's imagery—and letting any verbiage play a support role to the graphics.

Rehearsing

Good presentations require practice, and the entire presentation should always be rehearsed. This involves actually saying the words and going through the visuals in front of other people. Taking a quick look at some notes is not rehearsing—it is reviewing. However, taking the time to practice saying the words while moving through project graphics provides an understanding of pacing, highlights any potential weaknesses, and gives the presenter a solid feel for the material. It is the only way to become completely comfortable with the totality of the presentation.

Both students and professionals—even those with many years of experience—prepare for presentations by rehearsing. Design firms have even been known to hire presentation coaches and to require designers to make presentations to community members and schools in order to develop their presentation skills. The amount of preparation necessary relates directly to the type of presentation being made and the level of polish it requires: a student desk critique does not require many run-throughs, whereas a final design presentation made to support a long-term project may require extensive rehearsal. In the professional realm, presentations made to stakeholders and those made to market a firm's services may also require considerable practice. When in doubt, practice—it can only enhance a presentation.

A Few Words from the Experts

There are a number of excellent books on the subject of verbal and visual presentation written for business professionals. The best of them provide strategies for moving beyond the limitations of PowerPoint and focusing on the question posed at the beginning of this section: What is the purpose of this verbal presentation? A very brief statement about what three authors discuss follows.

Carmine Gallo

The author of *The Presentation Secrets of Steve Jobs* (2010), Carmine Gallo writes that all great presentations contain nine elements. Those elements most important to design presentation are boldfaced.

1. Headline: What is the big idea?

2. Passion statement: State why the speaker is excited.

3. Three key messages: Write out three important messages you want the audience to receive.

4. Metaphors and analogies: Use these to engage the audience.

5. Demonstrations: Let the audience see or experience things.

6. Partners: Use industry partners when possible.

7. Customer service or testimonials: Offer customer evidence.

8. Video clips: Similar to demonstrations.

9. Flip charts, props, show-and-tell: Appeal to a range of learning styles (visual, auditory and kinesthetic).

Of those in bold, the three most important for all design presentations are

Identifying a headline

Focusing on three key ideas

Demonstrations (All of the drawings, materials, models, and images in a presentation can be thought of as demonstrations and show-and-tell–type items.)

While not all design presentations can make use of all of these elements, it is worthwhile to consider each for every presentation. And it is advantageous to try to limit design presentations to three key messages, although this is not always possible.

Garr Reynolds

Garr Reynolds, the author of *Presentation Zen* (2008), breaks presentations into three parts: **Preparation**, **Design**, **Delivery**

What Garr describes as preparation and design are actually the planning and execution of the presentation, from its inception to its final visual form. Reynolds focuses on what he calls "crafting the story" and keeping visuals simple and straightforward. Garr gives some excellent advice: "As you prepare a presentation," he writes, "exercise restraint and keep these three words in mind always: simplicity, clarity, brevity" (page 43).

Reynolds also discusses the importance of working on analog sketches—that is, brainstorming and sketching by hand prior to moving to software. He believes that working without computers allows you "to see the big picture and identify…the single core message. This can be difficult unless you create a stillness of mind for yourself" (page 45).

Nancy Duarte

Nancy Duarte, the author of *Slide:ology* (2008), also discusses the importance of working with hand drawings in developing presentations, writing, "The best creative process requires stepping away from technology and relying on the same tools of expression that you grew up with—pens, pencils, and crayons. The goal is to generate ideas..." (page 26).

Duarte is an advocate of using Post-its or other kinds of sticky notes to generate ideas for presentations (see Figure 10–37). She continues, "Sticky notes allow ideas to be captured, sorted, and rearranged as needed.... [O]ne idea per sticky note is preferable" (page 28).

Duarte's book is particularly helpful to designers because it stresses drawing, rapid idea generation, and the use of diagrams and refined visual elements. Duarte also provides useful information about how to design effective presentation slides that "transform them into visual stories that support their message."

Anticipating audience needs is a key to creating strong presentations, according to Duarte. In the design of individual slides, she recommends that each one not have more than one main point and up to two subsidiary points, and that there not be more than three layers of information. In addition, Duarte suggests that how the slides flow graphically be considered so that the reader can follow the text comfortably (Figure 10–38).

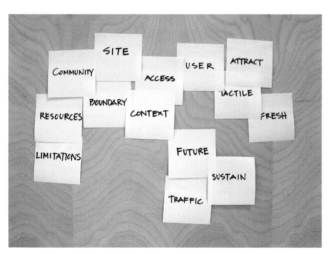

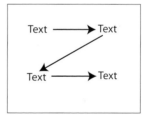

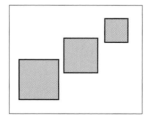

FIGURE 10–37
Each Post-it note should contain a single idea, according to Duarte. The notes can then be moved, juggled, and removed while preparing the presentation. The presentation script can actually be based on the structure uncovered through this process.

FIGURE 10–38
The design of each slide should facilitate the flow of information. The top image shows text-flow considerations (for readers of Western languages). The bottom image demonstrates that an item's size and placement can lead the eye, creating a visual hierarchy.

REFERENCES

Burley-Allen, Madelyn. *Listening: The Forgotten Skill.* New York: John Wiley & Sons, 1995.

Duarte, Nancy. *Slide:ology: The Art and Science of Creating Great Presentations.* Sebastopol, CA: O'Reilly Media, 2008. A fantastic book containing a wealth of information about design and strategies for making successful presentations. A must-have for design firms as well as anyone interested in making successful presentations.

Gallo, Carmine. *The Presentation Secrets of Steve Jobs: How to Be Insanely Great in Front of Any Audience.* New York: McGraw Hill, 2010.

Reynolds, Garr. *Presentation Zen: Simple Ideas on Presentation Design and Delivery.* Berkeley, CA: New Riders, 2008.

Tufte, Edward. *Beautiful Evidence.* Chesire, CT: Graphics Press, 2006.

————. *The Cognitive Style of PowerPoint: Pitching Out Corrupts Within.* 2nd ed. Chesire, CT: Graphics Press, 2006.

Weissman, Jerry. *Presenting to Win: The Art of Telling Your Story.* Upper Saddle River, NJ: Prentice Hall, 2006. While notions of "winning" are not always applicable to design presentations, this book has some excellent information on organizing and designing presentations.

Materials, Tools, and Equipment for Manual Drafting and Drawing

This appendix presents the materials, equipment, and tools used for manually drafted and freehand design drawings.

Figure A1–1 illustrates some commonly used manual drafting and drawing materials and equipment.

Drawing Surfaces

The drawing surface always affects the quality of the drawn image. Some surfaces accept pencil and ink readily and allow for clear, consistent imagery. Transparent papers facilitate diazo reproduction (blueprinting) and can be used as an overlay to continue a drawing by transferring details from one sheet to another. Drawings produced on non-transparent surfaces are reproduced by photocopying, digital reproduction (scanning), or photographic processes.

Tracing paper is the most common paper surface for sketching in-process design drawings and graphics. Known in various parts of the country as *trace*, *flimsy*, and *bumwad*, it is transparent and relatively inexpensive. Tracing paper is available in both cut sheets and rolls in a variety of sizes; rolls work well for interior design drawing because the drawing sizes vary. Tracing paper is available in white, buff, and canary (yellow); most designers develop a personal preference. Some use tracing paper to create actual presentation sketches (used to communicate with a client or end-user), while others use it only for personal exploration.

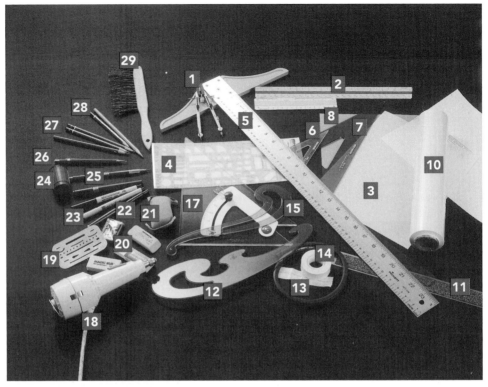

1. Compass	**9.** Vellum	**17.** Adjustable triangle	**25.** Lead holder
2. Architectural scales	**10.** Tracing paper (roll)	**18.** Electric eraser	**26.** Mechanical pencil
3. Drafting film	**11.** Cork-backed ruler	**19.** Eraser shield	**27.** Wooden graphite pencils
4. Template	**12.** Flexible curve	**20.** Erasers	
5. T-square	**13.** Drafting tape	**21.** Dry-cleaning pad	**28.** Layout pencils
6. Lettering triangle	**14.** Drafting dots	**22.** Disposable ink pens	**29.** Drafting brush
7. Triangle	**15.** French curve	**23.** Technical pen	
8. Appliqué film	**16.** French curve	**24.** Lead pointer	

Because it is inexpensive, tracing paper allows for exploration through the creation of many sketches and the generation of many ideas, and is therefore a good medium for developing preliminary sketches and in-process drawings. Tracing paper also works very well overlaid on drawings to be transferred and refined. Many layers of tracing paper are often overlaid as a design is refined or as a complicated perspective drawing is constructed. Images on tracing paper can be photocopied or scanned for inclusion in design presentations.

Final design drawings created manually and intended for diazo reproduction can be drawn on *drafting vellum*, a (usually) white transparent paper available in a variety of finishes and weights—although this medium is falling out of use. Drafting vellum should have a high rag or cotton content, which gives it a rich finish, strength, and stability. It is excellent for line work generated with graphite pencils. Good-quality diazo prints can be run from drafting vellum originals. Vellum can also be photocopied, scanned, and photographed.

In addition to vellum, *plastic drafting films* are used for final drawings and for some design presentations. Although they are expensive, plastic (and polyester) drafting films are tear resistant and do not generally react to fluctuations in temperature or humidity (as do many other kinds of paper surfaces). They accept ink beautifully and allow ink to be erased easily. Drawing on these films necessitates the use of special pencils. Drafting-film originals produce excellent diazo prints and photocopies. For years prior to the use of CAD, plastic film and ink drawings were considered the finest for reproduction.

A range of *art papers* is available (they are discussed in detail in chapter 5). These papers are made with a variety of materials and come in many colors, sizes, and finishes. Some can be used as a drawing surface or as a background or visual element within a presentation.

Adhesive reproduction film, also called *appliqué film* or *sticky back*, is used on vellum or bond drawings. Typed or printed images can be drawn or photocopied onto adhesive reproduction film. The film is then carefully measured and cut and applied to the vellum or bond paper.

Manually generated design drawings can be reproduced on large-format photocopying machines; however, CAD-generated drawings—printed or plotted on bond paper—are more commonly used. Many designers and design firms scan hand drawings and combine them with additional graphics using imaging software such as Photoshop or page layout software such as InDesign to create digital presentations like those in discussed in the "Digital Rendering" section of chapter 6.

Line- and Mark-Making Implements

In interior design drawings and graphics, lines and marks record spatial information, and line thickness and the type of stroke convey specific information. Thus the implements used to create lines and marks is key to successful manually drawings.

Graphite is mixed with clay and other materials to produce what are commonly called *lead pencils* (although they contain no lead). The ratio of clay to graphite is manipulated by manufacturers to a yield a range of hardnesses. Graphite pencils and replaceable "leads" are coded with a standard rating system: H stands for hard, and B stands for black; all black leads are softer than all hard leads. F (for fine point) leads fall in the middle. The number that precedes the H or B refers to the pencil's hardness or softness. For example, a 6B is softer than a 2B, but an 8H is much harder than a 2H. HB leads are slightly harder than B's and softer than F's. Softer leads are used for sketching and rendering; H, 2H, and sometimes F leads are more commonly used for drafting.

Graphite is used in a variety of mark-making implements. *Wooden drawing pencils* are made of a graphite mixture encased in wood and are sharpened like standard wooden writing pencils. *Mechanical pencils* are hollow instruments that hold very fine graphite leads; they are sold in a variety of lead widths that generate a range of line weights. *Lead holders* are hollow implements that accept thicker leads than mechanical pencils; although any given lead holder can only hold one lead width, it will hold leads in a range from hard to soft. Lead holders require the use of a special sharpener known as a *lead pointer.*

Specialized colored drafting pencils and leads can be used to develop drawings prior to hard-lining them. Lines made with *non-photo blue* pencils do not reproduce when photographed; however, they are sometimes picked up by photocopy machines. *Non-print* colored pencils do not reproduce in diazo prints. Both types of pencils can be used to lay out drawings prior to their completion.

One advantage to using graphite pencils is that it is easy to erase the marks they make. Marks made with harder leads are the most difficult to erase and may require the use of a plastic or film eraser, whereas soft pencil marks are easily lifted with gray kneaded erasers or pink erasers. A metal *eraser shield* is used to protect part of the drawing from being erased unintentionally. *Dry cleaning pads*, which contain *art gum powder* that is sifted onto drawing surfaces, are available for keeping drawings clean, by lifting tools off the drawing surface.

Technical pens have tubular points and refillable ink reservoirs. They are available in a range of point sizes that allow for the precise control of line weight. Because they employ black ink and metal points, technical pens create the finest line work of any drawing implement. They must be used with the ink specified by the manufacturer.

Disposable technical pens combine a tubular support with a felt tip and are available in a range of point sizes. These pens require no maintenance or cleaning, making them easier to use than traditional technical pens. Although disposable pens have been known to skip, causing inconsistent line work, the technology has improved a great deal recently and are they becoming very popular.

Felt-tip pens are available in a range of styles and point sizes; they are often used in sketching, exploration, and rendering. Felt-tip pens are not generally used for refined drafted drawings or working drawings.

Erasing ink marks is rather difficult and requires special erasers. Hard plastic erasers can remove ink. And sharp razor blades are sometimes used to scrape ink away from drawing surfaces. However, *electric erasers* with the appropriate eraser insert work best. Electric erasers must always be used with an eraser shield. Ink marks on film can be erased more easily than those on vellum. A *drafting brush* is used to remove eraser debris from the drawing surface.

A quality *drawing board* is necessary for the creation of successful drawings, and serious students should purchase a top-quality one. At a minimum, the board should accommodate paper that is 24″× 36″. Drawing boards should be covered with a specialized vinyl drawing surface, sold at drafting and art supply stores. The vinyl surface improves line consistency.

T-squares are used in conjunction with the edge of a drawing board to provide an accurate horizontal line or right angle for drawings. *Parallel rulers* can be attached to drawing boards using a system of screws, cables, and pulleys. This creates the sliding straightedge that is the standard in professional practice.

Triangles are used with a T-square to create vertical and angled lines. Adjustable triangles, as well as 45/45-degree and 30/60-degree triangles, are available. Triangles should be transparent and as substantial as possible. An *inking triangle* has raised edges and is required when using ink. It is also useful to have a tiny triangle on hand as an aid in lettering. Triangles should never be used as a cutting edge; this will ruin them because it is easy to cut into the plastic. A cork-backed metal ruler is the best edge to cut against.

Drafting tape or *precut drafting dots* are used to attach drawings to drawing boards. Unlike standard masking and household tape, drafting tape and dots are easy to lift from both the paper and the drawing board.

Measured interior design drawings require the use of a *proportional scale*, which allows for large areas to be reduced in size and fit on small drawings. An *architectural scale* is the standard scale ruler used in interior design drawing. In the United States, standard architectural scales employ imperial units (i.e., feet and inches). Standard architectural scales are marked incrementally with numbers running from left to right, with a number or fraction to the right or left of the incremental lines that indicates scale. For example, in ¼″ scale the ruler is marked so that each ¼″ measures 1″ in scale. Architectural scales have only inches marked below the zero marking; these are used to measure elements that are not exact to the foot. In transferring measurements, take care to record accurate dimensions. Do not draw against scale rulers; doing so will result in poorly drawn lines and damage the rulers themselves.

An *engineer's scale* or *engineering scale* is used for measuring larger-scale items related to building sites, roads, topographical features, and water and sewer lines. In the United

States, these scales are also based on imperial units. These scales are marked incrementally with numbers running from left to right; the number at the left of each incremental line indicates scale. Standard scales measure in parts to the inch—such as 1″ = 10′, or 1″ = 20′, and so on, up to 60′. To use an engineer's scale, multiply each value given by 10. For example, where the scale reads 1″ = 10′, the 1 actually represents 10′, the 2, 20′, and so on. Individual increments marked by small lines along the ruler (without numbers written next to them) represent individual feet. For example, two small line marks to the right of the 2 represent 22′.

Metric scales are standard throughout most of the world (with the exception of the United States) and measure in meters (m) and centimeters (cm) or millimeters (mm). Much like an engineer's scale, these are based on ratios, such as 1:50, where 1 millimeter scales up to represent 50 millimeters. The simplified, modern version of the metric system is properly called the International System of Units (SI), according to the U.S. Metric Association; this system includes other units of measurement as well.

Templates are most commonly constructed of plastic and are used much like stencils to draw various shapes, including circles and ellipses, and even furnishings and fixtures. The more expensive templates—constructed of heavy, durable plastic—are worth the extra money. Furniture and fixture templates work well for quickly laying out and plan spaces. However, in presentation drawings furniture and fixtures drawn from templates can appear artificial and monotonous.

French curves are drawn against as an aid in producing curved lines. *Flexible curves*, also known as *snakes*, are also used for drawing curved lines. These have flexible spines that can be bent to accommodate the desired curve; they also work well for transferring curves from one drawing surface to another.

A *compass* is used for drawing accurate circles and arcs and is especially useful if a template does not contain a circle of the required size. A good compass adjusts easily and accepts both drawing leads and ink heads.

Materials and Tools for Perspective Drawings

The tools and materials used in pictorial drawings are similar to those used in orthographic projection drawings and the other forms of graphic communication. Tracing paper—and lots of it—is probably the most important material in the making of perspective drawings. Its transparency and low cost make it very useful as a visualization tool: as soon as a drawing becomes confusing to sort out, a new sheet of tracing paper can be overlaid. When tracing paper is used as an overlay, colored pencils can be used as a visual aid in the construction of three-dimensional drawings.

Both pencils and pens work well in the construction of three-dimensional views when working by hand. Although the choice of implements is highly personal, quick-sketching methods are best accomplished with marking pens that provide immediate visual impact. Marking pens also eliminate the need for erasers, which actually helps with visualization. (This approach is tough at first but worth the effort as seeing one's mistakes can improve the final outcome.)

Hand-drawn, refined, measured paraline and perspective drawings are most often constructed in pencil on tracing paper; many layers of paper and a variety of colored pencils are often used before a final drawing is completed. These drawings can be drawn with the aid of drafting tools, although some prefer to draw them freehand. The final hard-lined, measured paraline or perspective line drawing is often done on high-quality vellum or drafting film, with drafting pencils or ink pens. This allows the line drawing to be reproduced by a variety of reprographic methods on a variety of papers. Once reproduced, the drawing may be incorporated into a presentation with or without rendering.

Blank Criteria Matrix

This blank matrix may be photocopied and used as necessary.

"Project Name" Room	Criteria	Adjacencies							Comments
1									
2									
3									
4									
5									
6									
7									
8									
9									
10									
11									
12									

Legend

1	Major Adjacency	○	Secondary Requirement
1	Minor Adjacency	Y	Yes, See Comments
●	Mandatory Requirement	X	Undesirable

Color Theory for Rendering

Color rendering requires a basic understanding of color theory—especially the properties of color and how to approximate these with various media or pigments.

Hue. What we often call a *color* should actually be referred to as a *hue*. Green and orange are both hues. Hue is changed only when mixed with another hue. Green mixed with blue changes the hue to greenish blue.

Value. This term refers to lightness or darkness. Adding white lightens a color without changing its hue; adding black darkens a color but does not affect its hue. *Value* also refers to the manner in which light falls on an object illuminating its surface.

Chroma. Also referred to as intensity or saturation, *chroma* describes a color's purity or level of brightness. Dullness or brightness are measures of chroma.

Hue, value, and chroma are all properties of color and are part of color rendering. When rendering a faded red chair, begin by selecting the correct hue: red. The red must be not bright, but faded, so the chroma will not be highly saturated. The chair must have light, medium, and dark values applied to various locations based on the light source.

When using markers, keep the following in mind to achieve the correct color:

Hue. If a desired marker hue does not exist, layering two marker hues can sometimes produce the appropriate hue. For example, red-orange is often created by layering orange and red. In some cases the hue can be altered with the application of colored pencil over the marker color. Hue is also changed by making a pool of color on tracing paper and picking it up with a colorless blender; the blender is then dabbed in the desired locations.

Value. The best way to create value with markers is to lay down gray marker prior to applying the colored marker. First locate the light, medium, and dark areas of the form; then underlay light, medium, and gray markers. Finally, apply colored marker on top of the gray to complete the values. Sometimes the complementary color may be underlaid in place of gray. A wash of gray or complementary-colored pencil may also be applied on top of marker.

To create highlights or light areas, wash over marker with light-colored pencil such as white or beige. Washes of dry pastel may also be used to lighten or darken value and to achieve value gradation. Small amounts of white gouache or Wite-Out pen (not the liquid from a bottle) also work for creating highlights.

Chroma. Marker chroma can be dulled by applying a layer of complementary-hued marker, colored pencil, or dry pastel; it can be brightened by applying a similar hue of marker, pencil, or pastel. For example, to brighten dull green marker color, apply a brighter green colored pencil layer on top of the marker.

Experiment with multiple layers of markers, washes of pencil, and pastel to vary hue, chroma, and value in order to enrich a rendering.

Index

Bold page numbers refer to definition or introduction of key terms.

B

Balsa-foam, **220**, 221, 232
Balsa wood, **219**
Baskerville typeface, 275
Basswood, **219**, 229, 231, 232
Bentley, 28, 187
Berol Prismacolor™ pencils, 154, 163, 179
BIM (Building Information Modeling) software, **28**
Blades, cutting, 193, 215, 224, 291. *See also* knives
Blocking diagrams, 33, 37, **44**–49
Boards. *See also specific types, e.g.* Paperboards
    bristol (bristol paper), **151**, 215, 218, 224
    chipboard, 186, 215, **217**, 218, 225, 233
    corrugated (cardboard), 215, **217**, 225, 233
    cutting, 216
    drawing, **291**
    foam (foam core), 51, **215**–218, 221–226, 228–233, 235,
        238–241, 244, 248, 261, 263
    Gator Board™, 51, **217**, 221, **241**, 242, 263
    illustration, **151**, 152, **229**
    mat, 162, 168, 215, **218**, 223–226, 229, 235, 238–241,
        247–249, 259, 260, 261
    mood (inspiration), **49, 50**, 60, 261, 269
    mounting (black), 151, 152, 215, **218**
    mounting (items to), 152, 217, 223, 241, 246, 247, 258
    museum, 215, **218**, 224–226, 228, 241
    nontraditional presentation, 243, 262
    paperboards, **214**–216, 218, 221, 223, 224, 229, 230, 238,
        247
    presentation, *see* Materials and finishes presentation;
        Presentations
Bodoni typeface, 275
Bold type, 274, 277
Bond paper, 150, **151**, 162, 289
    color rendering, 150, 151, 153, 161, 163–167,180, 183,
        260–262
    materials presentations, 238
    models, 230, 231
    Booklet (presentation), 255, 262, 263
Borders:
    for materials presentations, 238, 239, 243, 244, 246
    for presentations, *226*, 230, 254, 259, 261, 262
Boxes:
    enclosing, **81**–85, 89, 90, 95, 97
    in perspective drawings, 75–79
    with slanted surfaces, 79
Brainstorming, 36, 43, 258, 284

Branding,
    mood, inspiration boards, 50
    relating presentations to, 254
    Bristol board (bristol paper), **151**, 215, 218, 224
Bristol board (bristol paper), **151**, 215, 218, 224
Brush, drafting, 288, **291**
Bubble diagrams, 33, 37, **43**, 44, 46, 48
Building Information Modeling (BIM) software, 28
Bumwad, 287

C

Cabinetry,
    drafting conventions for, 11, 12
    drawing scale for, 16
    scale models, 228
CAD, 21, 28, 29, 46, 72, 69,124, 129, 130, 131, 134
Canson™ paper, 151-153, 238, 241, 248
Cardboard, *see* Corrugated board
Carpet,
    in materials presentations, 243, 245, 246
    renderings, 156, 168, 172, 174
Carpet tape, mounting samples with, 222, **248**
Centerlines:
    drafting, 11, 12, 22
    of ellipses, 81–83
Chalk, *see* Dry pastels
Cherry wood, 219
Ching, Francis, 31, 48, 79
Chipboard, 215, **217**, 218, 225, 233
Chroma, 297, 298
Circles, 82, 292. *See also* Ellipses
    on isometric drawings, 69
    on plan obliques, 65
Clear blender marker, 153–155, 168, 298
Clip files, 178
Color, in scale models, 213
Colored papers, 156, 244
Colored pencils, 64, 112, 150–155, 161–166, 168, 169, 177, 180,
    183, 185, 194, 290, 292, 293
Color movement, 163, **177**–179, 183, 205
Color rendering,
    by hand, **160**–168, 176–185
    in Photoshop, 196–210
    in Revit. 211
    in SketchUp, 188–196
    color theory for, 297, 298
Color variation, 155, **177**